Frankenstein's Daughters

FRANKENSTEIN'S DAUGHTERS

Women Writing Science Fiction

Jane Donawerth

Syracuse University Press

Copyright © 1997 by Syracuse University Press
Syracuse, New York 13244-5160

All Rights Reserved

First Edition 1997

97 98 99 00 01 02   6 5 4 3 2 1

Library of Congress Cataloging-in-Publication Data

Donawerth, Jane, 1947–
Frankenstein's daughters : women writing science fiction / Jane
Donawerth. — 1st ed.
p.   cm.
Includes bibliographical references (p.   ) and index.
ISBN 0-8156-2686-X (cloth : alk. paper). — ISBN 0-8156-0395-9
(pbk. : alk. paper)
1. Science fiction, American — Women authors — History and
criticism.   2. Science fiction, English — Women authors — History and
criticism.   3. Women and literature — Great Britain — History — 20th
century.   4. Women and literature — United States — History — 20th
century.   5. Shelley, Mary Wollstonecraft, 1797–1851.   Frankenstein.
6. Shelley, Mary Wollstonecraft, 1797–1851 — Influence.   7. American
fiction — 20th century — History and criticism.   8. English
fiction — 20th century — History and criticism.   9. Science fiction,
American — English influences.   10. Influence (Literary, artistic,
etc.)   I. Title.
PS374.S35D66   1996
813'.08762099287 — dc20   96-21139

Manufactured in the United States of America

For Woody, Kate, and Donnie,
my future

Jane Donawerth is associate professor of English and affiliate faculty in Women's Studies and Comparative Literature at the University of Maryland at College Park, teaching courses she has designed in science fiction by women, women writers of the English Renaissance, and the history of rhetorical theory. She is author of *Shakespeare and the Sixteenth-Century Study of Language* and coeditor of *Utopian and Science Fiction by Women: Worlds of Difference* (Syracuse University Press).

Contents

Acknowledgments

This book could never have been written without the enriching, supportive community of Women's Studies scholars, teachers, staff, and students at the University of Maryland and in science fiction, utopian, and Women's Studies networks across the United States. As a graduate student in English at the University of Wisconsin, I was educated in renaissance literature and history of ideas, and wrote my dissertation (directed by a marvellous scholar, Madeleine Doran) and my first book on Shakespeare. I read only half a dozen women writers in my entire five years of graduate study, although I was made aware of a rich tradition of women scholars. And of course, I read no science fiction in my classes — I read it at night while I studied "literature" during the day. Like many women of my generation, this, my second book, constitutes my continued education, my exploration of a literature that includes women.

Involved in activist and anti-war politics in college and graduate school during the years of the Vietnam War, I always thought of myself as a feminist but did not consider what that might mean for my literary discipline (although, thanks to the librarian, Doris Lusk, I did my high school senior thesis on Margaret Fuller and Elizabeth Peabody). I entered the world of feminist scholarship through teaching, on the issues of classroom climate and revisionist pedagogy, and soon realized that I needed an entirely new education to supplement that of my graduate work. At the same time, I discovered that I was choosing mainly women writers in my science fiction reading, and this question — what was so satisfying to me about McCaffrey as opposed to Anderson, or Le Guin as opposed to Heinlein? — brought focus to my reeducation.

I was especially fortunate to have as colleague, guide, and friend Virginia Beauchamp, a model for feminist scholars and activists, who has transformed all the multitude of activities she has entered — from curriculum at the university (she was our first, acting, Director of Women's Studies) to community politics (she has promoted recognition of women and women's history in many county and state organizations). When I asked her for a bibliography of the new scholarship about women, she also introduced me to the Women's

Studies Polyseminar for faculty and staff at the University of Maryland. And so began my reeducation: such a feast!

Through the polyseminar I entered a campus community that expanded into many forms of reading and study groups. I am very grateful to Evi Beck, Claire Moses, and Debbie Rosenfelt, who facilitated the polyseminar at different times; Margaret Palmer and Sandra Greer, who organized reading groups on feminist science; Laura Nichols, who kept us all organized and smoothed paths; and all the speakers who discussed their theories with us. I also want to acknowledge a special debt to Katie King, for her insights during the polyseminars and many lunches when we discussed science fiction by women or feminist theory. There are many other members of this community who have influenced my ways of thinking, foremost Judy Hallett, with whom I've worked on many projects, but also, and with great appreciation, Betty Day, Bonnie Dill, Lynn Bolles, Seung-Kyung-Kim, Gabi Strauch, Catherine Schuler, Sue Lanser, Sharon Groves, and Maria Lima. I could go on, if I had room: dozens of women's ideas and conversations have influenced these pages.

As a result of the polyseminar, I organized a reading group on feminist literary theory in my department. From this group, for conversation and for introducing new theorists or historical material, I wish to thank especially Stacy Steinberg, Ana Kothe, Linda Dove, Karen Nelson, Fran Gulino, Caroline Wilkins, Esther Birdsall, and Annette Debo. I also am grateful to Carol Mossman and Madeleine Hage from the French Department who participated in a cross-department group one semester.

This book has had many co-mothers ("coms" in Marge Piercy's future). I especially appreciate careful and tireless reading and commenting by Virginia Beauchamp, Susan Leonardi, and Carole Breakstone, suggestions from Debbie Rosenfelt, and advice on the introduction from Neil Fraistat. Andrew Weiner, Kathe Davis, and Donald Hassler have read sections of chapter 2 and suggested improvements. I am extremely grateful for the informed, supportive, and painstaking care with which Marleen Barr and Tom Moylan reviewed the manuscript for Syracuse University Press. I have further benefitted from many conversations with Carol Kolmerten, Carol Farley Kessler, Lee Cullen Khanna, Lyman Tower Sargent, and many other members of the Society for Utopian Studies, and Joan Gordon and other Science Fiction Research Association members. I further appreciate the correspondence, papers, and e-mail of Robin Roberts, Severna Park, Carol Emshwiller, Anne McCaffrey, Cecelia Holland, Joan Slonczewski, Emma Bull, Ursula K. Le Guin, Joanna Russ, Rebecca Ore, Judith Moffett, Phyllis Gotlieb and Eleanor Arnason, as well as the "fan" discussions I have had with Melissa Sites, Michelle Green, and Skeets London. I have been blessed with responsible and gifted research assistants, especially when my children were small and I needed them most: I thank Frank DeBernardo, Karen Nelson, and Jennifer

Rush. And I have had the great benefit of teaching "Science Fiction by Women" to undergraduates since 1983, often in double sections — hundreds of students have shared their ideas and responses to science fiction with me.

I further wish to thank the University of Maryland Department of English, College of Arts and Humanities, and Graduate School, for a sabbatical to begin this project, a Graduate Research Board Fellowship in the middle, and a semester off from banked overload to conclude it. I also appreciate very much the support of the Main English Office staff, especially Robin Evans for her computer expertise. In addition, I am grateful for the expertise of the editorial staff of Syracuse University Press and the support of the Executive Editor, Cynthia Maude-Gembler.

Finally, I thank my family — Woody, Kate, and Donnie — for the support, care, and joy that they bring to me.

An early version of chapter 1 was published as "Utopian Science: Contemporary Feminist Science Theory and Science Fiction by Women," in *NWSA Journal* 2, no. 4 (Autumn 1990): 535–57. Early versions of sections of chapter 2 were published as "Woman as Machine in Science Fiction by Women," in *Extrapolation* 36, no. 3 (Fall 1995): 210–21, and as "Mothers Are Animals: Women as Aliens in Science Fiction by Women," in *Graven Images: A Journal of Culture, Law, and the Sacred* 2 (1995): 237–47. I am grateful to the Ablex Publishing Corporation and The Kent State University Press for permission to make use of this material, and to Andy Weiner of *Graven Images* for letting authors keep their copyrights.

Throughout this book, whenever I first cite a work of science fiction, in parentheses after the title I give the original date of publication for the sake of historical comparison. If a second date appears in the parenthetical citation, that is the date of the edition of the work that I used, and will be the date the work can be found under in the Works Cited.

College Park, Maryland   **Jane Donawerth**
January 1996

Introduction

In this book I shall be exploring the strategies that women writers of twentieth-century science fiction in England and the United States have developed
for negotiating the constraints of the genre: the problem of masculinist science, which inscribes women as objects of study rather than scientist-subjects;
the representation of women's identities, manifest in their literal characterization as aliens; and the history of male narration. For male writers, these
conventions virtually define the genre of science fiction. For female writers
these conventions constitute a wall not only to define the boundaries of the
genre but also to keep women out. Women must climb over, tunnel under,
dismantle the wall—or else camp outside. These problems are not relegated
only to science fiction. Most Western women during their lives face them
often. The strategies that most women science fiction writers have adopted
to negotiate with the genre include creation of a utopian science formulated
by and for women, movement of the woman as alien from margin to center
to confront oppressors, and resistance to and subversion of male narration.
These political strategies are shared with women outside of fiction: utopian
revision, confrontation, and subversion and resistance.

In this introduction I hope to show why I chose to explore these issues,
and what links them together for women who write science fiction. By briefly
surveying what work has already been accomplished on women's science
fiction, I can explain part of my purpose, and I can explain the rest by
returning to the origins of science fiction in Mary Shelley's *Frankenstein*.

But first, I need to say a word about my method. This book is a feminist
study of popular culture. Biddy Martin urges that "A materialist cultural
interpretive practice insists that we read not only individual texts but literary
histories and critical discourse as well, not as reflections of a truth or lie with
respect to a pregiven real, but as instruments for the exercise of power, as
paradigmatic enactments of those struggles over meaning" (1988, 18). Even
though this book deals with contemporary Anglo-American popular culture,
whenever possible I have reminded us of the earlier history of utopias and
science fiction by women and its relation to that by men, of the state of

feminism in the decade of any text discussed, and of the culture-bound nature of the theoretical tools I use. In addition, I see the writing of these science fictions, the teaching of science fiction by women, and my own writing of a book about this subject as political interventions in patriarchal systems. I try, then, to learn from the politics of bell hooks, to hold to her definition of feminism: "By repudiating the popular notion that the focus of feminist movement should be social equality of the sexes and emphasizing eradicating the cultural basis of group oppression, our own analysis would require an exploration of all aspects of women's political reality. This would mean that race and class oppression would be recognized as feminist issues with as much relevance as sexism" (1984, 25).[1] Thus this book analyzes gender oppression along with many other forms of group oppression within the worlds depicted by these women writers.

My work depends in part on conceiving of science fiction by women as a continuous literary tradition from Mary Shelley until now — even from Margaret Cavendish until now — and, thus, on the work by feminist critics who have traced parts of this tradition. In particular, I am indebted to Betty King, who has surveyed women characters in science fiction; to Beverly Friend, Joanna Russ, and Ursula K. Le Guin, who have exposed the masculinist assumptions of male science fiction; to Lee Cullen Khanna, who has shown me the importance of Margaret Cavendish's seventeenth-century science fiction; to Carol Farley Kessler, Jean Pfaelzer, Nan Bowman Albinski, and Carol Kolmerten, who have traced nineteenth-century developments in feminist utopias; and to Pamela Sargeant and Susan Gubar, who have recovered some of the history of women who wrote science fiction before 1960.[2] Much recovery remains to be done, but that work lies outside the design of this book. Carol Kolmerten and I, with the help of our contributors, have outlined such a history in our recent book, *Utopian and Science Fiction by Women: Worlds of Difference*.

1. Because I think that we tend to assume a man behind a last name alone, in the notes I have included the first names of the authors whom I cite. bell hooks further defines feminism as "a struggle to end sexist oppression. Therefore, it is necessarily a struggle to end the ideology of domination that permeates Western culture on various levels as well as a commitment to reorganizing society so that the self-development of people can take precedence over imperialism, economic expansion, and material desires" (1984, 24).

2. See Betty King 1984; Beverly Friend 1972–73; Joanna Russ 1972a, 1980, 1984 and 1995; Ursula K. Le Guin, "American SF and the Other" in *The Language of the Night* 1979, 97–100, and "The Carrier Bag Theory of Fiction" in *Dancing at the Edge* 1989, 165–70; Lee Cullen Khanna 1994, 15–34; Carol Farley Kessler 1984, and 1990; Jean Pfaelzer 1984, 141–58; Nan Bowman Albinski 1988a, and " 'The Laws of Justice, of Nature, and of Right': Victorian Feminist Utopias" in Libby Falk Jones and Sarah Webster Goodwin 1990, 50–68; Carol Kolmerten 1994, 107–25; Pamela Sargent, ed., 1975, xiii–lxiv; and Susan Gubar 1980. On the history of utopias by women, see also Barbara Brandon Schnorrenberg 1982; and Nan Bowman Albinski 1988a.

My work also depends on that by feminist critics in the last twenty years who have helped to define contemporary science fiction or speculative fiction[3] by women as distinct from that by men. Joanna Russ and Ursula K. Le Guin, writers themselves, have been foremost in that project. Among many essays, Joanna Russ's 1972 essay, "What Can a Heroine Do? or Why Women Can't Write," offers science fiction as a genre where women writers may "escape from the equation Culture = Male" (17) and develop "myths of human intelligence and human adaptability" that "ignore gender roles" and "are not culture-bound" (18). Ursula K. Le Guin's 1986 "The Carrier Bag Theory of Fiction" has proposed that we get rid of the masculinist "linear, progressive, Time's-(killing)-arrow mode of the Techno-Heroic" in science fiction, and promote women writers who redefine "technology and science as primarily cultural carrier bag rather than weapons of domination" so that science fiction will become a "strange realism," "a way of trying to describe what is in fact going on . . . in . . . this belly of the universe, this womb of things to be and tomb of things that were" (1989, 170).

Other feminist critics have expanded and developed the conceptions formulated by Russ and Le Guin of a contemporary tradition of women's science fiction. Rachel Blau DuPlessis, in her article on feminist apologues (1979) and her chapter on speculative fiction in *Writing Beyond the Ending* (1985), has demonstrated how women writers of speculative fiction raise "the issue of the future [as] a way of trying to write beyond the ending, especially as that ending has functioned in the classic novel: as closure of historical movement and therefore as the end of development" (1979, 2). Natalie Rosinsky, in *Feminist Futures: Contemporary Women's Speculative Fiction* (1982, 1984) has outlined the experiments in narrative form and in democratizing heroism that make contemporary science fiction by women very different from that by men. In a 1985 essay, "A Manifesto for Cyborgs: Science, Technology and Socialist Feminism in the 1980s," Donna Haraway has presented the cyborg of feminist science fiction writers as "oppositional, utopian, and completely without innocence" (67), and as "a myth of political identity" (92) that depicts "the pleasure of connection of human and other living creatures" (68) and "permanently partial identities" (72). In a 1986 review, Susan Gubar has pointed out women writers' construction of "the liberation of a world elsewhere" in a "tradition of fem-

---

3. The term "speculative fiction" came into circulation during the 1960s and 1970s for several reasons: to suggest the fuzzy nature of the boundary between fantasy and science fiction, to recuperate the works of science fiction that were not part of the conservative space opera tradition, and to designate a body of New Wave science fiction that did not operate by the old rules. Since I shall try to maintain some distinction between fantasy and science fiction, and since I think the more sophisticated writers of the 1960s and 1970s have accomplished the rejuvenation of the term "science fiction," I shall stick with it. I will use "speculative fiction" only when I discuss another critic or writer who prefers that term.

inist speculative fiction often juxtapos[ing] a satiric critique of men's historical primacy with a visionary conviction of women's ontological equality" (1986, 79).

In addition, Marleen S. Barr, in *Alien to Femininity: Speculative Fiction and Feminist Theory* (1987), has further analyzed the contemporary "development of speculative fiction written by women" as "not hindered by the constraints of patriarchal social reality" and presenting "presently impossible possibilities for women" (xi). In her 1988 *In the Chinks of the World Machine*, Sarah Lefanu has studied the "subversive, satirical, iconoclastic" "strand within science fiction" that "offers [freedom] from the constraints of realism" and "a means of exploring the myriad ways in which we are constructed as women" (5). In *Feminist Fiction: Feminist Uses of Generic Fiction* (1990), Anne Cranny-Francis assigns feminist science fiction the tasks of presenting women, through estrangement, in new roles, and deconstructing literary conventions and, so, challenging women's subordination (42–43, 61); she suggests that the science fiction conventions of estrangement, scientific inquiry, extrapolation, and the alien may be adopted to denaturalize "institutionalized modes of behaviour, of representation and self-representation, in contemporary Western society" (74). In two recent books, *Feminist Fabulation: Space/Postmodern Fiction* (1992), and *Lost in Space: Probing Feminist Science Fiction and Beyond* (1993), Marleen Barr has further urged us to consider science fiction by women as part of postmodern narrative (1992, 151; 1993, 102), as "feminist fabulation," "myth which exposes, subverts, and rewrites patriarchal myth" (1992, xii) and which includes "the possibility of real-world change" (1992, xxvii) "by presenting revisionary power fantasies for women" (1992, 3). According to Barr, "Feminist fabulation is feminist fiction that offers us a world clearly and radically discontinuous from the patriarchal one we know, yet returns to confront that known patriarchal world in some cognitive way" (1993, 11). In *A New Species: Gender and Science in Science Fiction* (1993), Robin Roberts has argued against the conservative nature of science fiction (1), examining the ways that science fiction and illustration by men often subvert misogyny by its extreme presentation (3), and the ways that science fiction by women "can teach us to rethink traditional, patriarchal notions about science, reproduction, and gender" (2), and can "refashion . . . [scientific] myths that authorize the experience of women" (6). And in *Aliens and Others: Science Fiction, Feminism and Postmodernism* (1994), Jenny Wolmark has formulated science fiction by women as part of the postmodern in her argument that such fiction occurs at an intersection of science and feminism, a point "where discourses become openly contradictory," and so "boundaries flexible and subject to renegotiation" (3). As these quotations illustrate, these critics have stressed the freedoms that science fiction provides women writers to imagine an alternative world where the sex/gender system is different, or even nonexistent.[4]

Immensely indebted to this earlier work, I wish to take up in the present book a different but related topic: women writers' responses to the defining constraints within the genre of science fiction. These constraints happen also to be obstacles to women's writing: science, a defining term of the genre and a masculine preserve; woman as alien, a recurring image in both men's and women's science fiction; and the male narrator customary in the genre, who is retained in much of women's science fiction. Women's science fiction has been shaped not only by the freedoms offered by a genre set in the future or on alternative worlds, but also by the genre's conventional requirements for publication and, so, by the strategies that women writers develop to co-opt or circumvent those conventions. Along with Kate Ellis in *The Contested Castle: Gothic Novels and the Subversion of Domestic Ideology*, I "hope to demonstrate . . . that popular literature can be a site of resistance to ideological positions as well as a means of propagating them" (1989, xii).

I now turn to the history of the genre for women in order to show that the problems I propose to examine do, in fact, exist. At the beginning of the history of science fiction stands a woman writer, Mary Shelley, but ironically one who conceived of science fiction as a male story. Her *Frankenstein* defines the genre, but male critics have taken at face value her assumption of science fiction as male, writing her own contribution out of its history. Mark Rose, for example, explains that *Frankenstein* is not really science fiction because Mary Shelley did not name it that and the genre did not yet exist (1981, 5). And Darko Suvin dismisses *Frankenstein* as a "flawed hybrid," a portrait of failed proletariat revolution (1979, 127–37). Moreover, numerous editors of science fiction histories and encyclopedias have simply left women out of their works.[5] Nevertheless, women writers have continued,

---

4. Other works emphasizing the liberation for women writers of science fiction as a genre include Marleen Barr, ed., 1981; Barr and Patrick Murphy, eds., 1987; and Hilary Rose 1994, 209. In contrast, Lucie Armitt devotes one section of her collection to essays that explore "the extent to which these [women] writers have subverted the form [of science fiction] and its conventions for their own ends, and how they have contributed a specifically female voice to this seemingly patriarchal genre" (1991, 5). Work on feminist utopias (which overlaps the field of science fiction) with a similar purpose of defining as liberating contemporary work by women writers in the genre include Carol Pearson 1977; Marleen Barr and Nicholas Smith, eds., 1983; Lee Cullen Khanna 1984; Ruby Rohrlich and Elaine Hoffman Baruch, eds., 1984; Tom Moylan 1986; Frances Bartkowski 1989; Libby Falk Jones and Sarah Webster Goodwin, eds., 1990; and Angelika Bammer 1991.

5. Editors and historians were so sure that the barriers to women's writing of science fiction were unassailable that they did not look for them. Curtis Smith, editor of *Twentieth-Century Science-Fiction Writers*, for example, apologizes for the lack of representative women writers in the Golden Age by claiming that women were "present only as voluptuous and helpless objects

stubbornly, to write science fiction. They have returned again and again to the complexities of the questions that Shelley raised: making a science that does not exclude women, creating an identity for woman as alien, and finding a voice in a male world.

Indeed, these three crucial problems took shape in Mary Shelley's *Frankenstein*, suggesting that they are cultural as much as literary inheritance.[6] And just as men in the 1920s and 1930s pulps reprinted H. G. Wells, Jules Verne, and Edgar Allen Poe, modeling stories after them in order to constitute their modern genre, so women presented themselves as Frankenstein's daughters, alluding to Mary Shelley and *Frankenstein* in constituting their version of science fiction. In the 1920s and 1930s, allusions to Mary Shelley's *Frankenstein* occur in Clare Winger Harris's "The Artificial Man" (1929, 79, 80, and 82), Sophie Wenzel Ellis's "Creatures of the Light" (1930, 204); Kathleen Ludwick's "Dr. Immortelle" (1930, 536); and L. Taylor Hansen's "The City on the Cloud" (1930, 427). Even Charlotte Perkins Gilman's *Herland* echoes *Frankenstein*, rewriting Victor's jubilation: "she alone had founded a new race!" (1979, 57). In subsequent writers, Shelley's influence is equally important. In C. L. Moore's "No Woman Born" (1944) in *The Best of C. L. Moore*, the scientist Maltzer and the woman whom he has recreated, Deirdre, debate whether or not he is a "Frankenstein" (1975, 241–42). Faced with gender restrictions, Joanna, one protagonist of Joanna Russ's *The Female Man* (1975) cries, "I am a poet! I am Shelley! I am a genius!" (151). Phyllis Gotlieb includes a poem entitled "ms & mr frankenstein" in her collection

---

on the lurid pulp covers" (1986, viii). In fact, numerous women wrote for the pulps between 1926 and the 1950s, when paperbacks took over the science fiction market. But historians and editors who do include women may be found: see, for example, Thomas Clareson, *Some Kind of Paradise* (1985), and Peter Nicholls, ed., *The Science Fiction Encyclopedia* (1979), recently reissued in an even more inclusive second edition; and Brian Aldiss, for whom Mary Shelley's *Frankenstein* marks the beginning of the genre (1986, 18). As Joyce Carol Oates argues, "Where *Dracula* and other conventional Gothic works are fantasies, with clear links to fairy tales and legends, and even popular ballads, *Frankenstein* has the theoretical and cautionary tone of science fiction. It is meant to prophesy, not to entertain" (Oates 1984, 550).

6. And, I would add, as much cultural and literary problems as biographical problems. Thus my reading of *Frankenstein* is through its daughters, its literary offspring, not through its biographical precedents, which have inordinately influenced other readings of *Frankenstein*. Almost every critic "reads" Mary Shelley's life at the same time as he or she reads *Frankenstein*. But two classes of readings are especially clear: prefeminist readings, which emphasize the influence on Shelley of her father, William Godwin, and her husband, Percy Bysshe Shelley (see, for example, Muriel Sparks 1987, 159–62, and William A. Walling 1972, 48–50); and feminist readings, which emphasize the influence on Shelley of her mother, Mary Wollstonecraft, and the maternal experiences of her friends and herself (see, for example, Sandra Gilbert and Susan Gubar 1984, 222–23 and 242–46, and Barbara Johnson 1982, passim; the essay from Gilbert and Gubar is a revision of Gilbert's essay, "Mary Shelley's Monstrous Eve," 1978).

of short stories, *Son of the Morning and Other Stories* (1983). And Joan Slonczewski's Spinel fears that he is "becoming a monster" because of Shoran breath microbes (1987, 98). Robin Roberts further argues that Doris Lessing's *The Sirian Experiments* is a "revision of Shelley's *Frankenstein*" (1985, 21). In an essay on writing science fiction, Cherry Wilder claims that *Frankenstein* was a turning point in two ways, "one when I realised Frankenstein was written by a woman, and another when I realised that she was nineteen years old" (1992, 12). I suspect that the many monster stories by women, from Ellis's "The White Wizard" and Harris's "The Artificial Man," to C. L. Moore's "No Woman Born," Judith Merril's "That Only a Woman" in *Out of Bounds,* and Octavia Butler's "Bloodchild" are all to some extent reworkings of the issues of illegitimate birth and monstrosity that *Frankenstein* raises. These women's knowledge of Shelley as a predecessor quite probably enabled them to write. But they also then carried into their own works Shelley's problems with the genre. Even by the 1920s, an exclusively male science, first person male narration, and the woman as alien were established conventions in male "scientifiction." Mary Shelley's strategies for surviving the patriarchal and generic restrictions, therefore, were also helpful guides for women writers.

Let us begin with the science in *Frankenstein.* As Victor Frankenstein relates his story to Robert Walton, he gradually details a more and more disturbing picture of the male scientist. As a boy, Victor "delighted in investigating [the] causes [of things]" (1981, 22), and early felt "the enticements of science" (35). To him, "The world was . . . a secret" and he felt "gladness akin to rapture" through his "earnest research to learn the hidden laws of nature" (22). His "object of pursuit" (36) was "the inner spirit of nature" and "the physical secrets of the world" (23). As an adult he turns to the alchemists because he thinks that he has found men who "had penetrated deeper and knew more" (25). But he eventually learns that their knowledge is outdated. Not until college is he again stirred by enthusiasm for science: there he hears M. Waldman extoll "the modern masters" of science, who "penetrate into the recesses of nature and show how she works in her hiding-places" (33). The "master" and the "her" are crucial: for Victor Frankenstein, the scientist is male and nature is female; science is the domination of nature. The domination is erotic: the scientist pursues nature, uncovers her and unveils her, penetrates her, and rejoices in his mastery.

As the feminist historians of science, Carolyn Merchant and Evelyn Fox Keller, have pointed out, in the words of male scientists from Bacon to DNA specialists, the history of science is the history of male study of "female" nature, and erotic and patriarchal assumptions about controlling women inform science.[7] Nor is Victor the only male scientist in *Frankenstein* to use

7. See Merchant 1980, passim; Keller 1985, 33–42, and 1986b, passim.

these metaphors. Robert Walton admires Victor Frankenstein's "penetration into the causes of things" (1985, 14); he likewise hopes to achieve fame from science, exploring "over the untamed yet obedient element" (8), and aiming for a "knowledge" that would give "dominion . . . over the elemental foes of our race" (13). Exploration offers him "enticements" and the hope of "discovering [dis-covering?] a passage near the pole" or "the secret of the magnet" (2). Thus science is conceived of as an erotic act — Carolyn Merchant would say rape — and Victor Frankenstein's quest for life seems to typify the male scientist's activity. For Victor, science at times seems "a deformed and abortive creation" (27); at other times, the source of "immortality and power" (32). By "pursu[ing] nature to her hiding-places" (39) he "discover[s] the cause of generation and life" and experiences "the most gratifying consummation" of his "toils" (37). The result, he first imagines, will be "A new species," the scientist usurping both God's and woman's powers of creation, as well as experiencing his own self-sufficient consummation: "No father could claim the gratitude of his child so completely as I should deserve theirs" (39). With great horror Victor learns instead that his illicit intercourse with nature has produced a monster, an "abortion" (42, 204). Thus, as Anne K. Mellor has detailed, Mary Shelley in *Frankenstein* "challenged any conception of science and the scientific method that rested on a gendered definition of nature as female." [8]

For Mary Shelley, then, a significant constraint in the creation of her story was the exclusion of women from science in her culture, and the resulting image of a female nature as the object of male study. Indeed, Victor must leave the world of women entirely and enter the university world that excludes women in order to practice his science. These assumptions about the nature of science determine that scientists must be male, and that the quest, erotic and illicit, must be profane. Elizabeth, because she is a woman, cannot be a scientist, but she can have a different, holy, relation with nature: "in the majestic and wondrous scenes which surrounded our Swiss home — the sublime shapes of the mountains, the changes of the seasons, tempest

8. Mellor 1987, 287; see also 305–8, 310. Mellor develops her argument further in 1988, 110–12, 115, 122 and 139. Mellor's essays are the most developed analyses of Shelley's critique of masculinist science. Marina Benjamin sets the science of *Frankenstein* in the contexts of women writers on science between 1790 and 1840, and of debates between subjective Romantic science and conservative, descriptive natural science (1991). Other critics who have offered similar suggestions include U. C. Knoepflmacher, "Thoughts on the Aggression of Daughters" in Levine and Knoepflmacher, eds., 1979, 103; Kate Ellis, "Monsters in the Garden: Mary Shelley and the Bourgeois Family" in Levine and Knoepflmacher, eds., 1979, 141–42; Paul O'Flinn 1983, 198, 204; Robin Roberts 1985, 17–18; and Hilary Rose 1994, 210–11. On the vitalist controversy as a context for Mary Shelley's exploration of science, see Marilyn Butler 1993, 12–14.

and calm, the silence of winter, and the life and turbulence of our Alpine Summers—she found ample scope for admiration and delight" (1985, 22). "With a serious and satisfied spirit," Elizabeth can achieve a union with nature because women *are* nature.[9] Mary Shelley allows a brief glimpse of a utopian relation with nature. But she also allows the problem of science simply to stand: from its illicit eroticism her story derives much of its anguish, from what Margaret Homans calls Frankenstein's "oedipal violation of Mother Nature" (Homans 1987, 135). And from Mary Shelley, as well as from their patriarchal culture, later women writers of science fiction inherit science as a problem for women writing science fiction. Some women, like Shelley, detail the story of science as illicit intercourse. Many modern writers, as we shall see in the first chapter, alternatively construct a utopian science based on different metaphors, Elizabeth's metaphors—a science that places women as subjects at its center.

Intimately connected with the construction of science in *Frankenstein* is the depiction of woman as alien. The women of *Frankenstein* are all marked by difference. Elizabeth—found, not created by the Frankenstein family— seems "of a distinct species, a being heaven-sent, and bearing a celestial stamp in all her features" (Shelley 1985, 20). She provides "diversity and contrast" (22) to Victor, and is herself "saintly," "celestial," Victor seeing her function only in terms of this difference: "she was there to subdue me to a semblance of her own gentleness" (24). After her unjust condemnation for William's murder, Justine admits, "I almost began to think that I was the monster that he said I was" (71). Thus women in *Frankenstein*, as in much of Western literary history, are marked as either angels or monsters, both outside of normative society.[10]

This positioning of woman as alien is most strikingly presented in *Frankenstein* in the character of Safie. Although Safie's father is "the Turk" (Shelley 1985, 110) and represents the unjust prejudice that Europeans hold toward non-Europeans, Safie herself, always called "the Arabian" (102, 104, 110), functions in the novel more as a representative of gender difference

9. See Elizabeth Fee 1978, esp. 13–14: "Science itself was often claimed as 'masculine' by anti-feminist writers. Men's minds were scientific; women's minds were unscientific.... Stuart Glennie, for example, argued that each sex had its own intellectual attitude and conception of truth: 'The whole history indeed, of modern progress ... is but one continuous triumphant vindication of the masculine and scientific, as opposed to the feminine and priestly, conceptions of truth'.... Eliza Lynn Linton then urged the men of England to stand by male 'science and dominion' rather than by female 'poetry and aestheticism.' "

10. See Sandra Gilbert and Susan Gubar 1984, 240 on "monster woman" and "angel woman"; Mary Jacobus 1982, 135 on "the female monster" as female sexuality; and Devon Hodges 1983, 157 on the female author as "an alien presence that undermines the stability of the male voice."

than racial difference,[11] revealing Shelley's own racial prejudice. Like Elizabeth and Agatha, Safie is "angelic" (101), with a "complexion wondrously fair, each cheek tinged with a lovely pink" (101). She has taken from her Christian mother not only her complexion, but also her "higher powers of intellect and an independence of spirit" unlike that of other Muslim women (108–9). But this independence marks her for Shelley as different not only from Muslim women but also from the other Christian women we see in this novel: Safie alone of the women travels and adventures, exploring foreign lands, like the men of the novel. At the center of *Frankenstein*, then, is a hinted motif receiving much elaboration in later science fiction by women: the woman as alien. In *Frankenstein*, the alienation is simply represented and not developed into story; or, rather, it is developed by similarity to another alien—the monster.

Like the monster, Safie is marked by lack of the dominant language, and it is through Felix's teaching of Safie that the monster learns the language. Indeed, it is through Felix's teaching of Safie that the monster comes to a recognition of his monstrosity—"When I looked around I saw and heard of none like me. Was I, then, a monster . . . ?" (Shelley 1985, 105)—a recognition that might equally apply to Safie. Their quests are similar: the monster "an imperfect and solitary being" (95), a "stranger" (118) seeking through friendship to establish "intercourse" (105) with the cottagers; Safie, a "stranger" (102) seeking through marriage to remain "in a country where women were allowed to take a rank in society" (109). Thus Safie, like the monster cast out by her father-creator, freely chooses to alienate herself because of her bitter resentment. Indeed, both Safie and the monster suffer from their fathers' broken promises of intended mates.[12] Like the monster, Safie must learn a new language, a new culture, in order to find a voice, in order to enter society. And like Safie standing, voiceless, outside European society, all the women of the novel stand outside the narration, alienated, but with their feelings displaced by Shelley onto the monster—as many recent feminist critics have shown.[13] The monster, like the women of the

11. On Safie as outsider, see Kate Ellis, "Monsters in the Garden" in Levine and Knoepflmacher, eds., 1979, 125; and Kate Ellis 1989, 183 and 203. On Shelley's racism in the portrait of Safie, see Gayatri Chakravorty Spivak 1985, 256–58. Safie begins a long line of racist portraits of Arab women in science fiction by women, including the women of the Drytowns in Marion Zimmer Bradley's Darkover Series, and the women of Ka'abah in Joanna Russ's *The Two of Them* (1986b).

12. This idea was suggested to me by Beth Newman's analysis of promises in *Frankenstein* (1986, 153–55), although she does not explicitly draw this analogy.

13. On the monster as woman, see Marc Rubenstein 1976, 192–93; Sandra Gilbert and Susan Gubar 1984, 232, 235, 237 and 240; Devon Hodges 1983, 162; Marcia Tillotson 1983, 167; Mary Poovey 1987, 102; Robin Roberts 1985, 21; Margaret Homans 1987, 140 and 142–43; and Laura Kranzler 1988–89, 44. For a wonderful reading of the female monster as threatening because of the "resilient pluralism" of "female strength," see Marie Mulvey Roberts 1993, 67.

novel, is willing to "be even mild and docile to my natural lord and king" (84), if he, in return, is allowed to be king in his own home, to be given "a female who will accompany [him] in [his] exile" (133). However, unlike the monster and like many alien women who follow in science fiction by women, Safie is not inferior to the man she seeks to reach an understanding with across cultural boundaries: she brings her own gift of cultural difference across the border, singing "to him the divine airs of her native country" (109).

In *Frankenstein*, the problem of woman as alien is thus introduced into science fiction but displaced onto the monster and not resolved. In many later works of science fiction by women, as we shall see in the second chapter, the woman as alien is returned to, explored, expanded as a symbolic category, and sometimes transformed through equality of respect for racial, gendered, and personal differences. For help in interpreting the taxonomy of alien women that later writers develop, I shall eclectically draw on feminist psychology. In any case, the woman as literally an alien, but a subject with a culture of her own, calls into question the naturalness of male superiority.

If the woman remains an alien in science fiction by women, only recently in the genre does she share and then usurp the male human point of view. In the structure of male narration in *Frankenstein*, we can recognize the difficulties for a woman writer.[14] The story is told in letters by Robert Walton to his sister. This narrator is an adventurer, wending his way further and further north towards the pole and to discoveries, further and further away from his sister-reader, Mrs. Saville ("Civil")[15] and her "gentle and feminine fosterage" (Shelley 1985, 6). This narrator also travels further and further from the writer's own experience, the writer — Mary Wollstonecraft Shelley — lending her own initials not to the adventurer but to the supportive reader — Mrs. Margaret Walton Saville. Like Robert Walton, the second narrator, Victor Frankenstein, is male, a scientist who adventures into unknown realms not geographically but in his laboratory. Again, the spaces he inhabits, and the story he tells, are exclusively male: he must journey to the all-male university in order to make the monster. Finally, we hear in the middle of the tale from the monster, who is also male, despite his parallels to Safie. He,

14. Other critics who have studied male narration in *Frankenstein* as a problem for the woman writer include Devon Hodges, who sees the woman writer as continually disrupting the male narration she constructs, therefore "destabilizing narrative" and "its patriarchal message" (1983, 156–57 and 160); Mary Poovey, who studies "the narrative strategy of *Frankenstein*" as allowing "Shelley to express and efface herself at the same time" (1987, 93); Beth Newman, who argues that "the monstrous narrative is domesticated" by the triple structure (1986, 158–60); Margaret Homans, who analyzes Mary Shelley's portrait of herself as " 'devout listener' to the conversations of important men" (1987, 151–53); and Anne K. Mellor, who describes "The structure of the novel" as "a series of screens around [Shelley's] authentic voice" (1988, 157).

15. U. C. Knoepflmacher, "Thoughts on the Aggression of Daughters," in Levine and Knoepflmacher, eds., 1979, 107.

too, would learn patriarchy, congratulating himself on his superiority when he learns the language much faster than the woman (103). For Mary Shelley, male narration, of course, was a solution as well as a problem, as it has become for many later women writers of science fiction: male narration allows a woman to enact vicariously a tale of adventure, a triumph of science, in a sexist society that rarely allows the female person such freedoms.

However, for a woman writer, male narration is not only a freedom but also a constraint: where can we put a female voice when so much of the text is spoken by men? In *Frankenstein*, Shelley experiments both with male narration, and also with strategies for resisting it and subverting it. Several of these strategies become important to later women writers of science fiction. First, she interpolates a female voice: Elizabeth writes Victor two letters (Shelley 1985, 49 and 171). As in later experiments with female voice in science fiction before 1960, Elizabeth's letters represent a misplacement in science fiction because they are bound so entirely to gender, to the middle-class domestic details of women's lives. Elizabeth could perhaps write a novel by Mrs. Gaskell, but she could not write the science fiction novel that Shelley herself writes. Second, Shelley resists male narration by providing the monster as an alien voice, an abnormal male with whom female readers can sympathize. With his insistent "Listen to my tale. . . . Listen to me, Frankenstein. . . . Listen to me" (84–85), the monster interrupts and resists the tale that Frankenstein is himself telling Walton. In this subversion of male narration, the monster expresses "the barbarity of man" (91), standing outside his gender but still retaining some of its privilege and authority.

Finally, Shelley retains the male narrator but forces him to undergo a distinctly feminine experience. Again, like many later women writers of science fiction, Shelley imposes a feminine story on a male narrator-protagonist.[16] In *Frankenstein*, Shelley dislocates the story of illegitimacy, placing it on Victor Frankenstein. She can thus turn male narration into a conversion story; she can also explore the feminine story in terms not only of guilt but also of triumph.

The fiction of an aristocratic woman conceiving an illegitimate child

---

16. Critics who have discussed Frankenstein as undergoing the feminine stories of childbirth or of sexuality, include Ellen Moers 1963–1977, 91–99 (reprinted in Levine and Knoepflmacher, eds., 1979, 77–87); Marc Rubenstein 1976, 165, 173, 7–8, 180, 187 and 192; Sandra Gilbert and Susan Gubar 1984, 227 and 232–33; Judith Spector 1981, 22; Burton Hatlen 1983, 32–35; Mary Poovey 1987, 105; John Dussinger 1976, 53; George Levine, "The Ambiguous Heritage of *Frankenstein*" in Levine and Knoepflmacher, eds., 1979, 8–9 and 11; Robin Roberts 1985, 17–18; Gayatri Chakravorty Spivak 1985, 255; Margaret Homans 1987, 145; Barbara Waxman 1987, passim; Anne K. Mellor 1988, 41–43; Alan Bewell 1988, 116–18; and Laura Kranzler 1988–89, 43–45. None of these critics, however, has discussed Frankenstein's story as sharing characteristics with the eighteenth-century narrative of women giving illegitimate birth.

was common among women writers who preceded Shelley.[17] We may take as representative of Shelley's inheritance the story of Lady Emilia in Sarah Scott's 1762 novel, *Millenium Hall* (1986, 166–174). The Lady Emilia, in a moment of passion, conceives a child by her honorable fiancé, Lord Peyton. The next day she realizes her terrible mistake, refuses to marry him knowing that he could never respect her, bears the child secretly and gives it up in order to protect her family honor, and spends the rest of her life in penance separated from both her lover and child. After her lover's death, she reconciles with her child, revealing the truth only on her own deathbed. She is heroic because she has enacted sufficient penance, but she has, of course, also punished all those connected with her: her fiancé has been deprived of a wife and her baby of both parents, nor can her daughter marry once she learns her monstrous lineage. The story of the illegitimate mother is the story of a lifetime of anguish as a result of her secret creation.

Similarly, Victor Frankenstein, in "a moment of presumption and rash ignorance" (Shelley 1985, 64), creates the illicit monster, "the life I so thoughtlessly bestowed" (76). Like the Lady Emilia, he immediately sees his error, deserts the monster, and spends the rest of the novel in anguished, secret penance for the "wretch whom I created" (82). Like the Lady Emilia, Frankenstein has a "dreadful secret" (173, 176) that obstructs his marrying (138). Also like the Lady Emilia, Frankenstein avoids making himself known to his child until he dies (202), and so Frankenstein enacts the penitent woman on his/her deathbed. This narrative technique is, in fact, cross-dressing: the male narrator is wearing the story of the fallen woman with an illegitimate child. By displacing this feminine story onto the male narrator, Shelley enables male conversion: Victor Frankenstein eventually "felt what the duties of a creator were" (85) — not in the form of financial responsibility like Lord Peyton, but in the form of responsibility for the "happiness" of the creature, like the Lady Emilia (85).

Victor's conversion comes too little and too late, but again Shelley's strategy is extended and experimented with in many later novels by women. In Marge Piercy's *Woman on the Edge of Time* (1976), for example, future science enables men and women to engender life in the laboratory, and men undergo in a utopian setting the feminine experience of nursing. In Jayge Carr's *Leviathan's Deep* (1979) and in Octavia Butler's "Bloodchild" (1984), men are raped by alien females, and in Butler's story, men undergo pregnancy, caesarean section, and all the physical and emotional dangers of unwanted childbearing. In Shelley's novel, the satisfaction of the story derives not from Frankenstein's androgyny, since he never lives up to the calling of

---

17. See, for example, Aphra Behn, "Adventures of the Black Lady" in *All the Histories and Novels* (1698), and Hannah Foster 1986, *The Coquette* (1797).

mother, but instead, from the revenge of casting a powerful male in a woman's story, from making at least one imaginary male feel what many women had felt (including, perhaps, Mary Shelley, her mother, and her half sister — all of whom bore illegitimate children).

In creating the genre of science fiction, in fusing the romance with enlightenment rationality, Shelley created a genre that gave women writers enormous freedoms — to be adventurers and scientists, imaginatively, to be vicariously what their society denied them. But Shelley also created a genre inheriting the limitations of her patriarchal society: a society in which women were denied education and careers in science, in which women were constructed as aliens, and in which men retained the license to speak and control the stories. These, I think, are the limitations that women writers of science fiction have surmounted throughout the twentieth century in an infinite variety of ways. Their achievements are the subject of the rest of this book.

In the remaining three chapters, I shall treat in sequence the ways women writers negotiate these three constraints. It is remarkable how similar are the responses among varied writers. It is equally remarkable how unique each writer remains: this is not formula fiction in a mechanical sense. Consequently, I have organized each chapter into two parts. The first part addresses in general the solutions of women writers and the paradigms that women, writing in the tradition of science fiction, developed in concert. The second part offers readings of two or three fictions by women in the context of these paradigms, demonstrating each individual's unique response to what she had inherited and exploring what she contributed to the ongoing conversation.[18]

In chapter 1, I examine the creation of utopian science as a solution that most women science fiction writers offer to the problem of masculinist science: a woman-oriented science that works in partnership with nature, that depends on the subjectivity and empathy of the scientist, and that is organized in a co-operative and non-hierarchical manner. At the end of chapter 1, I look at Naomi Mitchison's *Memoirs of a Spacewoman* (1962), Barbara Paul's *Under the Canopy* (1980), and Octavia Butler's "Bloodchild" (1984) as fictions that variously construct, reject, and question the paradigm being established in women's science fiction. In chapter 2, I analyze the taxonomy of variations on the woman as alien that women science fiction writers offer as revisions to confront male stereotypes: the alien erotic female, the woman as animal, the woman as machine, and the minority woman. At the end of the chapter, I look at Joan Slonczewski's *A Door Into Ocean* (1986) and Carol

18. I have been strongly influenced by Christine Gledhill's feminist elaboration of the cultural materialist argument that resistance is always possible because ideology is not seamless, but conflicting, and so offers points of resistance. In her study of film, Gledhill examines ways in which resistance is possible at multiple points — in production, within the text, and at reception (1994).

Emshwiller's *Carmen Dog* (1990) as novels that place the woman as alien in the center of discourse, thus negotiating a new vocabulary of character types for women's science fiction to work with and respond to. In the third and final chapter, I examine the strategies by which women writers cross-dress as male narrators and subvert masculine dominance of narration in science fiction as a genre: parodying the male narrator's voice, converting or punishing the male narrator with feminine experience, disturbing the category of gender by multiplying narrators and, finally, recasting the author's own problems with double gender through cross-dressed or androgynous narrators. At the end of chapter 3, I look at Cherry Wilder's *Second Nature* (1982) and Emma Bull's *Bone Dance* (1991) as fictions that en-gender narrative, exposing and resisting the universal male narrative voice.

Frankenstein's Daughters

1

Utopian Science
in Science Fiction by Women

I may be out of date, but I always feel that biology and, of course, communication are essentially women's work, and glory. Yes, I know there have been physicists like Yin Ih and molecular astronomers—I remember old Jane Rakadsalis myself, her wonderful black, ageless face opening into a great smile! But somehow the disciplines of life seem more congenial to most of us women.
                                                        —Naomi Mitchison,
                                                Memoirs of a Spacewoman

The conception of science central to any science fiction is important to its literary effects, because science fiction as a genre depends for its reading pleasure not only on literary form but also on the satisfaction of scientific problem solving. As I outlined in the introduction in my reading of *Franken-stein*, this aspect of the genre becomes problematic for women writers because our culture defines science as a masculine endeavor. The issue of women as objects not subjects of science is resolved by the greater portion of women writing science fiction in twentieth century United States and Great Britain through the imaginative creation of utopian science. Were these women writers to rely on the science of their (male) contemporaries, their careers as science fiction writers, their female heroes' careers as scientists, and even the kinds of worlds they inhabit—all would remain implausible. As Simon Weil, writing as a feminist Marxist in the 1930s, explains, "equality is destroyed" by a "monopoly...made up of...scientific processes" as surely as when it is made up of "the religious rites by which man thinks to win nature over to his side"; and, even if "those in possession of [the monopoly] are called scientists and technicians instead of priests," their "magical and technical secrets...give a hold over nature, armaments, money, co-ordination of labour" (1958, 64–70). Rather than extrapolating from contemporary science, a strategy male writers can adopt, women writers must thus imagine a major rupture with science as it exists in the twentieth century in order to present themselves as scientific authorities and their female heroes as scientists, and in order to build a technology conformable to women's experience. Like Naomi Mitchison in 1962, we must still look forward to a feminist revision of science. But Mitchison's fictional Mary, who "writes" the quotation that heads this chapter, looks nostalgically backwards, from her vantage in a utopian future, to a history of science full of women.

Although each writer constructs a different vision, we can describe the paradigm of utopian science in science fiction by women because the writers share this obstruction to women's writing and overcome it in similar ways.[1] In this chapter, then, I shall outline that paradigm, drawing frequently on feminist science theory and discussing science in women's science fiction as utopian in several ways: women's participation in science as subjects not objects, revised definitions and discourse of science, inclusion in science of women's issues, treatment of science as an origin story that has been feminized, a conception of humans' relation to nature as partnership not domination, and an ideal of science as subjective, relational, holistic, and complex. After establishing that paradigm, we can examine individual responses to it by close readings of the science in Naomi Mitchison's *Memoirs of a Spacewoman*, in Barbara Paul's *Under the Canopy*, and in Octavia Butler's "Bloodchild."

"Utopia" (following a Greek pun by Sir Thomas More — "no place" or "happy-place") is a fictional, idealized place or system, created as a dialogue with and critique of contemporary social assumptions and practices. "Uto-

---

1. To my knowledge, no one has yet attempted to describe the paradigm of science in women's science fiction, although there are very fine discussions of science in some individual works by women. See Patrocinio Schweickart 1983, 198–211, who reads Dorothy Bryant's *The Kin of Ata Are Waiting for You* (1971) and Sally Miller Gearhart's *The Wanderground* (1979) as critiques of male science and logic, Marge Piercy's *Woman on the Edge of Time* (1976) as a gynocentric revision of science, and Ursula K. Le Guin's *The Dispossessed* (1974) as recovering an ideal science that does not exclude women's experience. Also see Donna Haraway 1985, 65–107, who argues that "a cyborg world might be about lived . . . realities in which people are not afraid of their joint kinship with animals and machines, not afraid of permanently partial identities" (72), and finds utopian models for such a world in Joanna Russ, Samuel Delany, James Tiptree, Jr. (Alice Sheldon), John Varley, Octavia Butler, and Vonda McIntyre (97–99); Donna Haraway in 1989a, 295–312, further reads Octavia Butler's *Dawn* (1987) as "science fiction as primatology," or "a post-nuclear, post-slavery survival literature" (307); Haraway elaborates this argument to Butler's whole trilogy, *Xenogenesis* (1989) in 1989b, 376–82. Robin Roberts is more concerned with the history of the female alien than with science in science fiction by women, although she argues that "Feminist science fiction can teach us to rethink traditional, patriarchal notions of science" (1993, 2); Roberts further suggests that science fiction by women sets masculine science against feminine magic (92–99), drawing on myths of female goddesses and on theories of psi (103–7). Finally, Hilary Rose discusses science fiction by women as response to science writings and debates and utopian dreams of a future science in 1994, 208–29, treating mainly reproductive technology and science in Cavendish, Shelley, Gilman, Le Guin, Piercy, Russ, Gearhart, and Butler.

pian" is also a term used by many feminists (following earlier Marxist practice) to criticize visionary writing as politically ineffective.[2] Both senses of the term may apply to this paradigm of utopian science in women's science fiction. Because almost no feminist science exists, many women science fiction writers and feminist science theorists have imagined an idealized system of science, creating it as a dialogue with and critique of contemporary scientific ideologies and practices.[3] Sometimes this creation seems politically effective, a way of scrutinizing current science and of modeling alternatives. At other times these writers have been better at erasing masculinist problems in science than at imagining what new problems would result from feminist science; thus they also create a sense that feminist science is unrealistic as well as unreal. I would like to keep both senses of the term in mind during this examination of the utopian science of these women writers.

Women's Participation in Science

By the middle of the 1990s in the United States and Great Britain, participation by women in science education and in science careers is still discouragingly low. In the United States in 1984, women composed 20 percent of the scientific staff in medical research, 9 percent of the academic appointments (but only 1½ percent of the faculty) in chemistry, and held less than 5 percent of engineering doctorates. Primatology is currently the only science where women approach 50 percent participation. Although women made up 45 percent of the workforce in the United States in 1983, they represented only 13 percent of the science and engineering jobs. College training for women in the sciences decreased from the 1920s to the 1960s, and the increases from 1970 to 1985 seem to have stopped (Sheila M. Pfafflin 1984, Judith B. Moody 1989). In Great Britain in 1986–87, only 11 percent of the students in engineering at universities were women and only 9 percent of the students at polytechnics. In computer studies, the percentage of women students in higher education decreased from 24 percent in 1980 to 10 percent

2. For feminists who use the term "utopia" to disparage visionary writing by women, see, for example, Elaine Showalter 1977, 4–5 and 29; and Gayatri Chakravorty Spivak 1988, 271–313. For current Marxist recuperation of the term "utopian," see Tom Moylan 1986, 1–28; Peter Fitting 1987, 101 and 113; Angelika Bammer 1991, 48–59; and Hilary Rose 1994, 213–15.

3. On feminist science as utopian, see especially Hilary Rose 1994, 231. I do not mean to describe feminist science theory as monolithic, however. For good surveys of the range and the controversies in feminist science theory, see Evelyn Fox Keller 1981, 414–19, and 1982, 589–602; Joan Rothschild 1981, 65–74; Cannie Stark-Adamec 1981, 311–17; Elizabeth Fee 1986, 42–55; Hilary Rose 1986, 57–76; Sandra Harding 1986, 136–96, and 1991, 6–16; the essays in Women's Studies International Forum 12.3 (1989), in honor of Ruth Bleier; and Lynda Birke 1991. On the danger of generalizing about women's science fiction, I am also indebted to Veronica Hollinger 1989b.

in 1987 (Rose 1994, 109). In 1988, Carolyn Merchant estimated that of United States degrees in science, women numbered 10 to 30 percent in the life sciences, 5 to 15 percent in the physical sciences, and 1 to 6 percent in engineering (Merchant 1988). In 1992, women constituted only 18 percent of engineers and scientists in the United States; only 14 percent of the bachelor's degrees in engineering, 31 percent of the bachelor's degrees in the physical sciences, and 34 percent of master's degrees and 28 percent of doctoral degrees in science and engineering went to women (Lipson 1994).[4]

The pattern is already set by high school. Reasons that feminist scientists and educators have suggested for these differences between female and male participation include overt discrimination, lack of encouragement from parents and teachers, scarcity of role models, and teaching methods uncongenial to female students; the higher the level of education or profession, the more extreme the discrimination against women (Jane Butler Kahle 1985, and Jan Harding 1986). Consequently, a major goal of feminist science has been equal participation by women in science. As Hilary Rose points out, even equitable participation of women in science is a utopian proposition in our century (1994, 113).

The concern for increased participation by women in science has an analogous utopian reflection in science fiction by women. Although science fiction by men generally lacks women scientists, women writers have regularly pictured women as scientists.[5] In Ursula K. Le Guin's *The Dispossessed* (1974), the female physicist Mitis is Shevek's teacher and hero. Moreover, Shevek is partner to the biologist Takver, who "had always known that all lives are in common, rejoicing in her kinship to the fish in the tanks of her laboratories, seeking the experience of existences outside the human boundary" (Le Guin 1975b, 18). Jeanne Velory, black physicist and astronaut in Vonda McIntyre's *Barbary* (1986), studied Navaho as a prerequisite for advanced physics in graduate school, because of "the way it deals with time" (McIntyre 1988, 20). Velory tells us that she has been in space "a couple dozen times," most recently as a member of the *Ares* mission that "returned with samples of Martian life, the organisms that all the robot missions had missed" (16). She accompanies the ship on the hero Barbary's first trip into space, explaining that she is part of a welcoming committee for first-contact with an approaching alien spaceship. Seventeen-year-old Hellene Ariadne, research scientist in Cynthia Felice and Connie Willis's *Light Raid* (1989), experiments with GEM biots, "little genetically engineered memory chips"

---

4. On the historical origins of science as a world of men, see Noble 1992.

5. Darko Suvin has rightfully pointed out the lack of women scientists in American science fiction (1979, 268), but failed to add that he had read almost exclusively science fiction by men. On women writers picturing women scientists in the 1920s pulp magazines, see my essay, "Science Fiction by Women in the Early Pulps" (1994). See Hilary Rose's discussion of the womanless science fiction of the 1950s and 1960s in 1994, 215.

(7), and with hydra, "the little water-pumping and cleansing organisms" capable of tapping water that mechanical pumps can't reach (8). Sent to safety out of the war zone, Ariadne helps to save her country with her biots when the originals are destroyed by sabotage.

There are many other examples of female scientists in women's science fiction. Mary, the hero of Naomi Mitchison's *Memoirs of a Spacewoman* (1962), is a biologist and specialist in alien communication. Kira, a biologist, M.D., is "the *de facto* head of her department at the university" in Pamela Sargent's *Cloned Lives* (1972–76). Margaret, the black computer expert in *Up the Walls of the World* (1978) by James Tiptree, Jr. (Alice Sheldon) rescues humanity by her empathic communication with a space-sailing alien. Varian is a veterinary xenobiologist and co-leader of the expedition in Anne McCaffrey's *Dinosaur Planet Survivors* (1984). And Dr. Marguerite Chase provides medical care to the small Quaker village rescued from holocaust by aliens in Joan Slonczewski's *The Wall Around Eden* (1989).

Nor do the examples begin only in the 1960s, with increased interest in feminism, although the number of women scientists increases then in works by women. Clare Winger Harris describes a woman scientist in a 1928 short story, "The Menace of Mars": Vivian Harley, chemist and astronomer, college-educated, is assistant to her father in his home laboratory and, after marriage, assistant to her husband (1928, 582 and 584). Louise Rice and Tonjoroff-Roberts, in a 1930 short story, "The Astounding Enemy," picture Mildred Sturtevant, one of their heroes, both as a career scientist working side by side with her fiancé in the laboratory, and also as an officer in The Woman's Party (1930, 83 and 91). Working as a scientist to find a way to save humans from giant insect hordes, Sturtevant heroically endures capture by the aliens. This early interest in women scientists must result not only from changes in women's careers but also from the struggle to secure education for women in the sciences in the late nineteenth century.[6]

Women scientists as characters in women's science fiction are thus a legacy of the earlier feminist utopias, which represented the dreams of women for education in the sciences. In Margaret Cavendish's *The Description of a New World, Called the Blazing World* (1668), for example, the first act of the newly crowned Empress is to gather philosophers together to discuss natural philosophy. With the philosophers, the scientist-empress disputes, among many topics, the circulation of the blood (sigs. F1^v-F1^r), the nature of color and optics (sigs. G1^v-G2^r), and the tiny "flies" seen under a microscope that carry the plague from one person to another (sig. H3^v).[7] In

---

6. On the nineteenth-century struggle to gain education for women in the sciences, see Margaret W. Rossiter 1982, 1–99, and Carroll Smith-Rosenberg 1986, 245–96. I am also indebted to Carolyn Merchant 1988.

7. On Margaret Cavendish's fictional portrait of herself as a great scientist in a utopian world, see Lee Cullen Khanna 1994.

Mary Bradley Lane's *Mizora* (1880–81), chemists and mechanical engineers make the all-woman society a technological utopia where only machines do housework (1975, 45 and 58). And in Charlotte Perkins Gilman's *Herland* (1915), female geneticists have bred crop-producing and disease-resistant trees, as well as quiet cats that do not kill birds, while other women have developed as sciences fields not so regarded by Gilman's contemporaries — language development, sanitation, nutrition, and a kind of psychology-history (Gilman 1979, 31, 49–53 and 105).

Both the feminist utopias and later science fiction by women allow us to see the possibility of a history of women in science, not just a few great women who seem to be historical anomalies. In one of the earliest feminist utopias, *Three Hundred Years Hence* (1836), written when most women were still denied college educations, Mary Griffith shows a future historian relating a woman's invention of a new power that replaces steam, as well as restoring proper credit to Lady Mary Wortley Montagu, "for introducing into England the practice of inoculation for the small-pox" (Griffith 1975, 72–73). By linking our real past with an imaginary future as also past, Griffith creates the possibility, for herself as well as other women, of this tradition of women's science. (Mary Griffith, who lived until 1877, was herself the first published woman physicist in the United States.)[8]

Such a vision of restoring women to the history of science is shared by Naomi Mitchison in *Memoirs of a Spacewoman*, in the quotation that serves as headnote to this chapter. In 1962, when many colleges were still effectually segregated by race, and when want ads were still separated into male and female occupations, Mitchison presents, as a matter of course, the participation of women of color in science. By making a utopian future a nostalgic past, Mitchison establishes entry into science for her contemporaries, her women readers. What these utopian and science fiction writers offer, more than portraits of individual women scientists, is a revision of past and future science history that includes women as rightful participants. In this way, they share a goal with current feminist historians of science.[9]

Thus the fantasy of utopian participation by women in science works not

8. As well as short stories and this utopia, Griffith (also spelled Griffiths) published articles and a book on optics. Although no one has yet in print determined the utopian writer and the physicist to be the same person, Margaret Rossiter also deduces that she was (personal conversation, 6 March 1990). On Griffith as publishing material on optics, see Margaret Rossiter 1982, 322n. 22; and Lina Mainiero, ed., 1984, 184. On Griffith's works as a short fiction writer and utopian, see David Hartwell's introduction to Griffith's *Three Hundred Years Hence* (see Griffith 1975).

9. For recovery work in the history of women in science, see especially *Hypatia's Sisters*, coordinated by Susan Schocken, developed by the "Women and Science" class of the University of Washington Women's Studies Program (1975); Anne Fausto-Sterling 1981, 41–50; Margaret Rossiter 1982, 1–99; and Hilary Rose 1986, 57–76.

to ameliorate society's exclusion but, instead, to expose it. This criticism is especially clear in those fictions, like Naomi Mitchison's *Memoirs*, Louise Rice and Tonjoroff-Roberts' "Astounding Enemy," and McIntyre's *Barbary*, which criticize the exclusion from science of people of color as well as of women. In addition, women scientists are the necessary first step of imagining women as subjects of science, not as its objects. By putting women as subject at the center of science, these women writers change its nature, creating the paradigm of utopian science that is the focus of the rest of this chapter. In addition, by making their scientific women heroes, these women writers expand women's possibilities, celebrating the adventures of discovery that rational, educated women may embark on. As anyone knows who has examined current videogames, the absence of depictions of females results in girls and women being less interested in the technology. By focusing on women scientists as heroes, these women writers further broaden the readership of science fiction, making a space for women readers to identify with the adventures and discoveries of science. Such a space is crucial for science fiction, since the genre depends for its pleasure not only on the conventions of the romance, but also on the problem-solving capacity of science.

Definitions and Discourse of Science

As Hilary Rose, a British feminist scientist has pointed out, the definition and boundaries of science change. What constitutes science varies from culture to culture and era to era (1994, 98). Dietary control was a large part of ancient Greek and renaissance medicine, but when women scientists in the late nineteenth and early twentieth centuries studied diet scientifically, their chemistry was consigned to home economics departments, and was not awarded the title of "science" by male scientists (Margaret W. Rossiter 1982, 65–68). For Western culture, the boundaries of science are mapped onto the boundaries of masculinity, but this is not necessarily the case for other cultures. Cleaning labs doesn't count as doing science, but perhaps it should, since many other cleaning and organizing projects in labs do count (Rose 1994, 98).

That the definition of science is tied to cultural difference is often recognized by women writers of science fiction. For example, many present communication as a science. In Mitchison's *Memoirs of a Spacewoman* (1962), women make better scientific communicators than men because of their biological capacities for empathy. Moreover, in this future communication has been studied as a science, enhanced through technological means, and humans have established an elaborate technical process for contacting and learning to communicate with other species — even some of their own terran species, like dogs and horses. In Marion Zimmer Bradley's *The Bloody Sun* (1964), and many of her other Darkover novels, Darkovan experts learn to communicate telepathically through use of a matrix crystal; such study is called "matrix science" (114). In Sheri S. Tepper's *After Long Silence* (1987) scientists only discover the crystalline aliens as sentient beings when they learn how to communicate with them — through music (258). Other examples include Piercy's *Woman on the Edge of Time* (1976), where people use ritual gesture to communicate with cats; Suzette Haden Elgin's *Native Tongue* (1984), where the family of Linguists have developed a scientific system for learning alien languages and so a monopoly on translation; Sheila Finch's *Triad* (1986), which features as hero the xenolinguist, Gia Kennedy; and Janet Kagan's *Hellspark* (1988), where future scientists study language for its nonverbal as well as verbal aspects — "proxemics" and "kinesics" as well as linguistics — in order to communicate with aliens. These women science fiction writers piece together suggestions from linguistics, personal rhetoric, parapsychology, and studies of empathy and of gesture in order to envision a utopian future that would include scientific knowledge of communication. In their futures, communication, traditionally assigned as one of women's roles, is legitimated under the title (and the economic support) of science, and directed nonhierarchically to all species.

The discourse of science that we take as fundamental, Hilary Rose points out, is socially constructed and often faulty. For instance, Rose sees contemporary genetics as a reductionist discourse explaining the human body (1994, xiii), since it leaves out social and physical environments in order to detail the body's workings by internal mechanisms (Rose 1994, 172 and 203–4). Indeed, in contemporary applications of genetics, this discourse becomes a means of blaming the victim rather than treating the cause of social problems: we spend money not to clean up streams but to engineer salmon to be able to live with pollutants (Rose 1994, 194). Rose further suggests that the abstract language of science is a cultural choice that enhances and mystifies the political effects of science rather than a scientific necessity; she contrasts this abstract discourse to feminists' taken-for-granted embodiment, and their understanding of the social construction of knowledge (1994, 22).

We can see this sense of embodiment and connection to other life (rather than an abstract discourse of science) in utopian fictions by women science fiction writers. In these writings the most common metaphor for the relation of humans to nature is "the web of nature." In Marge Piercy's *Woman on the Edge of Time* (1976), for example, Luciente warns Connie, "We're part of the web of nature," when Connie urges putting immortality, or at least longevity, as a major goal of science (Piercy 1976, 278). And in Joan Slonczewski's *A Door Into Ocean* (1986), scientists facilitate nature's own processes, "when the web stretches . . . to balance life and death" (1987, 287). The metaphor of the web suggests women writers constructing a utopian vision of nature and science in partnership.

Hilary Rose further suggests that who speaks science is determined by gender and class: historically, women speak through men (1994, 100), and working class or colonized men can be helpers but not witnesses of science (1994, 100). In the example of Marion Zimmer Bradley's Darkover, previously cited, the exclusion of women from science, but not its class bias, is corrected through matrix technology. In fact, Bradley uses and naturalizes class bias to promote women's participation in Darkovan science, the *laran* or telepathy necessary to matrix technology appearing only in the aristocrats of Darkover, generally marked genetically by their red hair.

Finally, Hilary Rose also criticizes the deterministic language of Western science, which leads us to see science as unstoppable, autonomous, as inevitable progress along one line to truth (1994, 176). "Biology is destiny" is one particularly virulent version of this deterministic discourse (Rose 1994, 173).

In many science fictions, women writers substitute a language of choice (what Hilary Rose would call the "respectful and responsible" discourse of love in utopian science, 1994, 30, 39–42, 49 and 231) for this deterministic discourse in their science. As example, let us look at Judith Moffett's *The Ragged World* (1991). One way in which this is a feminist novel is its dispersement of narrative authority among many points of view. One point of view is that of a female heterosexual biologist with AIDS, whose story provides much of the science of this science ficton novel. Another way in which this is a feminist novel is its careful revision of the definition and discourse of science.

In *The Ragged World*, Moffett avoids the reductionist discourse of genetics that explains the body only through internal mechanics. Moffett's portrayal of science is attuned to the many social and environmental factors that influence how the body operates. In the near future of this novel, a serum to prevent infection with the HIV virus is discovered just about the time aliens make first contact with earth. After the discovery of the serum, the witchhunts for AIDS victims stop, but many are still left to struggle with the threat of the HIV virus, or with the disease. Although from our viewpoint in 1996, inoculation against AIDS is a miraculous breakthrough, Moffett tells a science fiction story not of a miraculous cure but, instead, of learning to live with the virus by controlling one's environment for co-factors that might precipitate the deadly state of the disease: "general health, stress levels, lifestyle" (Moffett 1992, 86). Moffett even makes fun of the story of rescue from aliens (1992, 111), although eventually her hero is helped by the aliens. But long before the aliens arrive, Nancy "Sandy" Sandford, the female biologist who is the "I" for part of this novel, completely redesigns her life in order to make herself less susceptible to her disease: she takes a lower-stress college teaching job rather than a university research job; she joins a therapy group and practices daily meditation; she schedules her life around a rigorous routine of lots of sleep and lots of exercise; and, as a biologist, she grows her own crops to prevent exposure to environmental poisons. In her later research on a plant virus, the biologist finds that resistance in muskmelons varies, too, in response to environmental changes — in this case, the weather (Moffett 1992, 108).

Rather than presenting an abstract discourse about science, Moffett, through her biologist, stresses embodiment and connection to life: when the biologist finally does an experiment, she does so with melons and squash in her own backyard, not in her college laboratory, not even with commercially popular varieties. She plans a five-year experiment to raise muskmelon to resist cucumber mosaic, a virus that kills many of the squash-related garden plants before they bear fruit. Her first year, her hybrid melon plants do not do very well at all against the virus, but the single promising plant that she saves stands as a metaphor for her own struggle with HIV: "That one had managed to struggle to maturity and produce a crop despite its illness" (Moffett 1992, 108).

What caused the biologist to begin this experiment is recounted by Moffett in what Rose would call the "language of love" that current science lacks and a utopian science would discover. Despite her careful control of her life, the female biologist had still found something missing — a sense of contributing to society with her science that was a dream of her college study before she was infected. She finds the goal that satisfies her because of a dream of Mendel:

> In my dream Mendel had the mild wide face with its little round-lensed spectacles of the photograph in the college biology text I used. . . . He bent tenderly over a bed of young peas, helping them find the trellis of strings and begin to climb. . . . He looked up and smiled . . . — a smile brimful of love — and handed me his notebook and pen. When I hung back, reluctant somehow to accept them, he . . . drew me into an embrace so warm and protective that it seemed fatherly; yet at once I was aware of his erection where it arched against me through the folds of cloth, and of his two firm breasts pressed above my own. (Moffett 1992, 98)

In this dream, Mendel offers the female biologist a vision of a science that cares lovingly for the living beings of this earth, and that welcomes women as well as men: he cares for the peas tenderly, he hands a woman his phallic pen, and he himself is androgynous. The biologist's own research responds to her dream of Mendel: she does science in the garden, not the laboratory; she cares lovingly even for the beetles that carry the cucumber virus to her melon plants; and she herself transgresses the boundaries of gender in more than her aspiration of science, cross-dressing in many episodes. The result is pleasurable immersion in the material stuff of her experiment, not abstract conclusions: she had "never been so busy or interested or free of anxiety" (Moffett 1992, 109). When she finally succeeds many years later in raising a melon immune to the virus, she describes it with sensual love: "Its rind is tan and thin, netted like the rind of an ordinary cantaloupe, and its flesh is a beautiful deep salmon-orange, as sweetly, intensely delicious as any I have ever tasted" (130).

Finally, Moffett presents us with a scientific discourse of choice, rather than determinism. Her biologist chooses what kind of science to do, chooses and plans her experiment carefully, arrives at as many answers as she does hybrids, and chooses which ones might be of use. Because of alternative technologies (especially sheets of netting used commercially to prevent the beetles who vectored the virus from infecting the plants), no one else was working on this problem: there was no inevitability to her discovery. She further figures the environment into her experiment, and so rejects the idea of a determined outcome, explained only by internal genes. Moffett thus presents us with a utopian science that revises the definition of our science and offers a different vision, of science as full of choice (and accident), practised by loving caretakers who speak a language that includes connections to external environment as well as internal genetic mechanics.

In A Door Into Ocean (1986), by the biologist Joan Slonczewski, we can see another particularly clear example of revised definition and discourse of science in science fiction by women. In this novel, Slonczewski imagines an all female society, the Sharers, inhabiting a planet entirely water-covered, with rafts for homes. Slonczewski thus immediately does away with gendered science on this world—all scientists are female. By centering women as subject in science, she also realizes that the location of science must shift: all Shorans are caretakers and most are parents sharing equally responsibility for children, so spaces for science (and for all occupations) are intertwined with living spaces. When an occupying army from another planet (with science very like ours) looks for laboratories, they cannot find them because the laboratories look just like homes (Slonczewski 1987, 212–13). Thus who speaks science in this society is very different from the hierarchy of scientific speech in our society, and ethical or strategic questions about the development of science are discussed in community meetings along with other social issues. In addition, since science is part of home, what constitutes science is very difficult for the intruding, more Western-like culture to ascertain. In this society, the person who cleans the labs is very likely the same person who does the science.

Indeed, because the relation with nature for this scientific culture is cooperative rather than dominant, scientific libraries look like natural plants, which look like home: "The ultimate library was kept within raftwood: every living cell of every raft held a library within its genes, millions of units within a cell too small to see" (Slonczewski 1987, 270). Shorans thus speak a discourse of science that is not abstracted but embodied in their environment: they see themselves as "part of the web" (352, 369). Having inaccessible the materials of a mechanical culture — stone, metals, and fossil fuels — Sharers have developed on their water world an organic-based technology that uses animals for motor-power and light but not for food, and revises many creatures through genetic manipulation to their own purposes. They redesign bacteria and viruses for healing, for restoring ecological balance when the invading army pollutes the ocean with toxins, and for helping humans adapt to their environment, as in microbes that help Sharers retain oxygen for underwater swimming (53, 64, 98, 142, 243, 318). In making women the subject of science, Slonczewski finds that science must be redefined and its boundaries redrawn: the result is a utopian science that puts science in the home, that reconceives the home as organically related to the natural environment, and that thus is controlled by an ethic very different from our current science — a sharing ethic.[10]

A biology professor at Kenyon University, Joan Slonczewski defines her own writing process as similarly organic. She writes, she claims, "the way Nature does it, by accretion," writing down little ideas: first naked women, owing to the benign environment, then bacteria that bleach out with light (both included in *A Door Into Ocean*). In writing as in science, for Slonczewski, "Nature is wasteful and profligate" — only 10 per cent is saved in evolution, and much more is lost than saved in writing.[11]

Thus in science fiction by women, as well as in feminist science theory, science is seen to need redefinition in order to fit the story of women's experience and needs. Its deterministic and abstract discourse is reformulated into a discourse that is embodied, and full of choice.

Women's Issues in Science

Women science fiction writers, like feminist science theorists, often recognize that contemporary science is "a human construct that came about under a particular set of historical conditions when *men's* domination of nature seemed a positive and worthy goal" (Ruth Hubbard, Mary Sue Henifin, and Barbara Fried 1982, 209). Like historian Elizabeth Fee, women science fiction writers often see our current science as "a major social investment," for

---

10. By calling Slonczewski's science "utopian," I do not mean to call it ideal; ecofeminists, for example, might very well object to animals used for motor power, or to microorganisms redesigned for mainly human purposes.

11. Interview with Slonczewski (1989a).

"any society will attempt to generate the kinds of natural knowledge which best fulfill its social, economic, and political needs." [12] This realization prompts women writers to include women's issues in their utopian science and to offer critiques of our current science for neglecting them.

Both the inclusion of women's issues and the critique of our society in science fiction by women grow out of a recognition that scientific "fields" and measurement of "progress" in science are shaped by social ideology. Through her character Luciente, for example, Marge Piercy in *Woman on the Edge of Time* (1976) explains that in 1970s U.S. culture "only huge corporations and the Pentagon had money enough to pay for big science" (278). In Luciente's future, a different society decides communally how to invest in science, thus producing different kinds of science: "The councils. The town meetings. That's how general questions of science get decided" (277).

Similarly, Cynthia Felice examines science as a construct by presenting in *Godsfire* (1978) a feline society like that of late nineteenth-century Europe, with science in transition from minimal organization to a state-funded and university-supported enterprise. However, in this alternative feline history, women are educated as scientists in equal numbers to men. The ambitious female geographer and astronomer, Heao, has her researches co-opted by the warrior king who conquers her city and who, in order to consolidate his conquest, invests in the new technologies offered by science. Heao's desire to be funded for her learning leads her to see this process as progress. In a further irony, in fact, she mates with the capitalist entrepreneur who has followed his king to exploit the new markets. Not only is science exposed as a social investment, but also, by contrast with a slave race (actually second-generation lost Terrans), some of the limits of the feline science are traced to their comparative physical limitations — especially nearsightedness. Thus this novel presents a complicated interweave of utopian science that includes women as scientists, with a critique of capitalist exploitation of science to enforce class and racial difference.

Two issues related to women, which may serve as examples, resurface frequently in twentieth-century women's science fiction, both issues dependent on viewing gender as a cultural and material circumstance affecting modern science. Throughout the century, these writers depict experimentation with alternative methods of reproduction; and, since 1980, they refute the gendered premises of sociobiology.

In imagining alternative methods of reproduction, women science fic-

12. Elizabeth Fee 1981, 387. On science as contingent upon the material and cultural circumstances of its production, see Thomas S. Kuhn 1970; Fee 1981, 386–87; Donna Haraway 1978, 49; Haraway 1979, 206–37; Haraway 1983, 199–201; Evelyn Fox Keller 1985, 4–12, 70 and 78–79; Cannie Stark-Adamec 1981, 312–13.

tion writers acknowledge the repressive economics of twentieth-century reproduction: women do all the labor of childbearing and much of the labor of
childrearing, but they are not paid or valued for that labor.[13] As in Shulamith
Firestone's utopian feminist polemic,[14] many twentieth-century science fiction writers wish to relieve women of this labor in order to free them for
education and for their personal work.

The women writers of the early science fiction pulps repeatedly offer
alternative technologies of childbirth and scientific child rearing.[15] In Leslie
F. Stone's "Letter of the Twenty-Fourth Century" (1929), humans "have
discovered how to make child-birth a safe and beautiful function" (1929a,
861), and in Stone's "Out of the Void" (1929), aliens have invented a way "to
bring forth a child without a woman's help" (1929b: II, 549). The utopian
from Lilith Lorraine's "Into the 28th Century" (1930) tells her time-traveling
lover that "Birth is entirely different from the horror that it was in your day.
The embryo is removed from the womb shortly after conception and brought
to perfect maturity in an incubator" (258). In Sophie Wenzel Ellis's "Creatures of the Light" (1930), embryos are immediately put in an artificial
glass womb — "the Leyden jar mother" — for "the human mother's body does
nothing but nourish and protect her unborn child, a job which science can
do better" (213). In Stone's "Women with Wings" (1930), childbirth has
become so dangerous that all women are temporarily sterilized while scientists work to produce "our young through mechanical agencies" (989). As
these quotations show, women science fiction writers of the 1920s and 1930s
saw in science the hope for the abolishment of childbirth and its grave
physical dangers: until 1930 and the discovery of antibiotics, one maternal
death occurred in every 150 live births in the urban United States (Ulrich
1990, 170).

13. Classic feminist analyses of the repressive economics of reproduction are Charlotte
Perkins Gilman's *Women and Economics* (1898 — see Gilman 1966) and Shulamith Firestone's
The Dialectic of Sex: The Case for Feminist Revolution (1970 — see Firestone 1982). In *The
Second Shift* (1989) Arlie Hochschild with Anne Machung document by statistical and inter-
viewing techniques the distribution of labor in recent two-job families: at best (even in marriages
based on liberal ideology) women do two-thirds of the housework and childcare, men at most a
third. These authors also explore the lack of a functioning system of gratitude in such marriages
and the resentment felt by both partners over the issue of who does what in "the second shift."

14. I take the useful term "feminist polemic," for those treatises defending women and
asserting their rights and dignities in the face of misogyny or patriarchal restrictions, from
Catharine Stimpson 1989, 160.

15. Compare the early feminist utopias, Mary Bradley Lane's *Mizora* (1880–81) and
Charlotte Perkins Gilman's *Herland* (1915), where all-women societies have naturally evolved
alternative methods of reproduction and where professionalized childrearing is highly valued in
the society, with much scientific study devoted to it; the narratives, too, center their attention on
children and mothering.

These science fiction writers often add a reduction of childcare owing to scientific progress to the utopian abolishment of the dangers of childbirth. Ellis's "Leyden jar mother," for example, also shortens gestation, and special rays quicken growth so that child raising occurs in under a year. In Stone's *When the Sun Went Out* (1929), children are raised in "the City of Children" (1929d, 13), and in Stone's "Men With Wings" (1929), children from the age of five are raised by "educationalists," not by parents (1929c, 74). Thus women writers of science fiction in the early pulps hope for science to abolish both the physical dangers of childbirth and also the tiresomeness of daily duties of child-rearing. Their radical alteration or abolishment of birth and childraising (and in Lorraine's case, of sex) frees women from domestic duties for further education and for public responsibilities. Their imaginative sciences of reproduction, however, may be said to be utopian in the Marxist sense, since these writers displace their critique of the unfairly gendered social organization into unrealistic hopes for a science that will make the problem disappear.

Women's science fiction since the 1960s, while continuing the emphasis on alternative methods of reproduction, more realistically imagines their effects, and more effectively uses their imagined differences to denounce patriarchal institutions. In Joanna Russ's "When It Changed" (1971) and Joan Slonczewski's *A Door Into Ocean* (1986), pairs of women reproduce by combining ova, a technology within reach of our contemporary science (although scarcely a priority for government grants!). In Naomi Mitchison's *Solution Three* (1975), scientists are raising the first generation of cloned leaders, and old-fashioned heterosexuality and biological birth are discouraged. In Marge Piercy's *Woman on the Edge of Time* (1976), fetuses are genetically formed and grown entirely outside women's bodies in an artificial womb, so that women and men will be equal even in this task. In Sherri S. Tepper's *The Gate to Women's Country* (1988), reproduction depends on artificial insemination. In the all-women societies, those reproducing by combining ova or by artificial insemination, women are freed from control by heterosexual relationships like those in our current culture. In these, and in other science-fictional feminist societies, the scientific transformation of reproduction allows women more personal freedom. It also facilitates more equitable distribution of childcare among all members of the community.

But, as the observer Genly Ai, in Ursula K. Le Guin's *The Left Hand of Darkness* (1969), records of the androgynous Gethenians, "The fact that everyone between seventeen and thirty-five or so is liable to be . . . 'tied down to childbearing,' implies that no one is quite so thoroughly 'tied down' here as women, elsewhere, are likely to be — psychologically or physically. . . . Therefore nobody here is quite so free as a free male anywhere else" (Le

Guin 1976, 93–94). These writers acknowledge negative as well as positive results of altered birth technologies, and they explore personal problems attendant on communal responsibility for raising children: relationships between mothers and children are central, as in the early feminist utopias, although the answers to problems differ. These works further admit the fears — especially those that homophobia reveals — that surround women's monopoly on reproduction. In Russ's short story, and in Slonczewski's novel, men are unnecessary since women reproduce and raise children without them. In Mitchison's *Solution Three*, the majority of people have chosen homosexuality since heterosexual reproduction is no longer enforced. In Piercy's novel, women have to give up childbearing as the last vestige of unequal power so that men will no longer need other powers in compensation; consequently, most people choose bisexuality. These novels thus identify and examine the homophobia that in our culture lies behind the collusion of science with heterosexual ideology — the fear that, if women are not "tied down" to childbearing and childrearing, all of us will turn to same-sex partners.[16] Such stories graphically present the dependence of science on definitions of gender from within the social context that contains it, and the value-laden character of science itself as a social enterprise.

A second women's issue has surfaced in the science of many works by women in the last fifteen years: refutation of the premises of sociobiology. In a now ironic passage in *Sexual Politics*, Kate Millett called "Attempts to prove that temperamental dominance is inherent in the male . . . notably unsuccessful . . . [in] endocrinology and genetics" (1987, 39). Since 1969, when Millett first published her revolutionary study of literature, many scientists, mostly male, have made their living pursuing the question of a biological basis for gender difference, and an entirely new science, sociobiology, has captured enough public attention to convince most people that there are "scientific" reasons for gender categories. Much of current feminist science theory is focused on the refutation of sociobiology and other forms of biological determinism or gender bias in science. In *Myths of Gender: Biological Theories About Women and Men*, for example, Anne Fausto-Sterling, among many women scientists to enter this controversy, refutes the ideas that there is a genetic basis for boys' superior math abilities and girls' superior verbal abilities, that there are more male than female geniuses because of genetic differences, that hormonal fluctuations inhibit females' ability to function rationally and decisively, and that male aggression is a naturally evolved

16. In a chillingly homophobic solution, Sherri S. Tepper's *The Gate To Women's Country* alternatively has science do away with the "gay syndrome": "The women doctors now identified the condition as 'hormonal reproductive maladaptation,' and corrected it before birth" (1989, 76).

biological characteristic that accounts for the inevitability of patriarchy and war.[17]

Sociobiology has also inspired several recent dystopias by women. In *The Handmaid's Tale* (1985), for example, Margaret Atwood imagines a future United States that has accepted as scientific truth, and as a rationale for excluding women from citizenship rights and property ownership, contemporary sociobiological arguments for the natural limitations of female intelligence and for traditional male gender roles as innate. The use of "handmaids" as childbearers for men whose wives bear no children derives from biblical history, but also refers to the concept in sociobiology whereby men maximize reproductive potential through multiple matings. "As we know," says the future academic analyst of Gilead in the epilogue, "the sociobiological theory of natural polygamy was used as a scientific justification for some of the odder practices of the regime, just as Darwinism was used by earlier ideologies" (Atwood 1987, 388). To Offred, the handmaid, the Commander condescendingly explains, "This way . . . [women] can fulfill their biological destinies in peace" (284); "Nature demands variety, for men. . . . It's part of the procreational strategy" (308); "All we've done is return things to Nature's norm" (285). In her critique of sociobiology, Atwood reveals the ideological underpinnings of our contemporary science, exposing them as value-laden and aligning them with the dogmatic right-wing religion of Gilead. Atwood's novel explores the experience of one woman, offered as a refutation of her containment in the role of childbearer, the only role she is permitted to have in this society and by this science.

Similarly Suzette Haden Elgin's *Native Tongue* (1984), *The Judas Rose: Native Tongue II* (1987), and *Earthsong: Native Tongue III* (1994) are set in a dystopic future United States, where arguments about women's innate inferiority justify repealing women's right to vote, where females legally belong to the male head of their household, and where Reagan's birthday is celebrated as a national holiday. *Native Tongue* begins with the constitutional articles that encode the sociobiology of women's inferiority: "The natural limitations of women being a clear and present danger to the national welfare . . . all citizens of the United States of the female gender shall be deemed legally minors" (Elgin 1984, 7). The male characters constantly enforce the

---

17. For other studies of gender bias in current science that include critiques of sociobiology or biological determinism, see Ruth Bleier 1986, 147–64; Elizabeth Fee 1986, 42–55; Hilary Rose 1986, 57–76; Lynda Birke 1986, 184–202; Evelyn Fox Keller 1986a, 16; Helen Weinreich-Haste 1986, 113–31; Sandra Harding 1975–1987, 283–302; Helen Longino and Ruth Doell 1975–87, 165–86; Bleier 1984; Marian Lowe "Social Bodies" in Hubbard, Henifrin, and Fried, eds., 1982, 91–116; Cannie Starc-Adamec 1981; Linda Jean Shepherd 1993, 23 and 47–49; and Hilary Rose 1994, 19–21 and 43. For an argument that feminists may appropriate sociobiology for their own ends, see Sarah Blaffer Hrdy 1981, esp. 1–15.

scientific authority of their gender bias: "The *man* goes to the trouble of impregnating the woman. . . . To attribute any credit to the woman who plays the role of a receptacle is primitive romanticism . . . and entirely unscientific. Re-read your biology texts" (Elgin 1984, 11). They also, as this passage demonstrates, enforce this ideology on younger men who might show sympathy for their wives.

Indeed, during the 1980s, the sex-role reversal science fiction novel, which had formerly been used by male writers to cry up the dangers of women on top,[18] has been appropriated by female writers to expose the dangers of biological determinism. They do so by exploiting the irony of a future science that enforces reversed sexual bias as natural, showing the male to be inferior or limited in his role. In C. J. Cherryh's *The Pride of Chanur* (1982),[19] for example, the spaceship captain Pyanfar sadly reflects on her society's conception of the male as innately limited by his gender: "Nature. Nature that made males useless, too high-strung to go offworld, to hold any position of responsibility beyond the estates. Nature that robbed them of sense and stability. Or an upbringing that did" (1982b, 189). As a result of this view of the male's nature, Pyanfar's society limits males' education and refuses them access to careers in space. In Pamela Sargent's *The Shore of Women* (1986), the aristocratic Laissa reflects on her studies of history and science: "men had a propensity for violence that was both genetic and hormonal. The biological well-being of humankind as a whole required some of their qualities, but the survival of civilization demanded that women, who were less driven and able to channel their aggressiveness constructively, remain in control" (Sargent 1987, 90). As a result of this view of the male, Laissa's culture separates men from women. Women live in walled cities, and men are denied the education and benefits of urban technology. Sons are cast out of the cities at age five. These writers do not reverse the roles assigned to females and to males; instead, they reverse the bias in education and science in their worlds, imagining the roles as innate and the male role as limiting, destructive, and inferior.

Similar strategies are employed by Jayge Carr in *Leviathan's Deep* (1979), by Cynthia Felice in *Double Nocturne* (1986), and by Octavia Butler in her trilogy *Xenogenesis*, where the aliens rather than future matriarchs analyse human males as inferior.[20] Thus these novels expose gender roles

18. On sex-role reversal science fiction by men, see the wonderful witty article by Joanna Russ, "*Amor Vincit Foeminam:* The Battle of the Sexes in Science Fiction" (1980).

19. Cherryh's *The Pride of Chanur* (see 1982b) is the first of a series of five, all of which reinforce the lesson of role reversal in the first novel: *Chanur's Venture* (1984), *The Kif Strike Back* (1985), *Chanur's Homecoming* (1986), and *Chanur's Legacy* (1992).

20. See Carr 1979, 8, 25, 63, 65–66; Felice 1986, 29; and Butler 1987–89: *Adulthood Rites* 252, 256, 432, 455, 463 and 488, and *Imago* 517. Perhaps this strategy of using role reversal to question determinism is also Sheri S. Tepper's in *The Gate to Women's Country* (1988), but

as social constructs and our science as dependent on our society's gender expectations, helping us to doubt biological determinism. Indeed, in Carr's, Cherryh's, Sargent's, and Felice's novels, a major plot movement is the liberation of males from these social stereotypes, while in Butler's novel, the plot moves to liberate all humans from biological stereotypes dependent on both sex and race.

Science as an Origin Story

As well as introducing women's issues into the science of their novels, women science fiction writers also offer feminized visions of science as origin stories. Recent feminist science theorists have argued that science is not a body of facts dispassionately accumulated; instead, it is an interpretation, a story, frequently an origin story. Ruth Bleier speaks for most feminist science theorists and, indeed, for most post-Kuhn historians of science, when she reminds us that "As social movements threaten the social order, . . . corresponding scientific theories emerge that implicitly defend the *status quo*" (1984, vii). Extending this perception, Donna Haraway argues that biology is itself a story, "the science of life, conceived and authored by a word from the father" (1981, 470), and that anthropology and other "life sciences and social sciences . . . [are] story-laden, . . . composed through complex, historically specific storytelling practices" (1986, 79). Similarly, Anne Fausto-Sterling argues that the embryology of male and female as it is currently taught is a "story" —an "active story about the male, a passive or absent story about the female," the "cultural story of maleness or femaleness imprinted on our knowledge" (1988; see also 1989). Thus feminist science theorists have pointed out that the sciences tell cultural origin stories that reinforce current sex and gender dogma, and feminist scientists offer contesting stories — especially at the moment in primatology and anthropology.[21]

It is not surprising, then, that women science fiction writers also offer contesting stories. As Hilary Rose observes, "By contrast with the masculinist utopias and science fiction, these feminist visions of transformed natural and social worlds emphasize again and again that technoscience is not inevitable; as part of culture it is socially constructed and can be reconstructed" (1994, 228). Again, such revisions begin with the feminist utopias. In Charlotte Perkins Gilman's *Herland* (1915), the race of women tell a different story about their origins than do the visiting American males — in both a biological and a religious sense. In imagining an all-woman society, Gilman has to revise biology. She does so not merely in a cursory way, by creating a race of

---

by giving eugenics as the means of rectifying the situation to her women, she makes us question their superiority in a different way.

21. Misia Landau 1984, 262–68; Haraway 1989b, passim.

self-reproducing women without men, but in a more significant way, by challenging the assumptions of Victorian biology and its father, Charles Darwin.

Gilman's radical critique of nineteenth-century evolutionary theory is worked out in *Women and Economics: A Study of the Economic Relation Between Men and Women as a Factor in Social Evolution*, (1898) and given imaginative shape in *Herland*. Thus, in *Herland* the women take their origin not from a mythical first man, but from a historical first woman — "she alone had founded a new race" (Gilman 1979, 57). In her earlier sociological treatise, Gilman argues that the human female, not the male, is the primary sex; that gender roles were necessary in evolution to feminize men, to force them into nurturing and protective roles for women and children, in order to bring them up to the level of women's development; that traditionally feminine roles are unnaturally limiting for women; and that we have now outgrown those roles and are ready for the next evolutionary stage (126–31, 329–30). Consequently, in *Herland* "these ultra-women, inheriting only from women, had eliminated not only certain masculine characteristics, . . . but so much of what we had always thought essentially feminine" (1979, 57). The women of Herland are more rational and quicker than the visiting American men, as well as more caring and nurturing. Gilman's vision, which she made clear in *Women and Economics*, is not a primitive biological determinism but a vision of social development potentially influenced by human rationality as analogous to physical evolution. The sex roles that the men in the novel (and Darwin) assumed are biologically determined are, in fact, gender roles culturally induced and therefore changeable.[22]

---

22. For a contrasting view, see Jean Pfaelzer, who argues that Gilman "reifies gender" by presenting the achievements of Herland as resulting from "woman's nurturing instincts" (1983, 327). On the superiority and dominance of males in humans, see Charles Darwin, *The Descent of Man and Selection in Relation to Sex*, chs. xix–xx. A few passages that would particularly have provoked Gilman are worth quoting: "Man on an average is considerably taller, heavier, and stronger than woman, with squarer shoulders and more plainly-pronounced muscles" (Darwin 1884, 551); "Man is more courageous, pugnacious and energetic than woman, and has a more inventive genius" (552); men's superior characteristics would have been developed by the "Law of Battle" (556), "both in the general struggle for life and in their contest for wives" (558); "Woman, owing to her maternal instincts, displays these qualities [greater tenderness and less selfishness] towards her infants in an eminent degree; therefore it is likely that she would often extend them towards her fellow-creatures. Man is the rival of other men; he delights in competition, and this leads to ambition which passes too easily into selfishness" (558); "a larger number of female than of male infants are destroyed [among barbarians], for it is obvious that the latter are of more value to the tribe, as they will, when grown up, aid in defending it, and can support themselves" (586). (The editions of Darwin cited are nineteenth-century ones that Gilman herself might have read.) For further examination of Darwin's sexism, see Elizabeth Fee 1978, 75–76, and 1981, 379–80. For the nineteenth-century United States debate on Darwin's ideas about the sexes, see Louise Newman, ed., 1985, 1–53. Gilman's revision of evolutionary theory to delete gender bias did not include a deletion of racial bias and, instead, seems to support

As important as her challenge to male dominance is Gilman's challenge to another basic tenet of Darwinian evolutionary theory: that life as a competitive struggle is necessary for human evolution.[23] In *Women and Economics*, Gilman argues that social evolution toward altruism is as natural to humans as organic evolution to all beings (1966, 323–25). In *Herland*, where society is presented as having progressed beyond the United States male-dominated culture, the women are astonished to hear that competition in the men's world is thought a major motivating force for human industry and progress (Gilman 1979, 60). For the women, the means of development is "the literal sisterhood of our origin, and the far higher and deeper union of our social growth" "the fullest and subtlest coordination . . . [and] unanimity" (66–67). Visiting the state of Herland forces the male narrator to question his own Darwinian interpretation of what is natural: "here we found that the pressure of life upon the environment develops in the human mind its inventive reactions, regardless of sex; and further, that a fully awakened motherhood plans and works without limit, for the good of the child" (102). In Herland, the principle that "Life is a struggle, has to be" is "masculine nonsense" (99); and "based on the full perception of evolution . . . life to them was growth" (102). Herlanders have a different scientific story to tell, Gilman suggests.

Contemporary science fiction writers still find it necessary to challenge and revise Darwinism. In *Pennterra* (1987), Judith Moffett creates a sentient planet where all living beings are attuned to each other, where sex is constant and nonmonogamous during mating season but each living thing reproduces only once, and where each organic being offers itself as food when its life cycle is complete. "If nobody competes for food or sex," wonders Bob, a human observer, "then what is the evolutionary mechanism here? Because it can't be natural selection" (Moffett 1988, 130). Instead of our Darwinian biology, "every creature madly *struggling* to survive (eat, avoid being eaten) and to beat out the competition for breeding opportunities," Bob reflects, Pennterran life needs a biology to explain this "slow, coordinated dance of inter-and intraspecific cooperation" (131–32). Perhaps empathy is the key, Bob decides (132). These human scientists thus come to realize that they need a different science—a different scientific story—to explain alien life in this alien ecosystem.

---

eugenics and racism; on this point I am indebted to by Susan Sniader Lanser's lecture, "Feminism's 'Yellow Wallpaper' and the Transformation of Literature" (1988), later published as "Feminist Criticism, 'The Yellow Wallpaper,' and the Politics of Color in America" (1989).

23. On life as a competitive "Struggle for Existence," necessary to evolution, a "Survival of the Fittest," see Darwin 1899, *The Origin of Species by Means of Natural Selection*, I: 5, 77, 79, 108, 131–32 and 160; and II: 278. On the influence on Gilman of Herbert Spenser's extension of Darwin's ideas, see Ann J. Lane's "Introduction" to *Herland* (Gilman 1979, viii). For a good review of current feminist revision of evolution, see Ruth Bleier 1984, 115–61.

In *Emperor, Swords, Pentacles* (1982), Phyllis Gotlieb offers not only one revision of science as origin story, but a multitude. Each interplanetary culture, in fact, begets a different scientific narrative to explain it: there are stories for the Ungrukh, the Qsaprinli, the Praximpfi and, hovering in the background, for humanity, intruding in the novel as members of the capitalistic imperialistic megacorporation, GalFed.

The major culture invoked in Gotlieb's novel is the Ungrukh, a race of red panther-like cats inhabiting a desert planet, and the subject of a series of which *Emperor, Swords, Pentacles* is the middle novel (also including *A Judgment of Dragons* 1980, and *The Kingdom of the Cats* 1985). The Ungrukh explain their origins by a religious myth. But the Qumedni, a race of beings composed of energy rather than matter, one of whom wishes to intervene or perhaps control the Ungrukh, explain Ungrukh culture as the result of Qumedni bioengineering. Gotlieb does not resolve the puzzle of whose story is "true," but instead leaves them at odds. She thus foregrounds the motives that impel cultures to offer scientific stories about their origins: it is useful for the Ungrukh to explain their evolution as independent of other races, while it is useful to the Qumedni, who desire to enforce a relationship with the Ungrukh, to claim a prior relationship in their origin story. Here "science" and myth are equated, both used for political ends in a contest of dominance.

In *Emperor, Swords, Pentacles*, the action is set in the culture of the Qsaprinli, an amphibious race who developed mainly in tidal pools and still carry waterskins with them on their backs. Their version of origin story is Gotlieb's comment on Darwinian evolutionary theory. Qsaprinli believe that they evolved onto land because of population pressure and competition from their own species; that they evolved intelligence after developing fingers to dig for water in dry areas, which led to a language of vocal and gestural symbols; but that they developed civilization when "one venturer . . . picked up a stone in his small exact fingers and crept up behind [his enemy] . . . to bash his braincase in. . . . From there it was a short step to picking up stones and piling them in forts against attack. And civilization got born" (Gotlieb 1982, 70). As does the Darwinian model, the Qsaprinli model postulates evolution as a result of competition for scarce resources, and language as a result of group participation in food-gathering behavior. Unlike the Darwinian model for humanity, the Qsaprinli model of evolutionary development posits social tolerance as more advantageous than aggressive competition. Thus the discovery of weapons for the Qsaprinli is the end of warfare, not the beginning of its development. The Qsaprinli are, in fact, the most peaceful of the multitude of cultures explored in the novel. Both male and female Qsaprinli participate in raising children, the males carrying the infants in pouches after they have been fertilized in the females' eggsacks. Perhaps their peacefulness originates, Gotlieb may be suggesting, in their lack of overspecialization by gender. In any case, Gotlieb's variations on human evolution for the Qsa-prinli suggest not only that human evolution might have been different, but also that human evolution may be interpreted differently — perhaps the development of lethal weapons was not the impetus into civilization at all, but instead building walls to protect oneself from such weapons.

A culture on the margins of the novel, however, which most clearly demonstrates Gotlieb's purposeful play with science as origin story, is that of the Praximpfi. The Praximpfi are "the only organic shape-changing species," their culture constituting "a world of mystics who changed into their native plant and animal forms in religious ritual," "very jealous of their secrets" so that no outsider "knew what any of them really looked like" (Gotlieb 1982, 35). Gotlieb posits a culture, then, which lies outside the bounds of Western science simply because it contradicts — even deconstructs — all the assumptions of such a science. The culture is not known, is not knowable because the members guard their secrets and commit suicide if caught (35), and the mystical tenets of the culture stand in direct opposition to Western values of objectivity, rationality, knowability, and even the trustworthiness of physical data. Such a culture then becomes the test case for the xenobiologists of GalFed's Western science: if it can be explained, Western science is sufficient as origin story and we do not need other versions. But Gotlieb does not let Western science win: the planet

> Praximpf never seemed quite to obey the laws of nature. This was one reason for XenoBi's enthusiasm about it. Sometimes the globe was completely obscured by cloud, and sometimes what was seen from space did not coincide with what was found on land. The continents tended to slither, if they indeed were land-masses, and the temperature went cold at the equator and hot at the poles when the inhabitants wanted it that way. Seas changed from marsh to abyss at a yawn. Yet XenoBi did not believe that Praximf slid out completely from the fences of theory that contained [other] species and worlds. . . . All would be disclosed in the fullness of time — or maybe not. (Gotlieb 1982, 255)

By leaving unresolved the quest of Western science to explain in Western terms Praximpfi culture, Gotlieb contests the claims of science as a dominant discourse. If Western science cannot explain Praximpfi, then the stories science attaches to other cultures are also called into question. Praximpfi have no use for Western science, since it would negate their entire way of life. Gotlieb thus writes subjectivity into utopian science by suggesting that scientific truth might be judged as much by its usefulness to a culture as by its ability to explain physical evidence.

Rebecca Ore further suggests in *Becoming Alien* (1988), the first novel in her trilogy, that we must learn to accept multiple versions of origin stories as science if we are to learn to be tolerant in a multicultural universe. At a party on a distant planet, former enemies, still uncomfortable with each other, tell their culture's origin stories (1988, 126–29). Edwir Hargun, member of the ape-like Yauntry species, tells the "story" of molecules accidentally jarred together as cause of the origin of life—the story we would take as "science." Karriaagzh, member of a bird-like species, relates his theory that the development of life is inevitable, that mobile intelligence is what all molecules long to become—species may die, but intelligence lives on. And Black Amber, member of the bat-like Gwyng species, offers an origin story about time (not space or life) built around the Gwyng reproductive practice of pouching, coming out of and returning to the black hole of time. In the future, this novel suggests, life will become so complicated that we will not have the luxury of rigidly sticking to one scientific theory and discarding others that may be useful. We will need to incorporate even conflicting visions, not to find "truth," but simply to be able to continue life.

In Gotlieb's and Ore's novels, as Donna Haraway argues for science in general, "What determines a 'good' story" is partly decided by "the utopian quality" of the sciences, the "available social visions of . . . possible worlds" (1986, 80). There may be many stories and many sciences, instead of simply one.

Partnership with Nature in a Subjective, Relational Science

The transformation of science in science fiction by women is founded on a revision of a Western perception of nature. Feminist science historians have shown that male scientists from the seventeenth century on have conceived of nature as a potentially unruly woman to be mastered and penetrated for her secrets. "The image of nature that became important in the early modern period was that of a disorderly and chaotic realm to be subdued and controlled," argues Carolyn Merchant (1980, 127). Scientists understand nature as associated with women, according to Hilde Hein, and "Generally the sense of 'nature' which is assimilated to women is a primitive, disorderly state of affairs which must be overcome (by reason) and 'civilized.' Its spontaneity and irrationality are . . . fearsome, and so its control and subordination are regarded . . . as a spiritual mission and ethical imperative" (1981, 372).[24]

As an alternative to the destructive view of nature in traditional male science, feminist science theorists posit a revision of nature and humanity's

24. On this view of nature, see also Elizabeth Fee 1986, 44; Evelyn Fox Keller 1985, 30–34, 55, 64, 78, 124; Helen Weinreich-Haste 1986, 117; and Kirkpatrick Sale and Carol Moore 1987, 302–5. On the masculinist sexual imagery of the scientist penetrating and mastering nature, see also Hilde Hein 1981, 374; and Brian Easlea 1986, 139–50. I am also indebted to a lecture by Keller, 1989.

relation to her. "Women's identification with earth and nature," argues Joan Rothschild, must form "the basis for transforming our values and creating new ecological visions" (1981, 71). Such a new science would stress connection to, not domination over nature (Haraway 1985, 68); it would present nature not as passive but as resourceful (Keller 1985, 171); its structure would be "antihierarchical" (Merchant 1980, 140); and it would stress "the feminine value of harmony with nature" (Rose 1986, 65). Such a science would seek "new and pacific relationships between humanity and nature and among human beings themselves," argues Hilary Rose (1986, 59); and according to Keller, it would seek "not the power to manipulate, but empowerment—the kind of power that results from an understanding of the world around us, that simultaneously reflects and affirms our connection to that world" (Keller 1985, 166). According to Linda Jean Shepherd in Lifting the Veil, such a feminist science would be based on "openness to listening to nature and responding as in a conversation or as a cocreator with nature" (1993, 78).[25]

Such a vision of nature has long been implicit in women's science fiction, as we saw in the analysis of views of nature in Frankenstein in the introduction. In Andre Norton's Breed to Come (1972), humans return to an earth that their race had almost destroyed, and tell the intelligent felines who have risen to civilization, "Do not try to change what lies about you; learn to live within its pattern, be a true part of it" (Norton 1981, 287). The former Terrans are warning the current ones not to produce a destructive technology but to develop a partnership with nature. When humans arrive on the planet, in Judith Moffet's Penterra (1988), the native hrossa forbid them to expand beyond the initial valley of their landing site, and further forbid use of machinery except for some limited travel—none for agriculture or domestic convenience. The hrossa are protecting the finely balanced ecology of their sentient planet from human scientific intrusion.

Men's and women's views of nature in works by women are often sharply divergent. In Pamela Sargent's The Shore of Women (1986), women's scriptures record "the spirit of Earth, in the form of the Goddess" speaking to women: "You gave men power over Me, and they ravaged Me. You gave them power over yourselves, and they made you slaves. They sought to wrest my secrets from Me instead of living in harmony with Me" (Sargent 1987, 94). As a result, in Sargent's novel women assume political power and enforce

---

25. See also Elizabeth Fee, who observes that feminist psychologists argue that contemporary men show an inability "to integrate self-creative activity with a primary concern for others," and so an "inability to organize technology for human ends" that has produced "a scientific culture which . . . can only be recovered for humanity through a recovery of that part of human experience which has been relegated to the female" (1981, 382); and Hilary Rose, who urges feminist scientists to create "a new science and technology not directed toward the domination of nature or of humanity as part of nature" (1987, 273); as well as the rest of the chapter on "Receptivity" in Shepherd 1993, 78–95.

separation from men as well as limits on technology and reproduction to keep the ecology in balance.

Besides changing the conception of nature, by including women in science, feminist historians and theorists of science have argued, a revised science would express the culturally different qualities assigned to women. A feminist science will acknowledge subjectivity in its methods; it will look at problems not just analytically but also holistically; it will aim for the complex answer as best and most honest; and it will be decentralized and organized cooperatively. In all these ways, a feminist science is utopian, since these conditions, values, and goals do not describe contemporary science. Similarly, women writers of science fiction, in order simply to include women in their alternative sciences, have been unable to extrapolate from current science; instead they have had to reimagine science.

In feminist science theory, subjectivity as an ideal includes feelings, intuition, and values. "A feminist epistemology [for the sciences]," writes Hilary Rose, "insists on the scientific validity of the subject, on the need to unite cognitive and affective domains; it emphasizes holism, harmony, and complexity rather than reductionism, domination, and linearity" (1986, 72). In *A Feeling for the Organism: The Life and Work of Barbara McClintock*, Evelyn Fox Keller reads Barbara McClintock's scientific career as an example of allowing "the objects of . . . study [to] become subjects in their own right" (1983, 200), thus "fostering a sense of the limitations of the scientific method, and an appreciation of other ways of knowing" (201). A study by scientist Jan Harding suggests that girls in our society who choose scientific careers recognize more often than boys do that "science has social implications" (1986, 160) and that girls choose science as a means of developing "relatedness, capacity for concern, and an ability to see things from another's perspective" (165). Subjectivity in science must also encompass values and ethical context: science must be "context dependent" according to Carolyn Merchant (1988); connected to "social implications," according to Jan Harding (1986, 160); based on "relational thinking," according to Hilde Hein (1981, 372); grounded in women's experience and, so, a "labor of love," according to Hilary Rose (1987, 275).[26]

In the utopian futures of women's science fiction, subjectivity in all its aspects — intuitions and empathy, emotions, and values — is incorporated into good science. In Sheila Finch's *The Garden of the Shaped* (1987), Tagak continually reminds the other scientists who experiment with human genetics that "there exists no such thing as an impartial observer" (1987, 20), that "the experimenter becomes part of the experiment by the inexorable laws of the universe" (123). As the scientist Evelyn Fox Keller points out, the "questions

26. On subjectivity as valuable in feminist science, see also Linda Jean Shepherd 1993, 96–123 (on subjectivity), and 203–24 (on intuition).

asked about objects with which one feels kinship are likely to differ from questions asked about objects one sees as unalterably alien" (1985, 167). In this connection, a host of science fiction novels by women, in which the hero intuits the intelligence of another life form, are based on establishing communication with the aliens before "developers" destroy them and their planets — among such recent novels, Anne McCaffrey's *Dinosaur Planet Survivors* (1985), and Sherri S. Tepper's *After Long Silence* (1987). In Janet Kagan's *Hellspark* (1988), the hero rescues the planet from merchants hoping to harvest organic superconductors from its forests by proving that the native Sprookjes are an intelligent species who need protection: they can communicate, participate in gift exchange, and practice art in organic landscaping forms.

Along with intuition, emotions are given special place in the science of women's science fiction. Margaret, the black computer expert in *Up the Walls of the World* (1978) by James Tiptree Jr. (Alice Sheldon), at first seems to have succeeded in her scientific career by her machine-like repression of emotions; but it is her empathy, her feeling for the alien in the machine, that allows her to interact successfully with her computers and, later, with the giant space-sailing alien who threatens the destruction of earth. Tiptree imagines the union of logic and emotion, human and alien, in computer terms: "The strange symbiosis holds, the improbable interfaces mesh and spread. From spacebourne vastness through a small unliving energy-organization to the residual structure of a human mind with an odd relation to matter, information cycles. And power" (Tiptree 1978, 245). Similarly, in Barbara Paul's *An Exercise for Madmen* (1978), the feelings that the hero Jennie Geiss brings to her union with a machine, as the brain of a computer, will heal the scientific community and allow progress again.[27] In addition, large numbers of science fiction novels by women raise empathy itself to a science — especially the Witch World Series by Andre Norton and the Darkover Series by Marion Zimmer Bradley, but also such diverse works as Sally Miller Gearhart's *The Wanderground* (1979) and C. J. Cherryh's *Serpent's Reach* (1980).

For women science fiction writers, science also includes ethical contexts and values. As a result, women writers do not see "pure" or unapplied science as a necessary goal; instead, they imagine application as part of the process

27. On Barbara Paul's novel, see Jane Weedman Lynch 1987, 340–44, esp. 343: "The downfall of the society, it is clear, is not the expression of passion or emotion, but the repression of it — a total commitment to reason, to intellect which denies a place for the expression of the emotions." Many science fiction works by women also make fun of male scientific objectivity: see, for example, the film written by Floyd Byars and Laurie Frank and directed by Susan Seidelman, *Making Mr. Right* (1987), in which the male physicist loses connection with his world (at the end, literally) because of his view of science as based on objectivity, detachment, and repression of emotions; the android that he manufactures turns out to be more human than he.

of scientific inquiry. This way of thinking about science extends backward to the feminist utopias. In Mary Bradley Lane's *Mizora: A Prophecy* (1880–81), where the narrator compares her own world with the utopian one she discovers, she sees science as a means of social reformation: "Pallid and haggard women and children, working incessantly for a pittance that barely sustained existence, was the ultimatum that the search after the cause of cheap prices arrived at in my world, but here it traveled from one bevy of beautiful workwomen to another until it ended at the Laboratory where Science sat throned, the grand, majestic, humane Queen of this thrice happy land" (Lane 1975, 58). In Charlotte Perkins Gilman's *Herland* (1915), Herlanders develop science in the context of their limited space and in relation to the value they place on motherhood and children: genetics, for example, is developed in order to breed crop-producing trees; cats are bred who do not kill birds; and large animals have been allowed to die off because the country is limited in space. In contrast to these practices, the men from the United States describe their passion for dogs, yet admit that dogs spread rabies and bite children (Gilman 1979, 49–53). Thus in Gilman's *Herland*, genetics is applied not through the traditionally masculine values of hunting, competition, and individuality, but through the traditionally feminine values of nurturing and, more generally, creating an environment where no one will be hurt, "a pleasant garden, . . . but most of all . . . a cultural environment for their children" (94).

In the early *Mizora* and *Herland*, humans are still presented as the point of reference for ethical decisions, even by women writers. In later novels, women widen the context to include all species. In *The Dolphins of Altair* (1967), for example, Margaret St. Clair imagines a future where humans, because their destructive science poisons the oceans with radioactive and other wastes and because they torture and kill other species for experimental and military reasons, are deposed from their dominance by dolphins. Several more civilized humans achieve an empathic communication with the dolphins, aiding them in stopping the destruction caused by modern science. In Marge Piercy's *Woman on the Edge of Time* (1978), the people of the future Mattapoisett decide in town meetings issues concerning the direction of science, discussing "What could be consequences of the whole yin and yang of it" (Piercy 1976, 277).

For women science fiction writers, a science that incorporates subjectivity and sees humans in partnership with nature would also emphasize relational thinking and acknowledge a responsibility to understand the complexity of the whole. In Piercy's utopian future, Luciente explains that "We're cautious about gross experiments. 'In biosystems, all factors are not knowable.' First rule we learn when studying living beings in relation" (Piercy 1976, 97). "Elegant," a complimentary term in scientific culture for the explanation that offers simplicity with explanatory power, is not a compliment in science fiction by women, which values complexity. In Ursula K. Le Guin's *The Dispossessed* (1974), for example, physics is presented as based on relations, as aiming at complexity. The physicist Shevek reaches for a theory of time that relates the cyclical to the linear: "We don't want purity, but complexity," he urges; "A complexity that includes not only duration but creation, not only being but becoming, not only geometry, but ethics" (Le Guin 1975b, 182).

Such a new science, not analytical and objectively distanced, but holistic and connected to people and other living beings, would necessarily be organized differently from our current science. According to Joan Rothschild, it would question our current "technological ideals": "that bigness equals efficiency, that a high degree of specialization is always necessary, that value be placed on quantity criteria, that specialist elites must be created" (1981, 71). Such questioning is worked out at length in Naomi Mitchison's second science fiction novel, *Solution Three* (1975). There a future earth that has bred specialized plants finds its entire flora threatened by a virus. Its scientists must then be sent back to nature to gather a larger, less specialized gene pool. And much women's science fiction — from *Herland* (1915) to *Woman on the Edge of Time* (1975) to *A Door Into Ocean* (1986) — imagines technology as depending not on bigness but on a sustained yield, one which does not deplete the earth and its resources. "Our technology did not develop in a straight line from yours," says Luciente in Piercy's novel; "We have limited resources. We plan cooperatively. We can afford to waste . . . nothing. You might say our — you'd say religion? — ideas make us see ourselves as partners with water, air, birds, fish, trees" (Piercy 1976, 125).[28]

An emphasis on a science situated in a decentralized, nonhierarchical society, and operated as a craft industry creates a special problem for recent women novelists, who seem to traditional science fiction fans to be antiscience reactionaries. In Ursula K. Le Guin's *Always Coming Home* (1985), computer technology in the postholocaust Kesh society is used mainly for aesthetic purposes, and other sciences and technologies are developed in homes and through apprentice systems. In Slonczewski's *A Door Into Ocean* (1986), as we saw earlier in this chapter, the invaders from Valedon have trouble recognizing the scientists and the laboratories, since scientists are not labeled by dress, and science is practiced as a craft industry with organic rather than mechanical tools. The placing of science in the homes of these peoples is important symbolically for the authors: the place of science indicates communal responsibility for its outcomes.

28. On sustained yield economics and its relation to feminism, see Hazel Henderson 1978 and 1981. On the passage in Piercy's novel, see Hilary Rose 1986, 59.

Naomi Mitchison, Barbara Paul, and Octavia Butler: Questioning the Paradigm

No individual fiction reflects a paradigm in its entirety, the paradigm being a set of conventions of representation that is expressed in a group of stories and that defines a literary tradition — or a scientific tradition. In the remainder of this chapter, I shall look at two novels and a short story as participating in and responding to the paradigm of utopian science in science fiction by women. I have chosen Naomi Mitchison's *Memoirs of a Spacewoman*, Barbara Paul's *Under the Canopy*, and Octavia Butler's "Bloodchild" because they reflect a range of possible responses to such a paradigm of utopian feminist science. Naomi Mitchison struggles with the terms of her scientific utopia for women as she builds it, distrusting and hoping at once. Barbara Paul elaborates a critique of masculinist science by placing white women at the center of her scientific story and implicating them in its discourses. And Octavia Butler creates the feminist utopian vision of science — matrilineal, symbiotic with alien nature, performed at home — and shows it still to be oppressive.

Dedicated to the prize-winning geneticist, Anne McLaren, and published in 1962, Naomi Mitchison's *Memoirs of a Spacewoman* records an attempt to build a utopian science for women, at the same time as it offers an examination of problems that might arise in such a science. This text reimagines science, especially biology, along the utopian lines of the paradigm outlined in this chapter. First, women participate equally in science. For the protagonist Mary, a biologist and specialist in communication with other species, science on this future Earth is authored by men and women in equal proportions, and women are an integral part of the history of science as Mary recalls it (see headnote to this chapter).[29] Indeed, because of Mary's essentialist view of gender, women are seen in *Memoirs* as indispensable to the development of science. As Lynda Birke asserts, "it has sometimes been politically expedient for feminists to make [the] claim" of "an essentialist view of gender" (1986, 244). We have already discussed the passage where Mary situates herself in the history of women and science, arguing that "biology and, of course, communication are essentially women's work, and glory," and that "the disciplines of life seem more congenial to most of us women"

29. Naomi Mitchison is the daughter of the noted biologist J.S. Haldane and sister of a noted geneticist, John Haldane. In an interview, Mitchison recalls that she worked as her father's lab assistant as a child, and that she experimented with guinea pigs, but "I never had my brother's early understanding of [science], and I wonder, now, whether this was temperamental or whether certain avenues of understanding were closed to me by what was considered suitable or unsuitable for a little girl" (Caldecott 1984, 14–15). Perhaps Mitchison had a personal as well as social investment in wishing to see science revised to include women.

(Mitchison 1973, 9). Here Mitchison slyly appropriates discourse that has been used to limit women's achievements to a gendered sphere, in order to reconceptualize women as superior in these respects to men.

In addition, Mary sees women's traditionally feminine qualities as positive, not negative attributes. Adaptability, for example, and the empathy on which communication is based are innately feminine qualities to Mary: "I had, of course, like a dancer to adapt myself to my [alien] communicators. That's the kind of reason why, as I've said, I believe communication science is so essentially womanly. It fits one's basic sex patterns" (Mitchison 1973, 16). Mary sees intuition and adapting to others' needs as innately feminine qualities. However, in Mary's future, women are not limited by their biology but, instead, freed by it for special intellectual work. For example, in one set of experiments with grafts from an amoeba-like species from another planet, female humans and animals can establish a rapport with the graft and nurture it, but males cannot (86, 145–46). At the beginning of the experiment, Mary argues, " 'I don't believe this is a man's job. You ought to get a woman to do it. She'd get a better relation with the graft' " (44). In this novel, women are essentially different from men, but this difference increases the reliability of scientific knowledge — women are especially good at establishing communication with other species and at thinking through problems of biology.

Second, science in Mitchison's novel is utopian because the goal of science is not control of nature but, instead, partnership with earth species and noninterference with alien species. On earth, communication with animals has been achieved. As a result of communication with animals, the society has become mainly vegetarian: "there is no edible life in Terra which cannot evoke some slight empathy for any of us," Mary observes (Mitchison 1973, 10). Animals can no longer be used as objects for experimentation, and are subjects who must be asked permission before they participate in experiments (45–46, 165). Such communication also breaks down the hierarchy of objective observor and subject. "It was important that we all, Martians, humans, dogs, jackals and other species, should exchange as much information as possible," Mary tells us of one experiment (157). Indeed, Mitchison comes from that generation of British feminists who were very active in the antivivisectionist campaign (see Birke 1986, 250).

On other planets, Mitchison's stories of the ethical problems surrounding the rule of noninterference for her society's science offer a corrective to British imperialism (and to the imperialist assumptions of much 1960s science fiction). For example, in one episode, Mary and her research team must refrain from interfering in a culture where extremely advanced centipede-like aliens explain their diet of the lifeblood of humanoids. Mitchison's anticolonialism is clear. Of the Epsies, Mary observes, "The Epsies had colonised very vigorously, and at a period of moral crudity, which luckily humans had lived through and put behind them by the time they reached the technical excellence in space travel that the Epsies had achieved earlier" (Mitchison 1973, 25). As Mitchison writes this book, in 1962, the U.S. and U.S.S.R. are at the height of the space race, but the European colonial powers are also in the midst of conflict over colonies that desire home rule. Mitchison's Mary, as in the case of women's participation in science, looks nostalgically backwards to the solution of problems that appear insoluble in Mitchison's present: *Memoirs* portrays an earth where imperialism was given up long before human space travel was achieved. That Mitchison means to criticize her own British society in this episode is also clear. Mary wryly remarks of the Epsies, "Well, one has to make allowances for the colonist mentality. We know enough about it from our own history, but it was the first time I had met it in real life" (28). Thus, the Epsies, drinking the lifeblood of a people they share their planet with, represent British and other European imperialists, and Mitchison presents a utopia where such exploitation lies in Earth's past. But Mitchison furthers the anti-imperialist critique by the pacifist response of the research team. They cannot interfere violently even to save a people like themselves. We have only to remember all the times that Captain Kirk in the 1960s "Star Trek" violently interfered to save the humanoids or the democrats, to realize that Mitchison is criticizing the plots of traditional science fiction as ideology that justifies imperialism.[30]

Finally, Mitchison presents a science that is utopian because it is decentralized, nonhierarchical, and subjective. Much of the work is done in the field rather than in the lab. Instead of the two-tiered system of science in Mitchison's day (male scientists and female assistants), this science requires collaboration — not only between men and women but also between humans and other animals. This science further incorporates and values subjectivity in the form of empathy as the basic activity of biology, since establishing communication with other species is the first goal. Peder, a leading scientist, for example, compliments Mary for her empathy not her objectivity: "You've got the instinct for communication, Mary" (Mitchison 1973, 173).

Mitchison's portrait of women scientists, in fact, anticipates Evelyn Fox Keller's feminist analysis in *A Feeling for the Organism: The Life and Work of Barbara McClintock* (1983) of Barbara McClintock's work in corn genetics in the 1920s through 1950s as empathic and thus different from the work of male geneticists. In her extensive interviews and analysis of the geneticist's work, Keller found that McClintock "tells us [scientists] one must have the time to look, the patience to 'hear what the material has to say to you,' the openness to 'let it come to you.' Above all, one must have 'a feeling for the organism' " (1983, 198). In Mitchison's *Memoirs*, many of the scientists,

30. On the imperialism of 1950s and 1960s science fiction, see Mark Lagon's discussion of "Star Trek" and foreign policy (1993); and Hilary Rose's discussion of her dislike of early science fiction (1994, 212).

especially the women, have this "feeling for the organism." Such is Olga's experience, for example, in biology: "Olga's plant chemistry was becoming more and more sensitive, she seemed to know what a plant wanted from traces of evidence which were not apparent to the rest of us" (Mitchison 1973, 157). Like Keller's McClintock, Mitchison's Olga can "understand 'how it grows, understand its parts, understand when something is going wrong with it' " (Keller 1983, 198). Olga's "feeling for the organism" is so strong that she can anticipate a plant's needs the way humans anticipate their children's needs — with empathy.

Mitchison not only builds this utopian vision of science, which she shares with many feminist science theorists. She also begins in her fiction to sketch new problems that might arise from this reformulation of science. At the beginning of her *Memoirs*, Mary notes that she "sometimes . . . think[s] of [her life] in terms of moral problems" (Mitchison 1973, 5). If science is based on empathy, then scientists will be less often tempted by the dangers of control; and more often, by the dangers of losing their own identity, and so, their humanity. In A *Feeling for the Organism*, Evelyn Fox Keller, the feminist science theorist, presents such subjectivity as uniformly positive. Keller quotes McClintock commenting,

> "When I was really working with them I wasn't outside, I was down there. I was part of the system. I was right down there with them, and everything got big. I even was able to see the internal parts of the chromosomes — actually everything was there. It surprised me because I actually felt as if I were right down there and these were my friends. . . . And you forget yourself. The main thing about it is you forget yourself." (Keller 1983, 117)

In her novel, on the other hand, Mitchison builds and criticizes such a utopian vision at the same time. In one episode, Mary achieves such empathy with a radial starfish-like species that she loses her own ability to choose:

> Even while one admitted that moral and intellectual judgments were shifting and temporary, they had still seemed to exist. . . . But after a certain amount of communication with the radiates all this smudged out. . . . If alternative means, not one of two, but one, two, three, or four out of five, then action is complicated and . . . two or more choices could be made more or less conflicting though never opposite. (Mitchison 1973, 17)

Here Mary achieves communication with the aliens because of her empathy. Ironically, this very ability to communicate through empathy is destructive of her own identity — because of her identification with a species which operates differently, she is unable to function as a member of her own species. This general fear of empathy is expressed often in popular psychology — that by investing too much in another being, a person will "lose" her own identity. But Mitchison does not leave the problem at this negative stage. Instead, she sees it as part of a larger pattern in Mary's learning how to be a good scientist: "When I came to talk this over with others in my age group," Mary later recounts, "I found that personalities very often took a knock on their first expedition, and then re-stabilised more firmly" (Mitchison 1973, 23). Paradoxically, by experiencing extreme disorientation through empathy, the self grows not weaker, but stronger. The scientist does not lose her humanity through empathy, but strengthens her sense of self by her extreme identification with another kind of being. Fear of loss of self, then, is not the greatest threat to this new science, but instead, loss of the other, for this science recognizes the danger that an observer changes what s/he observes. Mary muses that one day scientists might have to find a way truly to be invisible to other beings in order to observe, for otherwise "we all commit [interference] when we go to other worlds merely by being there, by standing and staring, by collecting information" (138).

The British Mitchison develops the problems for a feminist science that might result from subjectivity by tying colonialism to the question of scientific objectivity: if one gives up as androcentric the concept of objectivity, does one have any place to stand? The policy of noninterference in Mary's culture is questioned in one episode, where Mary's science allows her to communicate with but not to aid a humanoid species that is rounded up and eaten by an insectoid species that is dominant on that world. But in another episode, where a member of Mary's scientific team interferes and kills to protect one alien from another, the analysis suggests that the alternative to noninterference is simply to repeat the mistakes of colonial interference.

So subjectivity provides the ground for as many problems as the older ideal of objectivity in science. So, too, in Mary's future, does the participation of women in science. When Mary joins an all-women expedition, for example, we can see clearly a model that makes science less hierarchical than in our institutionalized forms. Because of their empathy with other life-forms and their capacity for collaboration, the women form an ideal team for examining and puzzling out the complicated life cycle of an alien species, who also turn out to be all female. Like caterpillars and butterflies, the life-form goes through two stages, but these stages are estranged from each other: eggs hatch in an algal swamp where the caterpillars feed, copulate, and crawl out to make elaborate art forms from their excretions; then the caterpillars spin chrysalises from which butterflies hatch, some with the potential to become immortal. The caterpillars have their own culture but think of the chrysalis stage as death; they do not recognize a relation to the butterflies, except as enemy. The butterflies regard the caterpillars with disdain, and interfere with blame and instructions in order to promote the kind of life (one with little food, no art, and no sex) which they think results in immortal butterflies. The butterflies hate the caterpillars, not only for their sensual life, in direct contrast to the contemplative life of the butterflies, but also because egg-laying, resulting from the copulation while caterpillar, is the only cause of death butterflies know.

Utopian harmony is not the result of this all-women expedition. Instead, of all Mary's expeditions it is the most conflicted. In a troubling allegory, the women of the expedition split along generational lines, empathizing with butterflies or caterpillars according to whether they are mothers or daughters. Mary and Olga empathize with the overpowering joy of contemplation and the resentful grief at death in the egg-laying of the butterflies, while Nadira and Françoise feel sympathy only for the caterpillars, rejecting the butterflies' theories of immortality, and protecting the caterpillars' art and sex from attacks by the butterflies (Mitchison 1973, 92, 118 and 123). In one sense, this episode, with its mirroring of butterflies and caterpillars in mothers and daughters, is a psychological parable: unlike men, women until the mid-twentieth century, seeing death (from childbirth) more often than immortality through their children, gave up procreation in order to achieve a life of the mind. In another sense, however, this episode tests a utopian science based on empathy rather than objectivity: even though the puzzle of the species' life cycle is solved by empathy, the scientific team is also divided into resentful mothers and rebellious daughters by its empathy with different generations of aliens. Indeed, Françoise so empathizes with the caterpillars that she "commits interference," killing one of the immortal butterflies in order to prove to them that immortality is impossible *except* through procreation, that all creatures share death. By this demonstration of cause and effect, Françoise hopes to prevent further attacks of blame by the mother butterflies on the daughter caterpillars. Thus Mitchison sketches one side of a feminist science, empathy, as utopian, at the same time as she predicts what problems might result from incorporating such a faculty into science.

In another episode, where biologists observe symbionts from another planet by grafting them on Terran human and animal volunteers, female empathy becomes a limitation, not a benefit. Only females can achieve the graft, and Mary and the others initially see this as a boon: female biology provides a perspective impossible to male science (Mitchison 1973, 44). Furthermore, the episode explicitly denounces experiments on lab animals and offers a utopian vision in which the female lab animals are, through communication, part of the research team, not objects of research. During this experiment, for example, Mary comments that she has found out from Daisy, a canine fellow experimental subject, "a lot about canine aesthetic tastes" (159).

But again, at the same time that Mitchison builds a utopian vision of feminine empathy and biology as necessary to successful research, she also represents potential problems. The females become disastrously attached to their grafts. "Far down, almost smothered, there was still a very small quietly struggling observer. . . ," comments Mary, but "I had ceased to be a civilised scientist" (Mitchison 1973, 166). First, the grafts separate the hosts from their scientific community, offering "the feeling of hidden, but complete satisfaction" (161). In particular, the experience of hosting a graft is so gratifying that it separates the female from the male scientists: "How little he knows," Mary thinks, "of what kind this fulfillment is" (162). Finally, the female hosts try to further the next procreative cycle of the grafts by immersing themselves in water, which could spread the alien life form throughout the Terran ecological system. Under the influence of this foreign mandate to procreate the symbiont, the hosts even resort to violence: the jackals savage their keepers, and Mary bites a friend.

Thus this episode, a parody of the scandal of pregnancy, explores a feminine empathy that endangers one's own self. Mitchison is not suggesting the stereotypical fears of women's biology as a dangerous power that might overwhelm reason, fears that occupy men rather than women. Rather, she is exploring women's fear of pregnancy, the fear that the fetuses that they carry willingly and lovingly will take control of them and overwhelm their "real" selves: as my obstetrician cheerfully once assured me, "These babies are little parasites inside you." Mitchison airs the fears that pregnancy is in fact a kind of parasitism and motherhood a victimization — as legitimate problems of doing science. In this case, female empathy has been not a benefit, but a limitation. Science is seen in this episode as loss, not as an experience of transcendence over mortality, as it is often pictured in traditional portrayals of the glory of scientific knowledge overcoming death. Indeed, Mary and the other hosts experience "utter grief" (Mitchison 1973, 166) when their grafts are cut from them to save them from their influence. Such a feminist science, then, gains in the giving up of unwarranted power over other species, but loses, too, in its necessary letting go of the humanistic ideal of humanity's godlike powers of reason. Science may manage a slowing of time, through technology, as in their spaceflight, or through discipline, in which the elders of this future gradually skill themselves. Mitchison's scientists may achieve a self-reflective immersion in experience but not a triumph over time or mortality.

While Naomi Mitchison in *Memoirs of a Spacewoman* constructs an exploration and critique at once of such a utopian science as feminism might produce, Barbara Paul tests and criticizes modern anthropology and primatology as a means of defining women in *Under the Canopy* (1980). Donna Haraway, the feminist science theorist, has pointed out that anthropology takes its "birth from the distinction between primitive and civilized" and relates to "the Other as an object for appropriation, for observation, for visualization, for explanation" (1986, 91). Similarly, primatology, the study of apes and monkeys, "is about the simultaneous and repetitive constitution and breakdown of the boundary between human and animal"; and "it is not an accident that the objects of Primatology live in the Third World, [for] they are the preeminently tropic other, happily literally living in a vanishing garden" (1986, 92). Until very recently, of course, these sciences were authored almost completely by men, serving not as human self-definition, but as male self-definition (Haraway 1986, 78). In *Under the Canopy*, Barbara Paul subversively tests anthropology and primatology as myths of self-definition for women.

In her novel, Paul constructs a planet peopled by a preindustrial race who have established trade with a galactic capitalist empire. The novel opens with Margo Kemperer, Director of the Planet Gaea, appointed by the Colonial Office, about to welcome Stephanie Leeds, her new assistant, and the only non-native besides the director to stay on Gaea for years. What Paul has imagined, then, is the standard myth of colonialism but from the point of view of Western women, not men: Margo Kemperer is the director, defining herself by her civilized distance from the natives, dominating them for their own good; Stephanie Leeds is the assimilator, thinking she can become part of the native culture, but instead exploiting and abusing them by forcing on them her desires for integration.

To complete the womanization of the story of colonialism, Paul has borrowed most of the salient features of the Gaeans from Margaret Mead's portrayal of Polynesians. Like the Polynesians Mead popularized in her books, the natives in Paul's novel are a "primitive" tribe, copper-skinned, living on a river at the edge of a jungle that together easily provide them with food. Like Mead's Samoans, the Gaeans are gentle but with rare outbursts of passion, attentive to form and custom, promiscuous before marriage and generally faithful afterwards, lacking our versions of adolescence, accepting of death as a familiar part of nature, and cherishing the dance as their most important ritual and art form. In an echo of Mead's interpretation of Samoan adolescence as smoother because lacking the Western identity crisis, Paul's Stephanie resentfully observes of a native coworker, "Sipoh probably wouldn't know an identity crisis if she tripped over one" (Paul 1980, 100). Moreover, the book reads like a popular anthropological account, full of attention to the social customs of the Gaeans and descriptions of the local plants, animals, and insects.[31] Since the book is told from the points of view of Kemperer and Leeds, the result is a construction of the Gaean culture as utopian in the way that early twentieth-century Western anthropology constructed Polynesian peoples as utopian.

The initial conflict in the novel occurs between the two outsider women.

31. See Margaret Mead, *Coming of Age in Samoa: A Psychological Study of Primitive Youth for Western Civilization* (1961). The subtitle could be a subtitle for Paul's novel. Although her writings have been used to construct a patronizing view of Polynesian culture, Margaret Mead disavows such an attitude in her definition of the word "primitive" as simply lacking script: see Mead 1975, 151.

They represent what Haraway calls "the distorting mirror twins" of colonial origin stories: "mystic love of nature and the desire for limitless instrumental power" — "contemplation and exploitation" (1986, 82). Haraway analyzes this pair of destructive ideologies as part of her analysis of anthropology and primatology. She points out that both viewpoints distort observation and impose imperialist assumptions on the primates or peoples observed.

In Paul's novel, Kemperer complacently assumes the right to judge, control, and rule over the Gaeans, while Leeds's attempts to commune with nature and the natives turn into endangerment of the community and sexual exploitation. For example, Leeds is enraged when Kemperer hires two natives to be servants for Leeds: "I don't care how primitive this planet is, I'm not going to treat these people as my inferiors" (Paul 1980, 15). Kemperer responds by explaining that Leeds fails to understand Gaean culture, in which low-status service in Leeds's eyes is actually high-status indoor work in Gaean eyes. Furthermore, advises Kemperer, Leeds will need servants to do specialized housekeeping tasks in order for Leeds to have the time to do her own job well (15). Thus Leeds has self-righteously declared herself "like" the natives but has refused to acknowledge their cultural difference, while Kemperer has masked her role of domination with the rationalization that each person is filling a necessary function in society.

While Stephanie's democratic vision seems at first more attractive, her sexual exploitation of the Gaean male Imi and her demands on her servants to adopt her values and lifestyle expose her desire for communion as another form of desire for control (Paul 1980, 124–25, 128–31). What one hopes throughout the first half of the book is that the two perspectives will correct each other, that Leeds will teach Kemperer not to judge and that Kemperer will teach Leeds not to interfere. Instead, the two turn out to be the same, "distorting mirror twins."

The second half of the novel becomes a critique of Leeds's quest for self-definition as a human and, by extension, of Western science's definition of the human by contrast with Third World peoples and with nonhuman species. Leeds fails to achieve integration with the primitive river tribe. On a work expedition she becomes lost in the jungle, there encountering other races and exploring the boundary of her humanity. Leeds first travels with a race of small copper-green people who have barely developed fire and language and whose spare existence leaves no room for compassion: in a particularly feminized image, a mother eats her dead infant (Paul 1980, 200). Leeds again fails at communion but translates what she learns from this new people into the principle of merciless Darwinian competition for survival. This tribe then encounters a *bulu*, a white killer ape, and here, crossing the boundary from "human" to "animal," Leeds at last finds kinship: as she and the tribe kill this attacker, she admits first that it is "a dangerous, foul-smelling parody of man, of man who devours his own kind" (217); then that "Physically, the *bulu* and I were closer to each other than to the small folk" (218); and, finally, when she later sees the *bulu*'s skeleton, "It was a human skeleton" (220). In her desire for communion, for return to the garden of nature as part of her own self-definition, Leeds has imposed her own fantasies as a form of dominance on the races of Gaea. When she realizes that her vision of the descent of woman is false, that we are not basically innocent in origin, she goes mad, interpreting the natural relations of the food chain as a justification for her own violence and lack of humanity.

Paul does not offer the positive revision of science for women that Mitchison had. *Under the Canopy* rejects the self-definitions of modern anthropology and primatology for women, yet it implicates Western white women in their exploitative ideologies. Paul seems to be saying that women are bound by the tragic roles of imperialism and domination over nature and other races, even though women do not author the texts.

In *Under the Canopy* Paul thus exploits science as myth, using the stories of twentieth-century anthropologists and primatologists not only to structure her science fiction story but also to criticize the world they have helped to create. In addition, Paul may be further criticizing utopian visions of feminist science fiction in the person of Stephanie. Donna Haraway argues that the "mirror twins" of colonialism have a more general analogy in the ways Western culture approaches difference: besides antagonistic opposition, more common are either "functionalism" (Margo Kemperer's position) or "dream of community" (Stephanie Leeds's position). Both are dangerous, functionalism because it masks domination by its appeal to separate roles for each, dream of community because it refuses to acknowledge difference. The latter failing, Haraway suggests, is more common to feminists. What Haraway hopes, instead, but which the women of Barbara Paul's *Under the Canopy* are not able to envision, is reacting to difference through "partial connection," through "a politics of shared and partial realities that value serious difference" (1986, 86).

Thus, by examining the novels of Mitchison and Paul, we can see the degree to which individual writers interrogate and alter the paradigm of utopian science while advancing it. But I suspect that this paradigm is limited not only by its distance from the practice of individual writers but also by very particular social circumstances: those of privileged white women with science educations.[32]

Certainly, the most prolific contemporary black woman science fiction writer does not share this utopian vision of science. Octavia Butler seems, instead, to critique this vision of white feminists, especially in her short story "Bloodchild" (1984), where she presents a future society reaching the utopian

---

32. For critiques of feminist science theory based on cultural relativism, see Sandra Harding 1986, 136–96; and Zuleyma Halpin 1990, 285–93.

goals of the paradigm outlined in this chapter, but remaining a dystopia. In "Bloodchild," females have equal participation in science, but only because both male and female humans are reserved for reproduction and denied education, and science is in the keeping of female aliens resembling giant centipedes. The science of the story revolves around women's issues — reproduction and rights to one's own body — since the alien Tlic require human males to carry their eggs in the males' abdomens and human females to reproduce as many humans as possible in order to have a supply of hosts for the alien young. Science on this world has been feminized. The world is a matriarchy, because only the female Tlic survive to adulthood, the males perishing after rapid maturation and a brief adolescence of reproductive frenzy. Finally, the view of nature promoted by the alien Tlic is one of symbiotic partnership between species: "I had been told all my life," the young male narrator says, while watching the emergency surgery that takes Tlic grubs from the abdomen of a human host, "that this was a good and necessary thing Tlic and Terran did together — a kind of birth. I had believed it until now. I knew birth was painful and bloody, no matter what. But this was something else, something worse" (Butler 1985, 203).

As the narrator's reflections show, instead of symbiosis, humans experience a kind of exploitation modeled on female and racial exploitation, especially on that of black women in the United States under slavery. Humans are kept on a "Preserve" for their protection and only recently have been allowed to live together as families, allotted a status above animals in this society. They are required to reproduce for both themselves and the aliens, yet others own the children who are the products of their bodies. In "Bloodchild," Butler thus creates a future where feminist utopian goals in science are met but one still depending on hierarchy and exploitation. Butler extends this critique of utopian science in her novels, as well. In her most recent novel, *Parable of the Sower* (1993), the female hero begins the story in a walled compound with her middleclass family, who work most of the time inside their homes, for fear of the violent gangs of unprivileged and hungry unemployed who roam the streets. The novel underscores the point of technology for the few that Butler made in a lecture at the University of Maryland: we talk about the far regions of the world connected by technology, but how many families own computers in the United States? In her 1980s trilogy, *Xenogenesis*, the Oankali aliens each have equitable access to science because for them it is biological — their computer-like memories record data without error or loss of information, and their bodies have the biological capacity to analyze and integrate foreign genetic material, combining it with their own to create new kinds of beings. The Oankali, however, despite their achievement of an equal rights science for themselves, still exploit other species, calling what they take by force or coercion "trade."

Butler's short story, and often her novels as well, thus call into question the paradigm of utopian science as represented in feminist science theory and the works of white women science fiction writers. I do not think that our only recourse, however, is to abandon the reformulation of science. Instead, I share the hope of Zuleyma Halpin for broadening the critique: "An analysis that includes race, class, and sexual orientation, and that recognizes the commonality of women, racial minorities, sexual minorities, and the poor as 'the other' in science, can help us to better understand the underlying dynamics of scientific oppression." (1990, 293) This analysis can perhaps help us to construct a more inclusive vision of utopian science. As Hilary Rose observes, "believing in the possibility of other and better futures is a social precondition for bringing them into existence" (1994, 188).

2

Beautiful Alien Monster-Women—BAMs

Remember that the female has always been a formidable enemy both of society in general and of man in particular, as well as a formidable enemy of the rational. And now they are blundering onward, a menace not only to civilization and to life as we know it, but even to themselves.

Besides, they are all sisters. They are in this together and here it clearly doesn't matter what sort of beast you are, or came from, or will one day be. How wonderful, Pooch thinks, to be whatever one really is, even if half dog and even if something of the savage wolf, as has proven to be the case with her.

— Carol Emshwiller,
Carmen Dog

Aliens in SF invariably possess a metaphorical dimension," argues Patrick Parrinder in an essay on "The Alien Encounter" (Parrinder 1979, 155). In science fiction by men, the woman as alien has generally symbolized the erotic victim of masculine dominance who is a threat to reason and order (Russ 1980)—the position taken by the doctor and parodied in the first quotation above from Carol Emshwiller's *Carmen Dog* (1990). Just as traditional science fiction has frequently displayed racial fear of difference under the guise of BEMs—bug-eyed monsters—so traditional science fiction has also displayed fear of women under the guise of BAMs—beautiful alien monster-women. As I outlined in the introduction in my reading of *Frankenstein*, these negative associations with the woman as alien create a generic constraint: what perspective can a woman writer claim, if by this convention women are given only an alienated position in the text? This constraint is negotiated by the greater portion of twentieth-century women writers of science fiction through appropriating the convention of alien woman to their own ends, often as spokesperson in confronting the Terran custom of masculine domination.

In science fiction novels by women, female aliens often represent the experience of woman-as-other.[1] As the philosopher Simone de Beauvoir argued half a century ago, "Humanity is male and man defines woman not in herself but relative to him. . . . He is the Subject, he is the Absolute — she is the Other."[2] As other critics have explored — especially Robin Roberts, Marleen Barr and Jenny Wolmark — women writers have borrowed and transformed the goddesses, monsters, and witches of men's science fiction. These writers have developed a whole taxonomy of women aliens that must be read differently from the women characters as alien that male science fiction writers construct, and that many critics have deconstructed.[3] In this chapter I shall explore four categories of the woman as alien: woman as humanoid alien, woman as machine, woman as animal, and minority women as aliens among us.[4]

In the first headnote to this chapter, a male scientist in Carol Emshwiller's *Carmen Dog* ponders the terrifying transformation that has occurred in his alternative world: gradually over the course of one year, women (housewives, at least) have transformed into animals, while female pets, grow-

1. The most extended treatment of the woman as alien in science fiction is Robin Roberts 1993, passim, which explores woman as goddess, witch, or monster in science fiction by both genders; her discussion has been very helpful to me, although I have set up a different paradigm. The idea is mentioned in Le Guin, "American SF and the Other" in 1979, 99; Gregory Benford "Aliens and Knowability" in Slusser, Guffey, and Rose, eds., 1980, 55; and Spivack 1987, 14. Catherine Podojil, in "Sisters, Daughters, and Aliens," treats men as aliens in science fiction by a few women writers (in Riley, ed., 1978, 70–86). Carolyn Wendell's article, "The Alien Species" (1979), discusses the lack of strong, individualized women characters in most science fiction. Marleen Barr mentions, in a discussion of a short story by James Tiptree, Jr. (Alice Sheldon), that even human females are "alien in our culture which insists that 'to be human is to be male' " (1987, 31); and Barr further discusses woman as alien in 1993, 98–100. Despite its broad treatment of aliens, *Aliens: The Anthropology of Science Fiction*, ed. George E. Slusser and Eric S. Rabkin, 1987, does not treat women as aliens at all. In an essay on C. L. Moore, Sarah Gamble points out in an aside that "The science fiction genre . . . is a literary form which is eminently suitable for the expression of this [gynocentric] viewpoint, for, in these stories, the unbridgeable differences between the male and female protagonists are strongly foregrounded by making them literally different species" (1991, 35–36). Most recently, Jenny Wolmark has discussed the woman as alien in works by Octavia Butler and Gwyneth Jones in *Aliens and Others*, chap. 2, arguing that "The science fiction convention of the alien attempts to present otherness in unitary terms, so that 'humanity' is uncomplicatedly opposed to the 'alien'; both Jones and Butler focus on the way in which that opposition seeks to suppress the others of both gender and race by subsuming them within a common-sense notion of what it is to be human" (1994, 46).

2. de Beauvoir 1974, xviii–xix. See Molly Hite 1989, 6, who relates this passage from de Beauvoir to women writers' narrative techniques.

3. On men's treatment of the woman as alien, see especially Beverly Friend 1972–73, Joanna Russ 1980, and Ursula K. Le Guin "American SF and The Other" in *The Language of the Night* 1979, 97–100; for Roberts', Barr's, and Wolmark's work, see n. 1.

4. See Demaris S. Wehr on Jung and feminism: "even more powerful than concepts are images, because they are more primary." Wehr argues that images do not have to be treated as universal, but may be contextualized and politicized (1984, 124).

ing humanoid, have taken over housekeeping and childcare. This transformation was exactly what the men, it turns out, had feared all along: women have always been untrustworthy, different, animal-like, irrational, uncivilized, the other to men's attributes. In the second headnote, Pooch, a dog becoming a human female, reflects on a rally of the transformed in a wonderfully sympathetic parody of the women's movement. Among her sisters, Pooch relaxes from the demands of being human and becomes her "essential" self: a woman, animal-like, irrational, uncivilized — different from men, but joyful instead of unhappy in her difference. At this moment Pooch embraces, rather than suffers from, her difference. In the first passage, Emshwiller satirizes an essentialist misogynistic stance, creating within her text a view of gender as socially constructed. In the second passage, Emshwiller presents a comic but sympathetic portrait of women as they discover their similarities as women. Here the text views women as essentially different in valuable ways from men. Emshwiller is having it both ways.

In her essay "Coalition Politics: Turning the Century," Bernice Johnson Reagon points out that the women's movement is a coalition, that we do our work on the street, and that "home," where one is nurtured by women like oneself, is an illusion. Nevertheless, it is a valuable illusion. Each of us needs both "home" and "coalition," both the feeling of valuing our essential differences as women (and as working class, or African-American, or lesbian, and many more) and the satisfaction of changing society because gender, racial, class, and sexual roles are socially constructed. Thus the symbology of women as alien can be used to political ends, both to nurture in women a sense of the value of their differences, and also to reveal to them that the inequities they suffer are socially constructed, not natural, and so can be resisted.[5]

Throughout this chapter I shall turn to feminist psychology in interpreting the woman as alien. Since I am examining literary representations, not establishing a pattern of human development, I do not limit myself to one authority, but draw eclectically on many feminist psychologists and psychoanalysts — Jungians, neo-Freudians, object relations theorists, and others — to interpret these tropes of the woman as alien.[6] This eclecticism allows me to assume that psychology is not universal, but limited to our century and culture, and perhaps also to the middle class from whom almost all these

5. This symbology of the woman as alien, then, does not restrict women writers to either socially constructed or essentialist interpretations of women's roles. Although I have benefited very much from his perceptive readings of individual works, I am here taking issue with Peter Fitting's readings of feminist utopias in the 1970s and 1980s as politically dangerous because essentialist: see both articles by Fitting (1987 and 1992), as well as "On Peter Fitting's 'Reconsiderations,' " a response by Pamela Sargent (1992).

6. On the state of feminist psychology as "a multiplex account," cf. Nancy Chodorow 1989, 5.

writers come. Nevertheless, the theory of psychoanalyst Jessica Benjamin will serve as a unifying field for this chapter, because a recurring plot line associated with the woman as alien is the movement that Benjamin explores, from male dominance to a "mutual recognition" between the sexes (Benjamin 1988, 8, 27–29). I shall first set up and explore the paradigms for women's science fiction that create a different symbolic landscape from that in science fiction by men, and then offer interpretations of two novels—Joan Slonczewski's A Door Into Ocean and Carol Emshwiller's Carmen Dog—as examples of how individual women writers adapt and react to these paradigms. Because this symbology is produced in specific historical contexts, it is in constant metamorphosis as each writer adapts it to her own goals.

Alien Women and Sadomasochistic Erotics

In her explanation of the definition by men of woman-as-other, de Beauvoir includes the question: how it is that women are "submissive enough to accept this alien point of view?" (1974, xxi) In much science fiction by women, earth men meet strong alien women who do refuse to accept our culture's view of women, who see themselves as subject, not as other. In this section, I shall explore the woman as alien in novels by Andre Norton, Jane Gaskell, Marion Zimmer Bradley, Anne McCaffrey, and Jayge Carr, writers who overturn the sadomasochistic erotics of the romance plot, transforming the story into a problem-solving science fiction.

   In literary terms, the women authors move the woman as alien, a convention of much science fiction by men, from margin to center, from minor character to point of view through whom we see events. To better understand this difference between male and female writers, we may compare Andre Norton with Poul Anderson. Both published their first science fiction in 1947, and both are prolific writers with preferences for quest plots, for individualistic heroes who battle real evil, for minority characters, and for populist political ideals. In the 1950s, both wrote novels that included virtually no women—for example, Norton's Star Man's Son (1952) and Anderson's Planet of No Return (1956). In the 1960s, both introduced strong secondary alien women characters, but Norton let them share point of view, while Anderson retained exclusively male point of view—for example, Norton's Web of the Witch World (1964) and Moon of Three Rings (1966) and Anderson's Ensign Flandry (1966). In the 1970s and 1980s, Anderson included the woman's point of view, but Norton moved the alien woman into the role of protagonist with the man now a secondary character not sharing point of view—for example, Anderson's Dancer from Atlantis (1971) and A Midsummer Tempest (1974) and Norton's Ice Crown (1970), and Forerunner (1981). This movement of point of view carried with it political consequences, or, more accurately, reflected political positions. In Anderson's novels, women's roles remained subordinate to men's with marriage a reward at the end of the male hero's quest. Andre Norton, on the other hand, led the way for other women writers in revising how women are represented in science fiction. Her main tool in this revision was the appropriation of the literary convention of the woman as alien.[7]

But it is not only the female perspective that makes significant this centering of the woman as alien. In men's science fiction, the plot of the alien woman engenders sadomasochistic erotics — the alien woman falls in love with a human man as his reward for conquering the planet. Women writers, in contrast, manipulate the figure of the woman as alien to represent a fantasy of mutual recognition between men and women.[8] They resist the sadomasochistic scenario by insisting on the alien woman's subjectivity, by moving her to the center of the story, and by giving her a voice — often a telepathic voice.

In *The Bonds of Love: Psychonalysis, Feminism and the Problem of Domination*, psychoanalyst Jessica Benjamin posits that healthy psychological human development requires "*mutual* recognition, the necessity of recognizing as well as being recognized by the other" (1988, 23), "the reciprocity of self and other, the balance of assertion and recognition" (25). In our culture, however, this process occurs, in particular, in the context of gendered relations that idealize the father as the symbol of differentiation and subjectivity (105, 109, 123) and the mother as the symbol of symbiosis (158). "Neither state of mind," warns Benjamin, "represents real relationships or the truth about gender — each is merely an ideal"; and "Either extreme, pure symbiosis or pure self-sufficiency, represents a loss of balance" (158).

In Andre Norton's *Witch World* (1963), for example, the Terran Simon Tregarth and the alien witch Jaelithe share adventures and gradually fall in love. But Simon at first feels "no male interest at all" in her (20); instead, he experiences mutual recognition with her, often represented in the story by the meeting of their eyes: "and he glanced up to know an odd lift of spirit as he met a level gaze which was more than mere recognition of his identity" (198). In return, Jaelithe tells Simon her name, kept secret by all witches in her world: "her name, that most personal possession in the realm of the Power, which must never be yielded lest one yield with it one's own identity to another" (221). In this novel Simon and Jaelithe are the idealized and opposed figures of father and mother, of differentiation and symbiosis.

7. See Robin Roberts 1987, for a history of male depiction of strong female aliens in both stories and illustrations of the 1940s and 1950s science fiction pulps; she argues that these strong alien women were "protofeminist."

8. Leslie Rabine has noted a similar goal in Harlequin romances, where the heroine "wants from the hero . . . recognition of herself as a unique, exceptional individual. In addition to acknowledging her sexual attraction and her professional competence, he must also recognize her as a subject, or recognize her from her own point of view" (1985, 250).

Simon, representing self-sufficiency, finds Jaelithe's gaze at first "discon-certing" (18), his memories of her disturbing—"they possessed for him a hidden excitement he shrank from defining or explaining too closely" (197). Jaelithe, a witch who reads the thoughts and nature of people before they speak, exhibits a telepathy that represents her special capability of symbiosis (35, 216). Their exchange, then, of acknowledging glances and of names represents the mutual recognition of each other's identity.

But in our gendered culture, this desire for mutual recognition often results in a sadomasochistic, alienated version: "The fantasy of erotic domina-tion embodies both the desire for independence and the desire for recognition. . . . The process of alienation whereby these desires are trans-formed into erotic violence and submission. . . . is a paradox in which the individual tries to achieve freedom through slavery, release through submis-sion to control" (Benjamin 1988, 52). It is this alienated version, Benjamin points out, that is promoted as ideal by popular movies and romances.

While the alien woman is often represented in science fiction by men as masochistic victim, she is only rarely so represented in science fiction by women. Indeed, women's stories more often offer a critique of the sadistic Terran hero from a female point of view. For example, in *Strange Evil* (1957) by Jane Gaskell, whose great-great-great-great aunt was the nineteenth-century writer Elizabeth Gaskell (Tuck 1974, 182), the human hero Judith, named for the Biblical warrior, finds herself in love with a fairy and trans-ported to his world where she is the alien.[9] Initially attracted to Zameis, she eventually rejects him for his sadistic views of pleasure (Gaskell 1957, 105). In the novel the sadism is modestly displaced onto other fantastic beings and onto the landscape. When Judith desires Zameis, a male fairy haunts her, whose "sexual enjoyment lies in watching the reaction of others to themselves for the first time" (80). In later scenes, after almost being raped, Judith finds herself in a dangerously phallic landscape, where "Horrible snakes, . . . blotched and unwholesome. . . . moved ponderously along the boughs and over the yielding plants" (205), and where, "startled" by "a great pouring sound," she is "drenched and defeated" by a "great waterfall" (209–10). The

9. Presenting the woman as alien "unmetaphors," renders literal the social custom of the woman being shipped as a commodity into a new family, a new culture at marriage. The term "unmetaphoring" is proposed in Rosalie Colie's *Shakespeare's Living Art*: "an author who treats a conventionalized figure of speech as if it were a description of actuality is unmetaphoring that figure" (1974, 11; see also 145–52). In Eleanor Arnason's *To The Resurrection Station* (1986), for example, Belinda is suddenly withdrawn from college by her guardian and told that she is half native and must marry a man she has been promised to since childhood. Her designation as half-breed alien "unmetaphors" or literalizes the status of women in traditional societies, who could be transferred without consent to another family: "you are a native, my sweet. According to treaty, you are subject to native—not human—law. . . . Reconcile yourself to the situation," explains her uncle-guardian, the patriarch of the family (Arnason 1986, 17).

novel ends when Judith destroys the god of the fairies, a great Baby, whose infantile desires and destructions (224) represent the arrested state of the fairy people, who can not grow out of self-absorption into mutual recognition. At this point, Judith is rewarded with an adult relationship characterized by mutual recognition and symbolized, as in Andre Norton's novels, by eyes: Judith's new love has "alien purple eyes which looked at her strangely and yet with a warmth which was both yearning and thrilling" (212).

A frequent corollary to the story of a female alien meeting an earth man is the creation of an anachronistic world, lacking our technology but advanced in arts and "sciences" alien to our culture, a nostalgic world where traditional roles of women are truly valued. Such is Andre Norton's Witch World, Marion Zimmer Bradley's feudal Darkover, Suzette Haden Elgin's Ozark in *The Ozark Trilogy* (1981), or Vonda McIntyre's nontechnological world in *Dreamsnake* (1976). Although essentialist, these anachronistic worlds can be read as empowering and liberating.[10] Psychologist Jean Baker Miller has argued that characteristics traditionally associated with women's roles — vulnerability, emotions, cooperation, giving, accepting change, and serving others — are actually strengths, not weaknesses:

> Women have always had to come up with a basis of worthiness that is different from that which the dominant culture bestows. They have effected enough of a creative internal transformation of values to . . . believe that caring for people and participating in others' development is enhancing to self-esteem. In this sense, even women who live by all the old stereotypes are in advance of the values of this society. (Miller 1976, 44)

In Miller's sense, these anachronistic worlds celebrate women's traditional traits as strengths and recover an alternative portrait of heroism.[11]

This recuperative reworking of the woman as alien descends from earlier

10. For a different analysis of Bradley's opposition of a "rational, technological, bourgeois, male, artificial and heterosexual" Terran society with "an alternative [Darkovan] society in which intuition, instinct, feudalism, femaleness, and homosexuality are associated with naturalness," see Linda Leith 1980, esp. 32.

11. These fictions of the alien woman exploit nostalgia for a time when separate spheres encouraged greater appreciation for women's gendered roles; see Gerda Lerner 1979, 164: "Thus, women often participated in their own subordination by internalizing the ideology and values that oppressed them and by passing these on to their children. Yet they were not *passive* victims; they always involved themselves actively in the world in their own way. Starting on a stage defined by their life cycle, they often rebelled against and defied societal indoctrination, developed their own definitions of community, and built their own female culture." The symbol of such heroism in science fiction by women, based on a nostalgic idea of women's gendered roles, is often childbirth, as in Gillmore's *Angel Island* (1914 — see Gillmore 1984) where the female hero dies giving birth to the first winged man, or when the Lady Rohana in Bradley's *The Shattered Chain* (1976) nurses her sister during her childbirth and resulting death, and recalls her own heroic and conflicted response to childbirth. These portraits of anachronistic worlds of alien women seek to recover a history of women as heroes in their traditional roles, not as

utopias by women.[12] Similar valuing of women's culture and validating of women's traditional roles occur in Mary Bradley Lane's *Mizora: A Prophecy* (1880–1881), Inez Haynes Gillmore's *Angel Island* (1914), Charlotte Perkins Gilman's *Herland* (1915), and the early science fiction utopia, Minna Irving's "The Moon Woman: A Tale of the Future" (1929). These utopias explore alien societies on earth whose women are more moral, more nurturing, and more independent than the United States societies with which they are contrasted. In Gillmore's and Irving's science fictions, the women are literally aliens, winged versions of the Victorian angel of the house. In Gillmore's *Angel Island*, four United States men shipwrecked on an island meet four winged flying women and, in order to domesticate and marry them, cut off their wings; the women yet achieve a unified community different from the men's, rebelling from their house-bound roles when their daughters reach an age to fly. In Irving's "Moon Woman," winged women descend from the moon, choose Terran male spouses, and elevate life by taking over government, making the earth a moral, technically advanced, and healthy place to live.

Female aliens in novels by women often have special telepathic powers which men of their race do not usually possess. Andre Norton's sorceresses, for example, live in a world where empathy is heightened to telepathy by a female science that is not technological and that seeks to work with, rather than to dominate nature. For example, in Norton's *Witch World*, as in our culture, where "feeling" has been assigned to the female role, only women like Jaelithe possess the gift of telepathy, until Simon Tregarth is shown also to have this power (Norton 1963, 138 and 145). This empathic power represents the attunement to others that Benjamin argues is expected of women in our culture, an idealized representation of the symbiosis we attribute to the mother.[13] Hélène Cixous celebrates such idealized symbiosis as a political

---

exceptions: heroic women cooking, nurturing, giving birth. As Ursula K. Le Guin writes, "It is hard to tell a really gripping tale of how I wrested a wild-oat seed from its husk, and then another, and then another, and then another, and then another, and then I scratched my gnat bites, and Ool said something funny, and we went to the creek and got a drink and watched newts for a while, and then I found another patch of oats. . . . I said it was hard to make a gripping tale of how we wrested the wild oats from their husks, I didn't say it was impossible" ("The Carrier Bag Theory of Fiction" in *Dancing at the Edge* 1989, 165–66 and 169).

12. On feminist utopias that validate as heroic the characteristics of women's traditional roles, see especially the work by Carol Pearson and Lee Cullen Khanna (listed in the introduction n. 3). Compare Bartkowski's discussion of Christiane Rochefort's *Archaos* as a "nostalgic" utopia (Bartkowski 1989, 111 ff.).

13. Jessica Benjamin 1988, 27 and 253 n. 29: Benjamin points out that much of psychoanalytic theory posits differentiation as the goal of adulthood and sees symbiosis as regressive, while she argues that adulthood must balance independence and attunement to others, and that early symbiosis with the mother is thus the basis of adult capacities for cooperation and recognition of others. See also Chodorow 1978, 92–93, 102–3, and 206–7; Chodorow further connects symbiosis with the figure of the witch or fairy godmother 1978, 122.

value: "that which is ours breaks loose from us without our fearing any debilitation. Our glances, our smiles, are spent; laughs exude from all our mouths; our blood flows; . . . we never hold back our thoughts, our signs, our writing; and we're not afraid of lacking" (in Marks and de Courtivron 1980, 248). In much science fiction by women, telepathy represents the permeable boundaries of women deriving from empathy: they never hold back their thoughts; they do not defend the borders of their identities because they are not afraid of lacking.

Such a science fiction is Marion Zimmer Bradley's *Two to Conquer* (1980), set on Darkover, a feudal world where magic is a science and where only women can be Keepers (those who empathically link a group of adepts into a network to perform the most difficult magical tasks). In this novel, telepathy seems further linked to gender because the female characters — Melora, Melisendra, and Carlina — possess greater abilities in the science than do the major male characters — Bard di Asturien and Paul Harris. Melora's rapport with birds, for example, is called "a woman's art" (Bradley 1980, 49). The women's telepathy symbolizes their attunement to the needs of others: Melora, a pacifist, is the only woman who understands the soldier Bard, owing to her empathic abilities; Melisendra senses a caring Paul under his brutal exterior; and Carlina works out her bitterness against Bard by joining a women's group who worship the Goddess and provide birth control, abortions, infertility cures, and health care for women.

Two to Conquer multiplies through many characters the sadomasochistic transformation of the quest for recognition. Paul and Bard, both sadists, are literally doubles, Paul from a future earth and Bard from Darkover. Jessica Benjamin thus describes the sadist's quest for recognition:

> erotic domination expresses a basic differentiating tendency that has undergone a transformation. . . . Violation is the attempt to push the other outside the self, to attack the other's separate reality in order finally to discover it. . . . The thrill of transgression and the sense of complete freedom for the sadist depend on the masochist's survival. When the masochist endures his unremitting attack and remains intact, the sadist experiences this as love. (1988, 68)

Bard, illegitimate and feeling inferior, repeatedly rapes women, violating and attacking them to prove his own manly differentiation from them and to still his anxious fears of unworthiness. Attacking his fiancée Carlina, he justifies himself as establishing his manhood through difference from women:

> How dared she refuse him now, as if he were nothing to her? He would not be un-manned twice on mid-winter night by some damned woman's whims!

He dragged her into the gallery, gripping her so hard that she cried out, and forced his lips down on hers. . . . This time he would not submit to her meekly, but he would impose his will on her! (Bradley 1980, 93–94)

Bard also rapes Lisarda, Lilla, and Melisendra. Similarly, Paul justifies rape by its usefulness in establishing his own male identity as different: "He didn't play the stupid games women tried to make men play. . . . Her mother had probably taught her that you had to make noises about rape, unless the man got down on his knees and pretended to be a capon, a gutless wonder who'd let a woman lead him around by the nose. . . . Hell, he knew better than that. That was what women wanted and they loved it" (8). Although Bard gives his concubine Melisendra to Paul to humiliate her, Melisendra resists Paul passively: "She lay passive under his caresses, . . . simply acting as if he were not there at all. Damn the woman, he didn't want her that way, he would rather she'd scream and fight him than accept him as a loathsome duty!" (218). Melisendra's passive acceptance of him as a duty fails to establish his identity, making him "not there at all." But a woman who fights and still is dominated would establish him as other to her, with a will and identity of his own; she also would establish herself as a survivor, one who endures Paul's violence and remains intact, which he may experience as a substitute for love.

In *Two to Conquer,* the threat is always present that women will choose a masochistic role to complement the sadism of the men. Jessica Benjamin thus describes the benefits of masochism:

> The "masochistic" child has endured . . . retaliation, in the form of either punishment or withdrawal. . . . The masochist despairs of ever holding the attention or winning the recognition of the other, of being securely held in the other's mind. . . . The masochist's wish to be reached, penetrated, found, released . . . is the other side of the sadist's wish to discover the other. (1988, 72–73)

While Melora successfully refuses Bard, and Carlina and Melisendra retreat from his sadism — Carlina physically to the island of the goddess, Melisendra into apathy — Melisendra seems on the verge of such a masochistic compliance with Paul after his rape of her: " 'I have always wanted [Bard] to be this way with me. . . . I thought, better the cruelty that I knew than new cruelty from a stranger. . . . But you have taught me otherwise' " (Bradley 1980, 219). Bradley thus exploits the erotic potential of the sadomasochistic romance by acknowledging its attraction.

Women writers exploit this erotic potential, but they also use the sadomasochistic romance to explore sexuality as a form of power. Catharine MacKinnon points out that

> Women and men are divided by gender, made into the sexes as we know
> them, by the social requirements of heterosexuality, which institutionalizes
> male sexual dominance and female sexual submission. . . . A woman is a
> being who identifies and is identified as one whose sexuality exists for
> someone else, who is socially male. . . . Is women's sexuality its absence?
> (MacKinnon 1982, 245)

In Bradley's *Two to Conquer*, Bard makes us aware that sexuality is a form of
power, because of his definition of erotic sex as rape, and because Bradley
gives him the ability to cast a "glamour": Bard can not only rape women
because of his greater strength but can also take over their minds to make
them come to his bed against their own wills (36). As MacKinnon describes
it, sexual "objectification is [a] social process. It unites act with word, construction with expression, perception with enforcement, myth with reality"
(1982, 253). Bard's ability to cast a "glamour" represents the powerful influence of socialization on women, who acquiesce to men's desires against their
own wills, what Kate Millett calls "interior colonization" (1987, 33). In *Two
to Conquer*, Melisendra comments, "I have come to know that many women
lie with a man under a glamour, and sometimes they do not even know it"
(Bradley 1980, 268).

But the women of Bradley's novel do not react with masochism to Bard's
sadism. As aliens, as colonized, females have a special perspective on the
events of their society. Their special knowledge ironically derives from their
alienation, and allows them to resist the men's sadistic definitions of their
relations to women. Carlina and Melisendra respond by defining female
sexuality as absence: Carlina by her chastity in service of the goddess, Melisendra by her refusal to respond sexually to Bard. Lilla responds by adopting
the norms of male sexuality, free and uncommitted sexuality. Although Bradley portrays these women with sympathy, she presents these choices as
limiting.

Thus Bradley uses sadomasochistic eroticism but through subversion
resolves it into a safe space. Like many other women science fiction writers,
she constructs a fantasy of the man who gives up sadism *because* the woman
has given up masochism, because she has a voice to tell the man her pain
and her desires. In *Two to Conquer*, this voice is represented by telepathy, by
the traditionally feminine ability to share feelings with a man so that he
cannot avoid or deny them. When Bard rapes her for the second time, rapes
that Bard justifies by their former engagement and by his belief that "in your
hearts you [women] desire a man who will take you, and master you" (Bradley 1980, 269), Carlina reverses her special power of empathy, making Bard
feel her pain telepathically:

> Mortal terror, and awful humiliation, as she lay with her clothes torn off,
> impaled, tearing pain, but worse than the pain, the horror of knowing
> herself only a thing to be used. . . . self-hatred and horror that she had not

forced him to kill her first. . . . the fear and knowledge . . . that she would be no more than a womb for his child, . . . a horrid, hateful parasite that could . . . take over her clean body. . . . Bard did not know that he was on the floor, writhing, that he screamed aloud, in the depth of this violation. . . . The world was darkness and his own sobs as he felt with Carlina the horror of being taken again, used again, that *he* had dared to find pleasure in this horror (272–73).

Since Bard will not believe women who tell him they do not desire him, that they recognize his rape of them as violation to shore up his own sense of power, the telepathic communication with Carlina forces Bard to *feel* what he has done, so that he truly hears what the women have said to him.

After this experience, when Carlina seizes the power of her telepathic voice to resist the role of masochist, Bard is no longer a sadist. He recognizes Melora as an independent person whom he loves, and he offers what restitution he can to the other women he has harmed. His new abilities are symbolized by his own growing telepathy: he now can securely hold a woman in his mind; he has the capacity for mutual recognition. This is a utopian fantasy about a man's sudden change. But it is a compelling and useful fantasy about women's continued resistance until at last they have an effect, about a woman speaking her self in many different voices until she achieves a change.[14] Bradley, who elsewhere valorizes homosexual and lesbian relationships, in this book presents Melora with Bard and Melisendra with Paul, those who achieve a heterosexual relation based on mutual recognition, as central models.

Thus the female aliens of women's science fiction demand from men, and teach men to give, recognition, an ability these male characters had been unable to learn from other humans. Often the female alien's culture has

14. In Jane Yolen's *Cards of Grief* (1984), the woman's voice is represented not by telepathy, but by the feminine art of grieving through poetry and song. The alien woman Linni, formally called the Gray Wanderer, is the Queen's Own Griever in a matrilineal culture where women excel in the major art of the culture—grieving. Grieving is an art, explains Linni, of speaking "in symbols what I feel here, here in the heart" (17), and another female Griever ritually claims, "My work is firm, firmer than sleep or the Cup that carries it, firmer than the strength of heroes" (53). When the Terrans come, from a future earth culture still sexist although more equitable than ours (70, 74), the Terran Aaron falls in love with Linni. What they give each other is mutual recognition, Linni teaching Aaron how to grieve, Aaron teaching Linni how to love; they are both punished by their societies for the exchange, although through it their cultures share an understanding otherwise impossible. In this novel, then, the pattern holds: the story's goal is mutual recognition between a heterosexual man and woman. The differences in desires of men and women are here represented by the alien status of the woman, but the symbiotic feminine ideal is represented by the art form of grieving, rather than telepathy. In the novels where symbiosis is represented by telepathy, and also here where it is represented by the poetry and oral performance that are the manifestations of grieving, the arts are *women's* arts. They indicate that in these alien cultures, women have the voices to tell their feelings which are traditionally not allowed in Western earth culture.

already always given her recognition, so that she knows to expect it. These writers, then, offer a story where boy meets girl, falls in love, but must learn a different cultural pattern of heterosexual relationships in order to achieve that love.[15] This revision of character transforms the love story into a problem-solving story, which is essential for science fiction. As Joanna Russ has pointed out, science fiction as a genre revolves around problem-solving: "The myths of science fiction run along the lines of exploring a new world conceptually . . . , creating needed physical or social machinery, assessing the consequences of technological or other changes. . . . These are not stories about men *qua* Man and women *qua* Woman; they are myths of human intelligence and human adaptability" (1972b, 18).

For example, in Anne McCaffrey's *Dragonflight* (1968), the love story of Lessa and F'lar becomes the problem-solving story of ridding the planet of "thread" (destructive plant spores that rain from the sky). Both Lessa and F'lar are dragonriders but, although both are of Terran stock, Lessa is a descendant of those who have "Power," who can cast a "glamor" to influence people against their wills, as well as speak telepathically to all dragons, not only to the dragon she has "impressed," or bonded with. Here again an alien woman, Lessa, represents symbiosis, the idealized mother; and a human man, F'lar, represents independence, the idealized father, "incapable of emotion" (McCaffrey 1982a, 21). Since Lessa has grown up dodging blows of a sadistic tyrant, Fax (13, 18, and 49), a warning to the reader of what kind of man F'lar might become (69), the story derives suspense and sadistic eroticism from the possibility that Lessa and F'lar might fail to achieve intersubjectivity, that they might remain in the sadomasochistic relationship that F'lar has culturally been taught and that Lessa fears. F'lar's potential sadism is indicated by his rape of Lessa during the dragon mating, and by his repeated shaking of Lessa when she "disobeys" him (54, 112, 123–25, 141, 152, 168,

---

15. Note the similarities and differences between these science fiction romances centering on the woman as alien and "drugstore" romance fiction as interpreted by women readers in Janice Radway's *Reading the Romance: Women, Patriarchy, and Popular Literature* "it is essential to point out that Dot and many of the writers and readers of romances interpret these stories as chronicles of female triumph. . . . Dot believes a good romance focuses on an intelligent and able heroine who finds a man who recognizes her special qualities and is capable of loving and caring for her as she wants to be loved. Thus Dot understands such an ending to say that female independence and marriage are compatible rather than mutually exclusive. The romance she most values and recommends for her readers are those with 'strong,' 'fiery' heroines who are capable of 'defying the hero,' softening him, and showing him the value of loving and caring for another" (Radway 1984, 54). However, in the drugstore romances, the relatively passive methods of the heroine's changing the hero (78) are very different from the gender-defying activities of the alien women of science fiction. In addition, the science fiction by women exploits the erotic sadomasochism only to deny it, unlike what Rabine finds in the Harlequin romances, which "sexualize her impotence": "the heroine's restraint [by the hero] becomes on the one hand intermittent, and on the other hand emotionally and sexually gratifying" (1985, 256).

171, 194–95, and 253). The reader anticipates the author's depicting Lessa as masochist, one who might respond to F'lar's sadism. As Benjamin explains of sadomasochism in general, "The ideal lover's power calls forth the freedom and abandon that are otherwise suppressed, he offers an alienated version — an 'ever-ready look-alike' . . . — of the safe space that permits self-discovery, aloneness in the presence of the other" (Benjamin 1988, 131). Rather than sexual pleasure, the masochist thus achieves sexual abandonment only at the price of physical or psychological pain. Certainly Lessa has been suppressed while growing up, literally in hiding from the tyrant Fax who killed her parents, and at first we expect F'lar to become the typical sadistic lover for her.

But because Lessa refuses to be a victim, McCaffrey offers the reader a different outcome. The novel exploits the sadistic eroticism of the alienated form of love: the rape occurs because dragon-riders telepathically experience the dragons' sexual arousal and Lessa abandons herself to this experience — "The mating passion of the two dragons at that moment spiraled wide to include Lessa. . . . With a longing cry she clung to F'lar. She felt his body rock-firm against hers, his hard arms lifting her up, his mouth fastening mercilessly on hers as she drowned deep in another unexpected flood of desire" (McCaffrey 1982a, 124). This is a rape despite Lessa's arousal because, whereas F'lar knows that riders' sexual desires are heightened by telepathic contact with their dragons, Lessa does not expect this outcome, and so has no chance to say "no" to F'lar. For Lessa and F'lar, as Benjamin explains for other sadomasochistic couples, the man desires sadistic violation of the other's body in order to test her survival, and the woman is in danger of accepting the violation because she identifies vicariously with the power of the sadist. "The masochist's wish to experience [her] authentic, inner reality in the company of an other parallels the sadist's wish to get outside the self into a shared reality" (1988, 73), suggests Benjamin. Man and woman, Benjamin posits, desire mutual recognition, but choose alienated versions in the sadomasochistic relationship because these are all they have known. That Lessa and F'lar experience sexual union *through* the dragons indicates the alienation of their relationship.

In McCaffrey's novel, however, the dragons offer an alternative model for relationship, for they telepathically exchange mutual recognition with their riders. When Lessa first met F'lar's dragon Mnementh, "He arched his neck so that one eye was turned directly on the girl" (McCaffrey 1982a, 57); this is the exchange of glances symbolizing recognition that we have seen in other novels, although displaced here to F'lar's dragon. Moreover, when she impresses her own dragon Ramoth, "A feeling of joy suffused Lessa; a feeling of warmth, tenderness, unalloyed affection, and instant respect and admiration flooded mind and heart and soul. Never again would Lessa lack an advocate, a defender, an intimate, aware instantly of the temper of her mind

and heart, of her desires" (83). Similarly, Lessa watches F'lar with Mnementh, and muses, "She had, of course, heard of the strange affinity between
rider and dragon, but this was the first time she realized that love was part of
that bond. Or that this reserved, cold man was capable of such deep emotion"
(72). The equality of female with male that Lessa desires is acted out and
vindicated, as well, by the dragons. To the former leader, Lessa vindicates
herself by asserting that queen dragons can also fly (91). F'lar indicates his
potential for growth when he teaches Lessa to fly Ramoth and recognizes her
abilities equal to his: " 'Of course they can fly,' he assured her, his voice full
of pride and respect. 'That's why they have wings!' " (143)

The love story, however, is not the only story of *Dragonflight*, and this
second story, centered on problem-solving, provides the means of change for
Lessa and F'lar's relationship. In *Dragonflight*, the problem is how to rid the
planet of threads, when people have stopped believing in their existence and
allowed dragonkind to dwindle. Although some aggression and independence is required for this task, more important are adaptability and collaboration: how can F'lar achieve collaboration between all the peoples of the
planet Pern so that they can fight threads together? The problem of threads
thus also defines a goal for Lessa and F'lar's relationship: how can F'lar grow
out of his sadism and Lessa out of her fear in order to collaborate as adults
who support each other?

Very gradually, F'lar comes to respect Lessa for the same strengths he
respects in the men he fights along side of, and to allow himself to show
the "feminine" emotions indicating to Lessa that he recognizes her as an
independent other. F'lar feels the desire to comfort Lessa (McCaffrey 1982a,
158) but does not, hugs her in response to her sympathy for him while they
work together (212), smiles "down at her, his eyes glowing" (215), and kisses
her while asleep "With a tenderness he would never show her awake" (246).
Finally, when she returns from her dragonride between times, he kisses her,
hugs her, holds her, "all his careful detachment abandoned" (275). This
change in F'lar is linked to Lessa's heroic accomplishments and to her heroism, as a refutation of the argument that women need to be protected. "If
Lessa could jump four hundred Turns *between* and lead five Weyrs back, she
could take care of herself" (284), F'lar eventually realizes.[16] Thus, in this
story, the alien woman Lessa, who already combines male and female
strengths, in refusing to become the victim that F'lar desires, teaches him to

16. Compare Norton's *Web of the Witch World* (1964), where Jaelithe reminds Simon that
Loyse does not need special protection; "Loyse was no helpless maiden," Simon realizes, "but
had a mind, will, and skills of her own" (17). This realization by men that women are not
helpless is frequently indicated in science fiction novels by women's outrunning men;
for example, Simon is outrun by two women: "He doubted if he could match her pace,
though Jaelithe was not too far behind her" (Norton 1964, 162). See also, Charlotte Perkins
Gilman 1979, 17; the female panthers in Phyllis Gotlieb's series also run faster than their

become the balanced man whom she desires, the man who can recognize her abilities as she recognizes his. This outcome, of course, is a fantasy, but a useful one, which might reinforce in women readers their own attempts to avoid the role of victim, even though men around them may not change as easily as F'lar.

In a final example, in Jayge Carr's *Leviathan's Deep* (1979), an alien woman and a Terran man form a relationship to save the woman's planet from drug smugglers. Much of the story, however, exploits sadistic eroticism despite the gender ideologies that separate them. Neill is the Terran male, who seeks revenge on his former alien prison guard by trying to rape her once she helps his escape. He is astonished to learn that she cannot be raped, that a membrane physically protects her from penetration unless she desires it:

> "I was fine, naturally," [thought the alien woman]. "When you bang your head against a stone wall, it's your head and not the wall that gets hurt. . . ."
> He broke the silence. "It's your choice." He sounded almost accusing. "Isn't it? Truly, physically, your choice?" (Carr 1979, 62)

But this physical protection is further accompanied on the planet Delyafam (a pun, *de la femme*) by an inversion of gender roles: children are nurtured

---

mates. In a letter in response to reading my interpretations of her novels, Anne McCaffrey wrote:

> I can't imagine where you derived the notion that F'lar was sadistic, since I certainly never thought of him as more than just aloof, or at the worse self-centered since he intended to use *his* candidate if she was successful, to bring the Weyr round to his knowledge of the imminence of Thread. He was more of a crusader, devoting most of his energy to the "lost cause" of preparing his planet when he is the only one who perceives a threat. *Dragonflight* is basically a love story, a romance, not the "eternal struggle of women to be equal to men" and Lessa is a victim who becomes a survivor. Your analysis of the psycho-sexual interaction may well be correct, given the tenets you adopt to scrutinize the yarn with; but that aint the way I wrote it, nor the purpose I wrote it for.

Anne McCaffrey also cautions that my interpretation of *The Ship Who Sang* (which I discuss later in this chapter) is a misconstruction:

> I also fail to see Helva in the role of servant since she is far more powerful within her ship-self than any one of her brawn partners could possibly be. In fact, she feels sorry for those who cannot share her ineffable strength and abilities. But then I don't see "being needed" and "serving a need" as detrimental to a personality. So many people crack up because they are "not needed," feel "unneeded, unwanted": being/feeling useful is a basic human desire/need. Helva was to show people, as I often like to do, that there are many ways to overcome handicaps which can lead to success in a totally unexpected direction.

in the pouches of male hosts and the women rule, exploiting men in many of the ways that human men exploit women (8, 25, 53, 63, 65–66, 166–67, 124). "Every now and then, we have an Equality for Women movement," Neill explains about earth to the alien woman, "but they usually peter out, sooner or later, because of physical reality. Man is the natural provider, the master . . . the sexual commander" (62).

Thus when Val and Neill confront each other on the island they escape to, they vye with one another about who will be the sadist: after the attempted rape of Val by Neill, Val fantasizes, "I could force you, if I wanted to bother" (Carr 1979, 67). Neill knows that "The best, the best, . . . and it's rare, . . . is equality. Two people, mutually contributing, mutually caring for each other, loving each other, doing for each other" (66). Both Neill and Val are held from forming such a relationship by their desires for dominance, based on their cultures' mirror-reversed gender ideologies. This novel, then, plays with the tradition of the woman alien: Neill imagines himself as hero of the male space opera, who can rape and so conquer the aliens. The alien woman, however, views herself as dominant, not the victim; literally she cannot be raped. Since the female cannot be victimized, the sadomasochistic problem is doubled in this novel: how can two such limited persons learn to work together? As in the other novels, the author makes it happen—when Val is injured and Neill nurses her back to health. Despite her culture's restrictions, Val comes to see Neill as "friend as well as partner, a mental equal, a mind delectable to explore, a dear, loving comrade" (187). Yet this novel ends tragically, with the ideal of mutuality only a dream; Val kills Neill since he unknowingly possesses a secret about her race that, when used by other Terrans, would make Delyenes vulnerable to imperialist exploitation. As a rebel, Val successfully keeps her planet unprofitable for Terran exploitation. Nevertheless, because of her own, and Terran, gender ideologies, she fails in learning to trust another as her equal: on the final page, the novel gestures toward a son with Neill's blue eyes as hope that a future Delyene might accomplish such trust and recognition.[17]

In science fiction by women, the plot of the alien woman thus brings together self-sufficient men, potential sadists, with symbiotic women, potential masochists, but it disrupts the expected heterosexist conclusion with mutual recognition and problem solving—what Rachel Blau DuPlessis calls "writing beyond the ending."[18] Although women writers play with the erotics

17. See Lefanu 1988, 45–48, from whose reading of Carr's novel I have benefited, but who emphasizes the duality of the gender reversal that contaminates the politics.

18. See also Monica Hughes's *The Keeper of the Isis Light* (1980). In Hughes's novel, the female hero Olwen shares narrative point of view with the earth man Mark London, the plot involving Olwen's gradual understanding that she is alien, altered surgically and genetically, and thus different from the humans who settle her planet: "Perhaps you are right in thinking of me as an alien. I know I am different from you. You see—I do not kill" (Hughes 1984, 116). Olwen

of the sadomasochistic relation, they create alien women who resist that plot and, instead, insist on their own subjectivity and pleasure.[19]

Woman as Machine

The machine in science fiction, Mark Rose argues, may be "a positive image . . . of the power of reason expressed through science," "serving as the agency through which man explores and protects himself from the cosmos"; the machine may also be a negative image "of the nonhuman, . . . a threat to humane values" (1981, 139). Mark Rose's "man," although unintentionally excluding women, is accurate. In our society, and in traditional science fiction by men, science and technology have been male territory, and the machine has been seen as male. When a woman is represented by male writers as a machine, as in the famous science fiction short story, "Helen O'Loy" by Lester del Rey (modeled on the Greek tale of the sculptor Pygmalion who falls in love with his statue), man's superiority is indicated by his link to science; woman's inferiority by her mechanical body. Both the positive and the negative meanings of the machine in men's science fiction are often represented as negative in women's science fiction.

The machine as male is used by women writers to represent negatively science as the power of reason, and science as nonhuman. For example, as do male writers, female writers see man as machine as negative: alienated, mechanical, living without love or joy. In science fiction by women, however, man as machine is not representative of all humanity, but only of the masculine gender. In Joanna Russ's *Picnic on Paradise* (1968), "Machine," an alienated teenaged boy cynically wears earphones to keep out the trivialities of his human companions, aiming to develop a machine-like freedom from emo-

---

is stronger, faster, better adapted to the planet and more tolerant than Mark, with whom she falls in love. In a twist of the convention, which shows final acceptance by the man of the alien woman, Mark proposes, but Olwen rejects, marriage. In rewriting the ending of the heterosexual romance, Hughes resists conservative readings of her novel.

19. These novels, then, represent the peculiar process by which women come to know themselves, both as "other" to dominant men from men's perspective, and as subjects who in constructing themselves have effects in the world. For reflections on this double mode of knowing, see Weiler 1988, 58. Other science fictions by women that follow this alien woman plot, besides many of the other novels by Norton, Bradley, and McCaffrey, include Marcia Bennett's *Shadow Singer* (1984); Dorothy Bryant's *The Kin of Ata Are Waiting for You* (1976); Octavia Butler's *Survivor* (1978); the second and third novels of C. J. Cherryh's *Faded Sun* trilogy, *Shon' Jir* (1978), and *Kutath* (1979); Suzette Haden Elgin's *Communipath* trilogy—*The Communipaths* (1970), *Furthest* (1971), and *At the Seventh Level* (1972), published together as *Communipath Worlds* (1980); Ann Maxwell's *Fire Dancer* trilogy—*Fire Dancer* (1982), *Dancer's Luck* (1983b), and *Dancer's Illusion* (1983a); Doris Piserchia's *Star Rider* (1974); Margaret St. Clair's *Sign of the Labrys* (1963); James Tiptree Jr.'s (Alice Sheldon's) *Up the Walls of the World* (1978); and Sydney Van Scyoc's *Star Mother* (1975).

tions and vulnerability. In Tanith Lee's *The Silver Metal Lover* (1981), a machine makes the perfect musician and lover for women, enacting mechanically all the right sexual moves; the female hero of the novel by her love gives him a soul, making him fully human. In the film *Making Mr. Right* (1987), directed by Susan Seidelman and written by Floyd Byars and Laurie Frank, the look-alike robot made by the male scientist is more human than his maker, who lives only for work, without love or joy; at the end of the movie the scientist, less human than the robot, flies off into space, the robot remaining on earth to take up a human place through love of the female hero. Both the powers of (masculine) reason and the inhumanity of modern science are criticized in these portraits by women of male machines. Women in these stories, unlike men, are not machines; indeed, they can awaken humanity in the soul of the male machine.[20]

In novels by women offering portraits of the woman as machine, moreover, the subordination of woman-as-machine does not carry the proof of man's rational powers that it does in science fiction by men, for the mechanical women created by women writers will not stay in the servant mold men have designed for them. Ursula K. Le Guin's commentary on the portrayal of the other in science fiction offers a helpful path for discerning the import of the woman as machine in women's science fiction: "If you deny any affinity with another person, if you declare it to be wholly different from yourself—as men have done to women, and class has done to class, and nation has done to nation—. . . . You have made it into a thing to which the only possible relationship is a power relationship. And thus you have fatally impoverished yourself" (1979, 99).[21] The machine in science fiction by women often represents both dehumanized male science, from which women are excluded, and also the woman-as-alien, the object which differs from the dominant norm, the other literally objectified. The woman-as-machine in science fiction by women is not dehumanized as men are, by technology and modern life, in the masculine gender role that requires suppression of feelings. Instead, the woman-as-machine is dehumanized, rendered mechanical in her responses, by the scripts she is expected by society to play: she is dehumanized by the function of servant. The trope of woman-as-machine exposes the objectification of women as the machinery of society that carries out men's desires.[22] Like other women aliens in women's science

20. For further analysis of men as aliens in science fiction by women, see Catherine Podojil, in "Sisters, Daughters, and Aliens," in Riley, ed., 1978, 70–86.

21. Cf. Karen Horney, 1967, "The Dread of Woman," 133–46: men dread women because of the original power of the mother, an anxiety transferred to fear of the vagina and of engulfment; therefore men seek to protect themselves by seeing women as inferior and so not to be feared. See also Chodorow's development of Horney's concepts, 1989, 34–35.

22. May Irwin, turn of the century actress and feminist, argued in "My Views on That Ever-Interesting Topic—Woman," that women are seen by men as "household slaves, piece[s] of household machinery" (1912, 1057–58). My thanks to Sharen Ammon for this reference.

fiction, she is an ironic reversal of male norms. Constituted as a mechanical servant to men, she yet achieves humanity. Inferior and defective, she is more human than her masters. In this section we will look at women writers — C. L. Moore, Anne McCaffrey, Barbara Paul, James Tiptree, Jr., and Tanith Lee — who literalize the inferiority attributed to woman by presenting her as machine, but who then endow the machine with the humanity to contest the value placed on her services.

C. L. Moore's novella, "No Woman Born" (1944), reprinted in *The Best of C. L. Moore*, exemplifies the contradictory meanings of woman as machine. In her story, which alludes frequently to Mary Shelley's *Frankenstein* (Moore 1975, 232–33, 235, 241, 242), Deirdre, a dancer nearly destroyed in a fire, has had her body entirely recreated as a machine by the male scientist Maltzer. Deirdre's body, unlike Frankenstein's monster's body, is a flawless creation of science, and at first she appears proof of man's rational powers. As the feminist analyst of culture, Naomi Wolf, points out in *The Beauty Myth: How Images of Beauty Are Used Against Women*, "The specter of the future is not that women will be slaves, but that we will be robots. . . . [We will be subject to technologies that] replace the faulty, mortal female body, piece by piece, with 'perfect' artifice" (1991, 267).

Deirdre's body is also objectified — a thing — to the male narrator: her voice "was the voice of an automaton that sounded in the room, metallic, without inflection" (Moore 1975, 204); her body was "nothing but metal coils. . . . only machinery heaped in a flowered chair" (204). However, because of the grace with which Deirdre constitutes herself and moves, she seems fully alive and female. Through the detailed education she has gone through to become herself, Deirdre is an apt instance of what the psychologist Hogie Wyckoff calls "Plastic Woman" in *Scripts People Live*: "In an effort to obtain strokes, [a woman] encases herself in plastic," using the artifice of makeup, costume, and stylized movement to become an idealized sex object (Wyckoff 1980, 213). Even as a robot, Deirdre is such a being: "the machinery moved, exquisitely, smoothly, with a grace as familiar as the swaying poise he remembered"; her voice was still "the sweet husky voice of Deirdre," and "she was golden still" (Moore 1975, 205).[23] Indeed, this eroticism reveals the connection between the woman-as-machine and the humanoid alien woman discussed earlier. The woman as machine is erotic *because* she is a machine, deformed and objectified — this is part of her appeal to men fascinated by their own apparent superiority.

---

23. In her essay on C. L. Moore, Susan Gubar points out that "Deirdre had been a kind of golden girl of stage and screen; when her brain is planted inside a golden case, she paradoxically finds this metamorphosis less strange than she might, since both before and after the accident she was a woman created by and for men: a 'marionette'. . . . Unlike the 'mechanical dolls' in their human bodies who perform before her on the stage, however, she is now literally what she was before metaphorically: a living doll" (1980, 21).

The men—the scientist Maltzer and her agent and the narrator Harris —are also terrified of Deirdre, fearing that she is "not wholly human" (Moore 1975, 277), that they have brought "life into the world unlawfully" (276). Maltzer, especially, insists that Deirdre is defective: " 'She hasn't any sex. She isn't female any more. She doesn't know that yet, but she'll learn' " (218). Although Maltzer attributes her lack of humanity to her metal body, the eroticism of the portrait suggests instead that it is female sexuality itself that is not human: "surprised at the smallness and exquisite proportions of her," Harris realizes that she still would have "looked oddly naked" without clothes (207); and he admires "the long, slow, languorous rhythms of her body" (222), and "Her arms . . . pale shining gold, tapered smoothly, without modeling, and flexible their whole length in diminishing metal bracelets fitting one inside the other clear down to the slim, round wrists" (207). It is the sexuality of Deirdre, not her metal body, that make the men fear Deirdre, seeing her as grotesque.

The metaphor of woman-as-machine-as-entertainer that Moore constructs aptly exposes the situation of women as sex objects, machinery for arousing and satisfying men's desires. Influenced by the vamps of 1930s films, Moore has Deirdre in one scene enact the lighting of a cigarette: "She moved lithely across the room, . . . and stooped to a cigarette box on a table. Her fingers were deft" (Moore 1975, 231). As in the 1930s movies, the sharing of a cigarette symbolizes sex: Maltzer "let her put the brown cylinder between his lips and hold a light to it" (231). Deirdre's new mechanical body, however, allows her to expose herself as machinery, eliciting and performing desire. Harris reflects, "He had not sat here watching a robot smoke and accepting it as normal. . . . And yet he had. . . . And she had done it so deftly, so naturally, wearing her radiant humanity with such rightness" (236). Deirdre's convincing performance of the motions of desire and her laughter at the men's acceptance of the illusion force the men to the brink of questioning whether all women are merely enacting desire, whether the heterosexuality they depend on as natural is really performance.

In addition, Deirdre will not stay mechanical, will not serve the masters who made her. " 'I'm not a Frankenstein monster made out of dead flesh. I'm myself—alive,' " she claims (Moore 1975, 235). Wyckoff points out that the antithesis for the script of "Plastic Woman" is "to reclaim power over her life by taking responsibility for creating it. . . . She commits herself to being concerned with how she feels on the inside rather than how she looks from the outside" (Wyckoff 1980, 215). The first indication of Deirdre's rebellion against the men who wish to protect her comes when she makes this claim of internal autonomy: " 'since it's his own machine, . . . the body may be his work, but the brain that makes it something more than a collection of metal rings is *me*, and he couldn't restrain me against my will even if he wanted to' " (Moore 1975, 217). Deirdre asserts her autonomy over the men who made her, first, in returning to her career as an artist, next in her claim that she is "superhuman," "not sub-human" (287). The men see Deirdre's refusal to play to their desires as giving up her humanity; Harris worries about her "withdrawal to metalhood" (232). But Deirdre also asserts her autonomy by showing that she can act her sex *role*, that she can put on and take it off, perform it, that it is a "disguise" (236). As feminist theorist Judith Butler observes, "gender proves to be performative — that is, constituting the identity it is purported to be" (1990, 25).[24]

Moore's story, however, is not optimistic, for the last sentence still sees Deirdre through Harris's — the male — gaze: " 'I wonder,' [Deirdre] repeated, the distant taint of metal already in her voice" (Moore 1975, 288). The power of establishing a norm for what constitutes the human, the power to see women as defective even when serving men, is still in the hands (or the eyes) of men. Created to be an ideal, a union of science and art, male and female, Deirdre is not accepted by the men as human. She serves and offers pleasure through her dancing, yet she feels "unnatural" (286), alienated from those with whom she would like a partnership.[25]

Similarly, in Anne McCaffrey's *The Ship Who Sang* (1961 as story, 1969 as novel), a baby who would have grown up deformed is instead given the mechanical body of a spaceship. The ship is the female-as-object, a thing who serves and rescues and heals, but who is seen (covertly, at least) as defective. *The Ship Who Sang* begins with the sentence, "She was born a thing and as such would be condemned if she failed to pass the encephalograph test required of all newborn babies" (McCaffrey 1979, 1). When a pilot first enters the ship, he exclaims, "you beautiful thing" (8). As the psychologist Dorothy Dinnerstein explains, our culture encourages us to see "the female as a mutilated creature" (1976, 181). Psychotherapist Anne Wilson Schaef calls this "The Original Sin of Being Born Female": "to be born female means to be born innately inferior, damaged . . . there is something innately 'wrong' with us" (1985, 24). Woman as machine is frequently represented as already dehumanized by some deformity, before granted the machinery that saves her life yet still marks her as deformed.

In fact, the ship is dehumanized not so much by her initial physical

---

24. See also Judith Butler 1990, 136: "In other words, act, gestures, and desire produce the effect of an internal core or substance, but produce this *on the surface* of the body. . . . Such acts, gestures, enactments, generally construed, are *performative* in the sense that the essence or identity that they otherwise purport to express are *fabrications* manufactured and sustained through corporeal signs and other discursive means. That the gendered body is performative suggests that it has no ontological status apart from the various acts which constitute its reality. This also suggests that if that reality is fabricated as an interior essence, that very interiority is an effect and function of a decidedly public and social discourse, the public regulation of fantasy through the surface politics of the body."

25. For a reading that sees the negative ending as a result of Moore's own politics, rather than as a reflection of sexual politics, see Sarah Gamble's essay on C. L. Moore (1991, 46–48). On the male "gaze," see Laura Mulvey 1989.

defect but by the feminine role of servant. In *The Ship Who Sang*, Helva, the ship, is literally a member of the "Service," designed to "take care of herself, and her ambulatory half, in any situation already recorded in the annals of Central Worlds" (McCaffrey 1979, 7). "Conditioned for a partner, for someone to take care of, to do for, to live with" (101), Helva does all housekeeping and galley duty, handles piloting and navigation, and teaches herself to sing in order to provide her "brawns" (human partners) with entertainment. In *PartnerShip*, the sequel to *The Ship Who Sang*, Nancia Perez y de Gras, a "shellperson" who also wears a spaceship as her body, in a moment of recognition sees clearly the relation between herself and her father: "Just another man, seeing in her nothing but a tool to serve his plans, coming in to give her a rating on how well or ill she'd done for him. Were all men like that?" (McCaffrey and Ball 1992, 315)

But the female ship is also a combination of male and female cultural roles: technology with sentiments and conscience. In *The Ship Who Sang*, McCaffrey literalizes the romance of man and machine: the ship is paired with a human "brawn," almost always a male, and, if male, one who eroticizes her. To be paired with a ship, human pilots "court" her and compete for her choice (McCaffrey 1979, 129). Helva falls in love with her first brawn, Jennan (11), and she takes his name (JH 834, changed from XH 834). The language that the two speak to each other is sexualized: Jennan asks her "if there're any more at home like you" (12), and is forced "to defend the 834's virgin honor" (15). A later partner, Niall, openly states his desire: "I'd have to open that coffin they've sealed you in. I'd have to look at your beautiful face, touch that god-lovely smile, and hold you" (229). And Helva reflects on his desire for union with the machine: "There had been such desire in his voice, in the wiry body straining against the metal barrier" (240). The ship thus literalizes the union of rational man and (feminine) machine, of man's technological domination of nature.

But *The Ship Who Sang* also literalizes the mechanics of traditional heterosexual marriage, for, as Germaine Greer explains, "Romance sanctions drudgery, physical incompetence and prostitution" (1972, 198). Psychologist Anne Wilson Schaef analyzes "The Perfect Marriage . . . [as] two half-persons who could not survive without each other. Publicly, it appears that the man is a whole person and the woman is a dependent, childlike cripple. Privately, though, it is the other way around" (1985, 60). In *The Ship Who Sang*, Helva appears the cripple, but in private is the strong and capable one, making her "brawn" look good in public. Helva's drudgery in Service is recompensed by the "romance" between her and her brawn. Helva also offers a symbolic portrait of the alienated masochistic victim that suits the desires of the sadistic dominator: deformed and inferior, yet encased in metal, Helva will survive and so prove her "love."

Although Helva's recognition of her role is far from feminist, she yet recognizes herself as conditioned to be a machine who serves. Thus she claims a degree of self-consciousness and autonomy: "Now Helva could see that the subtle, massive conditioning she'd received in her formative years was double-edged. It made her happy as a shell-person, it had dedicated her to her life in Service, and it made Pay-off a mockery. What else could a BB ship do but continue as she had started . . . in Service?" (McCaffrey 1979, 205). Like the middle-class wife in a traditional midcentury United States marriage, Helva's job, serving others, gives her no autonomous options when those she serves choose to leave her. Rather than building on this insight, however, Helva's desires return to her eroticized relation with her human partners: "But surely there would be another man with qualities to recommend him" (205).

A union of woman and machine similar to Helva's occurs in Barbara Paul's *An Exercise for Madmen* (1978): Jennie, the only humanist on an artificial planet of scientists, offers herself as brain for the central computer in order to save the planet. As the only humanist, she sees herself as "the outsider, suffering loudly and dramatically from feelings of estrangement and alienation from my society" (Paul 1978, 78). She first "saves" the planet by welcoming in an alien who releases the humans' antirationalist Dionysian side. When that side grows destructive, she rescues the humans from their excesses: she volunteers to become a cyborg, to operate all the "services to sustain life" on the planet (21). The image is again ambiguous. Positively, the union of machine and poet is the union of science and humanism, of male technology and female empathy, "a union of mentalities" (167). Negatively, the union is achieved only by the woman's literal "sacrifice" (163). At least, offers an observer, Jennie has "escaped *her* stereotype" (167).

In James Tiptree Jr.'s (Alice Sheldon's) "The Girl Who Was Plugged In" (1973), reprinted in *Warm Worlds and Otherwise*, the woman as machine is a literalization and thus an exposé of internalized social mechanisms, of the damaging ways in which women's role is constructed by society. In this short story, P. Burke is born deformed: "she's the ugly of the world. A tall monument to pituitary dystrophy" (1975, 80). She is offered a "waldo" (92) or cyborg body, an organic human body grown from an ovum but modified by surgery so that Burke can be attached, long distance, to control the body through "eccentric projection or sensory reference" (86): this "melding of flesh and metal," this "Cinderella transistorized" (84) renamed "Delphi," is constructed by male scientists and business moguls to perform as a model consumer to stimulate sales. "To [the men in control] you're just a thing to get scratch with" (107–8), Delphi's friend tells her. Thus P. Burke, who eagerly accepts the role of "Plastic Woman" with a new body, represents the innately "defective" woman who must construct her "beauty" through consumerism; she is literally a social mechanism to stimulate consumption. As Naomi Wolf points out in *The Beauty Myth*, beauty is currently "commodified" (1991, 11), a "currency system" (12), "a destructive communal illusion" (17); "Like any economy, it is determined by politics. . . . It is an expression of power relations in which women must unnaturally compete for resources that men have appropriated for themselves" (12).

In such a role, Delphi represents Everywoman. The narrator cynically explains that Delphi "is just a girl, a real-live girl with her brain in an unusual place. A simple real-time on-line system with plenty of bit-rate — even as you and you" (Tiptree 1975, 92). As another character further explains, "They've got the whole world programmed. . . . They've got everybody's minds wired in to . . . want what they give them and they give them what they're programmed to want" (108–9). Thus the "thingness" of the woman programmed to her social role of consumer is exposed by this use of the woman as machine. Delphi is mechanical and erotic because she is the machinery of men's desires, a fantasy of the promise of sexual fulfillment if men and women only spend enough money.

However, Delphi refuses to be this automated consumer. She begins to evaluate the products she must recommend, and to reject those that are unsafe. Although her individuality is "rewarded" by the ability to love, Tiptree uses this plot move to expose the nature of romance also as social conditioning. Paul Isham is the "Man" (Tiptree 1975, 106), "divine flesh" (105), even if an angry young man with a social conscience. When he finally sees P. Burke, the inner woman behind the outer shell he loves, he rejects her as a monster. Her effort to be the doll he loves causes her death (118).

In Tanith Lee's *Electric Forest* (1979), we return to the woman as machine serving men's sexual needs. Magdala Cled, deformed from birth, inhabits a beautiful automated body identical to that of Christophine del Jan, in exchange for spying to further the plans of the handsome "mad scientist" figure, Claudio. Her real body hidden in a "cradle" equipped with life-sustaining services, Magdala in her new body still carries the secret knowledge that she is "ugly, crippled, deformed" (Lee 1979, 60). In her new body, she represents the plastic nature of women's beauty: she was a "robot — machine — synthetic simulacrum" (31); her new body was "a simulate woman" "a sensit dream" (32). In her new body, she also represents the construction of the feminine gender as machinery for satisfying men's desires: "She was a doll which could be bathed, with washable tresses. She was a doll who could walk and talk, and eat and drink and sleep, and have orgasms" (91). Claudio, who has made Magdala in the image of a woman he loved, is also metaphorically a machine — a cold man, willing to exploit women: "His profile . . . seemed machine finished. The long-lashed eyes shone translucent yet metallic" (10).

Electric Forest, of all the stories discussed in this section, most clearly exposes the connection between the objectification of women and sadomasochistic relationships between men and women. Because Claudio has constructed Magdala in the image of his desires, because she is a machine to "serve" him, he resorts to sadistic sex in order to dominate her, to prove his own reality. He reminds her frequently that she is "A freak. . . . An atrocity. . . . Not quite human" (Lee 1979, 23), and he sees her "as something he had constructed" (75). When she rebels to act autonomously, he "vandalize[s] whatever had become hers, all he had given her"; he is "thorough and sadistic" (69). When he has sex with her, she is "invaded" (71). Their relationship is not mutual recognition but a struggle for power.

The ending of the novel offers a twist: after Claudio has apparently destroyed Magdala's cradle and real body, we learn that all was performance: the actors playing Claudio and Magdala are actually married, and their roles were performed, Magdala's with reality-altering drugs. The scenario was a test, to try out effects on humans of the power to move to a new body. This twist enhances the readers' understanding that women construct artificial self-presentations to fulfill their roles as machines which satisfy male desires.

The portraits of woman-as-machine remain ambiguous at best. In "A Manifesto for Cyborgs: Science, Technology and Socialist Feminism in the 1980s," Donna Haraway has suggested that "by the late twentieth century, our time, a mythic time, we are all chimeras, theorized and fabricated hybrids of machine and organism; in short, we are cyborgs" (1985, 66):

> From one perspective, a cyborg world is about the final imposition of a grid of control on the planet, about the final abstraction embodied in a Star War apocalypse waged in the name of defense, about the final appropriation of women's bodies in a masculinist orgy of war. From another perspective, a cyborg world might be about lived social and bodily realities in which people are not afraid of their joint kinship with animals and machines, not afraid of permanently partial identities and contradictory standpoints. The political struggle is to see from both perspectives at once. (Haraway 1985, 72)

While they explore the ability of women to remake humanity continually out of the damaged identities of feminine stereotypes, the majority of women science fiction writers do not see the woman as machine as utopian. At best, perhaps we can see the woman as machine, in her assertion of autonomy, as Cixous describes woman: woman as the sex that can lose part of herself and not lose her identity; she "Derives pleasure from this gift of alterability. [She is] spacious, singing flesh, on which is grafted no one knows which I, more or less human, but alive because of transformation" (Marks and de Courtivron 1980, 259–60). At worst, the grotesquerie of the union suggests the machine as symbol of failed androgyny; the parts—technology and art, objectivity and subjectivity, man and woman — are too distant, too opposed, to fit together comfortably.[26]

Woman as Animal

In science fiction, women writers have adapted to other ends the generic convention, developed by male writers of the pulp magazines, of presenting women as alien animals. In this section, looking at science fictions by Rachael Marshall and Maverick Terrell, Phyllis Gotlieb, Naomi Mitchison, C. J. Cherryh, and Rebecca Ore, I shall argue that twentieth-century women writers depict woman as animal to explore psychological and social aspects of the mother in our culture.

In men's science fiction, women presented as animals generally represent women's sexuality, and "the male identity is preserved as a human, rather than a sexual one," to adapt a phrase from Kate Millett (1987, 72). Such a representation of woman is a particularly important negotiation in science fiction, where masculine rationality is seen as the wellspring of science, the savior of humankind, and the resolution of the plot; the portrayal of women literally as animals, associated also with sexuality, supports unstated assumptions that women must be dominated — for their own good and the good of humanity.[27]

We can see more clearly the problems of this masculinist convention of the animal woman for women writers if we examine the earliest story by a woman (with a man) I have found employing this convention. In Rachael Marshall and Maverick Terrell's "The Mystery in Acatlan," published in *Weird Tales* in 1928, the writers parody the masculine convention of animal woman representing destructive female sexuality. While in Mexico, Harvey Larrison rescues a dog from a bandit's cruel abuse, but the dog disappears at night, replaced by a Spanish woman who also begs asylum from abuse, and

26. Other unions of woman and machine include Margaret in James Tiptree, Jr. (Alice Sheldon), *Up the Walls of the World* (1978); Olwen in Monica Hughes, *The Keeper of the Isis Light* (1980); and Laenea Trevelyan in Vonda McIntyre, *Superluminal* (1983); a novel that plays with the conventions of both male and female machines is C. J. Cherryh's *Port Eternity* (1982a). See Donna Haraway on McIntyre's novel in 1985, 98–99.

27. The psychologist Dorothy Dinnerstein explains the basis for the fantastic dread of the woman/womb aroused by such stories by men: "So long as the first parent is a woman, then, woman will inevitably be pressed into the dual role of indispensable quasi-human supporter and deadly quasi-human enemy of the human self. She will be seen as naturally fit to nurture other people's individuality; as the born audience in whose awareness other people's subjective existence can be mirrored; as the being so peculiarly needed to confirm other people's worth, power, significance that if she fails to render them this service she is a monster, anomalous and useless. And at the same time she will also be seen as the one who will not let other people be, the one who beckons her loved ones back from selfhood, who wants to engulf, dissolve, drown, suffocate them as autonomous persons" (1976, 111–12).

in return enslaves herself to Harvey's every household need. Harvey falls in love and they marry, but when they exit the church, they are attacked by the bandit, whom Harvey kills; when Harvey wakes, the dog also lies dead beside him and never again does he see his wife.

The dog and wife, of course, are the same, and the confusion of woman with animal represents woman's illicit but attractive sexuality, parodied as male fantasy in this story. Harvey, for example, first feels sexual attraction to the dog, not the woman: "That is what first attracted me to the dog: its unhappy, beseeching eyes, bewildered with pain and fear and yet holding somehow to a dumb, blind hope" (Marshal and Terrell 1928, 583). And it is the woman who first brings him his slippers, not the dog (585). The woman is a young boy's fantasy of service, half child, half mother: "a young thing, hardly more than a child, staring at me with big, frightened brown eyes" (584)(so that the young man feels superior to her), yet "sewing buttons on my clothes . . . [with] only one idea—to be of service to me" (587)(so that the young man also feels mothered). This fantasy of the woman serving the man is further heightened by sadomasochistic erotics, made safe by attaching them to the bandit, made available by offering them for the enjoyment of the young man: "Words dissolved into sobs; her little brown hands clutched me; her tangled head dropped upon my knee. One shoulder of the loose garment she wore slipped back and down, and I saw across her back innumerable scars of the lash" (585). The bandit is the cruel cause of the scars, but Harvey may enjoy them safely as signs of the woman's subservience.

Marshall and Terrell's story is signaled as a parody by the language displaying the connection between woman and dog. The bandit shouts, "You steal my girl—I mean my dog!" (1928, 588), and a male companion visiting Harvey compliments Chulita with the praise, "She's a winner. . . . Some baby pup!" (587) "For some reason the old joke irritated me," Harvey comments (587). The convention is thus attached to the insensitive men, who easily see the connection between woman and dog, and the reader may enjoy the parody, as when the naive Harvey reports, "She rose and came to me, fawning at my feet, looking up at me with brown eyes of adoration and gratitude" (586). We see that his affection could apply equally to woman or dog until he finishes, "I patted her and pulled her ears" (586). Ironically, destructive female sexuality in this story destroys only the woman and her former illicit partner, not the young man, who learns from his experience to avoid dogs— and presumably also women.

In general, women writers have different fears than men and, to explore them, adapt the figure of the animal woman. As Kate Millett explains about gender roles in general, owing to "The limited role allotted the female" that "arrest[s] her at the level of biological experience," the "distinctly human rather than animal activity . . . is largely reserved for the male" (Millett 1987, 35). As the psychologist Dorothy Dinnerstein develops this idea, " 'I'ness wholly free of the chaotic carnal atmosphere of infancy, uncontaminated humanness, is reserved for man" by "projecting" the "mucky, humbling limitations" of our physical selves onto women (1976, 133) — especially onto mothers. In women's science fiction the mother's animal physicality is used to broach and repair fears of the messiness of pleasure, of damage mothers and daughters do to each other, and of the effects of carnality — death and change.[28]

Dinnerstein further explains that seeing women as lacking subjectivity results from perceiving the physicality of women's bodies through memories of early childhood and the physical experience of being mothered. Our "fundamental ambivalence" about women, Dinnerstein suggests,

> lies in the fact that the early mother, . . . is a source, like nature, of ultimate distress as well as ultimate joy. Like nature, she is both nourishing and unreliable. The infant loves her touch, warmth, shape, taste, sound, movement. . . . And it hates her because, like nature, she does not perfectly protect and provide for it. . . . Her body is the first important piece of the physical world that we encounter, and the events for which she seems responsible the first instances of fate. Hence Mother Nature, with her hurricane daughters. (1976, 95)

Women science fiction writers ironically turn the representation of woman as animal on its head: they portray the woman as animal, but as a rational animal who yet through maternity participates in the messy carnality of life; often the animal woman is seen consequently as more rational — and more human — than the reasonable man. In the animal mothers of women's science fiction — gibbon, butterfly, ant, and bat — these fears of the body, pleasure, and reproduction are emphasized.

In Canadian Phyllis Gotlieb's *O Master Caliban!* (1976), Esther, a talking gibbon, mothers an adopted mutant family — a philosophical goat and a four-armed human boy — along with a group of five castaway human children. Esther thus typifies the link between woman-as-animal and woman-as-mother: Sven, the boy she has raised, calls her "Mutti," and the castaways call her "Mama Ape" and "mama" (Gotlieb 1979, 1, 21 and 57). The novel opens with Esther, coaxing Yigal and the boy Sven to eat: "She thought he looked moody, and she sat on his shoulder, lifted the bowl to hook chunks out with her long black fingers and coax them to his mouth. 'Eat, darling, eat, sweetheart' " (1). Although not biologically a mother, she takes over all

---

28. Lisa Tuttle explores closely related issues in her essay, "Pets and Monsters," in Armitt, ed., 1991, 97–108. See esp. 97: "What does it mean for a woman to turn into an animal? . . . . It can represent escape into wildness and the delights of strength and sensuality, or it can express the limitations of a purely physical existence, the frustrations of being denied a share in human culture." Tuttle does not explore the symbolic relation between the woman-as-animal and mothering that I explore.

the gender roles of mother: cooking and feeding (1), housekeeping (10, 18, 58), anticipating bodily needs (44, 264), nursing (48), and comforting (122, 151, 264). She is perceived as the Ideal Mother, with no needs of her own: "giving love, all she wanted was to love" (188).

This link between woman-as-animal and woman-as-mother is illuminated by psychologist Dorothy Dinnerstein in a section entitled "The Mother as Representative of Nature: The Semi-Sentient 'She' ": "woman is the creature we encounter before we are able to distinguish between a center of sentience and an impersonal force of nature. . . . The ambiguity in our perception of the mother's subjectivity . . . is an important part of the reason why people — men especially, but women too — have such a partial, unsteady grasp on the fact that women are human, and find it so hard to show ordinary human respect for them" (1976, 105–6).[29] Esther the gibbon "unmetaphors" or literalizes our cultural conception of the mother as nonhuman, as tied to nature.

The attention to Esther's body in detailed descriptions (in comparison to the less frequent description of the human characters) reinforces this connection between mother and nature through bodily experience. Esther "had coarse thick hair and where she was not specked with color her body texture looked like charcoal, except for the skin that stretched and shone over the high bony vault of her forehead" (Gotlieb 1979, 11). While emotions are attributed directly to human characters, Esther's bodily responses are described: she kisses Shirvanian (151) and drums her fingers on Sven's shoulder (221); she swings "screeching with rage, from one to another [machine], dancing on wire probes, butting her heels at lenses, whirling in figure-eights around gripper tentacles till they tied themselves in knots grabbing for her" (153). Even her caretaking is presented as "natural," an outgrowth of her animalistic urge to groom (204, 230), an extremely physicalized maternal expression of affection: "Esther exploded. She threw arms wide and in one leap hooked her legs over Dahlgren's shoulders, . . . and plunged her fingers into his hair and began to scratch his scalp" (263).

The portrait of gibbon as mother thus emphasizes a central psychological experience for most Western children, the physicality of the mother, defined by touch and smell. As psychologist Demaris Wehr explains, "The experience of the mother is primary, built on touch, smell, nourishment, and the earliest experiences of self and other" (1987, 119).[30] For the other characters, damaged by their relation to their "natural" human parents, Esther's physicality

29. Cf. Sherry Ortner's argument that it is more useful to see women not as totally aligned with nature, but as an intermediary to nature, inferior to men who effect change by cultural means only, and more in need of control than men because women handle the dangerous task of bringing children from the realm of nature into the realm of culture (1974). Esther is in exactly this position in Gotlieb's novel.

30. Also see Wehr 1987, 111, and Chodorow on the mother's body as defining the infant's reality (1978, 57–70).

allows the nurturing of stunted emotions. Esther's feelings are attached to her animality by the very physicality of their expression. When Yigal the goat dies, Esther screams, and pushes "open one of his lids as if she might find his gruff stodgy spirit in the dark pool of his eye" (Gotlieb 1979, 171); after his last breath, she sits beside him, "stroking, grooming, touching" (177). She marks the grief on her own body: "Every so often she plucked a tuft of hair from her body, rubbed it between thumb and forefinger" (187). Esther's physicality provides other characters a safe place to grieve for their "lost" parents, and for their parents' incompetence. Especially with Shirvanian, the youngest, Esther offers rest. After nightmares and sobbing, "He pressed his head hard against her meager breast, and slept" (57); after another night of bad dreams for Shirvanian, Esther "crawled into bed with him, turned the light on, and clasped his grimacing face" (264–65). The end of the story for Esther is thus the end of mothering. She lets Sven grow up, commenting "he's not mine any more" (268). But Gotlieb also uses Esther to offer a parody of the romance ending. Although she must give up her children, the gibbon mother stays with the human father, Dhalgren, the cold machine-like scientist, to make him more human (266, 268).

Gotlieb's literalization of the animal-mother in O Master Caliban! does not reinforce a stereotype, however. The reader is offered continual surprise in the physical reality that a gibbon can talk, that Esther is physically, tangibly beautiful. Ardagh, one of the human children, realizes, "With her economy of grace and strength, her fine features and vivid character, even with the odd-colored spots on her dark fur, she was certainly beautiful" (Gotlieb 1979, 140). Thus, with her embodied physicality, as with the physicality of the mothers of our infancy, Esther lets the children and us accept the inevitable connection between messiness, disorder, animality, and the pleasures of life —food, affectionate touch, scratching, relieving of pains, appreciation of beauty—as physical presence. Gotlieb's gibbon mother further allows us to grasp that animal women—the mothers of our infancies—are "human," too, that we need to grant recognition of subjectivity across lines of difference.[31]

The representation of mother as animal in science fiction by women also allows writers to explore from a safe distance the damage that mothers and daughters can do to each other, in particular the physical damage of childbirth for mothers and blame for daughters. In order to examine this result of mother presented as alien animal, let us return to an episode from a novel already analyzed—the butterfly-caterpillar world in Memoirs of a Spacewoman (1962) by the English writer Naomi Mitchison. In this episode, an all-woman team explores a planet where intelligent life exists in insect form. In a juvenile cycle, androgynous caterpillars wallow in an algal swamp, eat and make art with their defecations, and enjoy intense polygonous sexual-

---

31. Gotlieb's Esther perhaps functions like Cherríe Moraga's dream of a new species, to reunite the human and animal worlds, representing a mixed race (1993, 127–28).

ity; in an adult cycle, female butterflies experience either transcendant meditative and blissful immortality or die in childbirth following the caterpillars'
previous sexual contacts. While earlier we analyzed this episode from the
vantage of theories of feminist science, now let us look at the psychology of
the woman as alien animal.

In *Feminism and Psychoanalytic Theory*, Nancy Chodorow argues that
"Blame and idealization of mothers have become our cultural ideology"
(1989, 90) and that recent feminists have sided with the child in a dangerous
"idealization of maternal life," or sided with the mother, in an equally dangerous "fear [of] the experience [of mothering] as all-consuming," of being
"devoured by their children" (92).[32] Both positions, Chodorow argues, depend on our culture's unrealistic expectation that mothering is perfectible.
Similarly, in Naomi Mitchison's feminist *Memoirs of a Spacewoman*, humans
side with butterflies or caterpillars, depending on whether they are mothers
or daughters.

In Mitchison's novel, all butterflies in the adult stage are female, and
ironically, the idealization of maternal life is represented by those unfertilized
butterflies who never lay eggs, who become immortal. When emerging from
their chrysalises, these butterflies project to Mary "a sensation of astonishing
joy . . . not only the delight of the new movement, of light after darkness, life
in a superb form, but also . . . a sense of justification, almost of complete
virtue" (Mitchison 1973, 104). But this bliss is achieved, according to the
butterflies, only through blaming their children, thus preventing behavior
that might deform their offspring's wings or cause them to die by egg-laying.
The human explorers share with the caterpillars, under attack by the butterflies, a "sense of guilt . . . [and] extreme resentment on behalf of the caterpillars, whose delight was shattered" (95). The caterpillars "seemed to shrivel as
from an inward searing" (95), experiencing "formless misery" and emitting "a
low moaning of guilt, yet clearly they did not know what they had been
guilty of" (97). The humans associate the feeling of blame with their own
experiences as children or mothers. Mary reflects, "I thought, suddenly and
guiltily—a quite irrational and disquieting feeling—of my own little children" (95). In Mitchison's novel the interaction between butterflies and caterpillars thus represents the potential for ideal motherhood ironically destroyed
by the need to oversee the growth of children through the tool of blame:
from the point of view of the butterflies, motherhood is achieved by denying
tender feelings for their children; from the point of view of the caterpillars,
the mothers are enemies who attack and destroy them, who physically abuse
them with their blame.

In addition, the cycle of caterpillar to butterfly to egg evokes the messy

---

32. See also Marcia Westkott on mothers and daughters: mothers ask daughters to meet
the needs of nurturing unmet in the mothers because of their own giving all the time; daughters
develop compliance in nurturing, rage at having to nurture (1986, esp. 217–19).

carnality of motherhood, and the fear for women of being overwhelmed by motherhood. In this hierarchical world, sexuality belongs to the province of the messy childish caterpillars, "wallowing in semi-liquid vegetable matter," (Mitchison 1973, 89), not to the adult butterflies, who fly above such animal concerns. But butterflies must still endure the consequences of sexuality. Sensing a "grief which was gradually beginning to overwhelm her" (115), the explorer Miss Hayes "felt a sense of irreparable loss, as though she had suddenly realised that her whole working life had been a dream" (116), and finds its source in a butterfly who is laying eggs and dying. Watching its death, Miss Hayes and Mary share the butterfly's "storm of grief," its "waves of grief and discouragement" (116). The butterflies believe that the artwork with defecation they do as caterpillars causes deformed wings in emergent butterflies, and that they are blameable for the sexual intercourse as caterpillars that causes their death as egg-laying butterflies (105). Watching the butterfly die in egg-laying, Mary realizes that "The enormous and beautiful something [of birth] which we knew was normally revolting to the butterflies. Its antennae drooped.... Shudders of colours, broken rhythms, went through its wings, and the eggs poured out, tearing its body and leaving a trail on the algae which gradually sank" (116). Since Mitchison was an early birth control activist in the 1920s,[33] and since she wrote this novel before widespread use of effective oral contraception, we may take this passage ironically: Mary in the future sees birth as the "beautiful something" because she has children only when she wants them, and she is not tied to caretaking; the women of Mitchison's time are closer to the butterfly, some still dying in childbirth, many still birthing children they do not want.

Thus in Mitchison's fiction woman as animal mother is associated with mortality and change: caterpillars changing into butterflies, some laying eggs and dying. Indeed, the caterpillars who turn into butterflies seem to be giving birth to themselves: first they are "stiff, still bodies, . . . in a rigor of death-like change" (Mitchison 1973, 102), then comes "the splitting of the dry old body which was now, so obviously, only a case or mask" (103), and finally the butterfly emerges, "with a birth damp which dried slowly away" (103). The older women identify with the butterflies, who offer a dangerous and compelling dream of changeless winged intellectual bliss if released from the messy necessities of birth and reproduction, from the body. The younger women of the expedition identify with the caterpillars, who model childish rage and blame at parental control. When Françoise enacts the blame, killing one of the immortal butterflies, she takes the position of child, acting out the rage and resentment against mother as nature or fate that Dinnerstein explores in her psychology.

33. On Mitchison's involvement in early birth control activism, see the interview by Leonie Caldecott 1984, 23–25.

In contrast, the insect mothers in *Serpent's Reach* (1980) by United States writer C. J. Cherryh, emphasize woman as alien and nearly unknowable nature, and so the mother's affinity with death and change. This distancing of the mother allows Cherryh to treat the private as public, and to examine the politics of reproduction in broad terms.

In *Serpent's Reach*, Raen, a human girl, seeks asylum with ant-like matriarchal aliens, the majat, when her family are murdered by a rival political faction: "the majat, the power under-earth, native here where men were newcomers. She had touched the Mother who had lived under the hill since before she was born" (Cherryh 1980, 31). The alien species possesses multibodied but centralized intelligence, and there are only four intelligences on any planet, immortal ones by human standards. The center, or queen, is woman as mother as insect, another version of the woman as animal. Raen finds protection with the Queen of greens on her planet. The queen's title is "Mother" — constantly producing eggs, the Mother is an exaggerated version of woman as her reproductive function. But the Mother also represents the ordering function of the role of mother,[34] and Raen is molded as well as protected by the ant queen: "She was aware of Mother. There was a Presence within the hive which sent Workers scurrying on this mission and that, to touch her and depart again in haste" (24); "Mother accepted; Mother had ordered" (186).

As in other versions of the woman as animal, woman presented as insect emphasizes the body in ways that recall not only the mother's reproductive function but also the early infant's physical communication with the mother: "the sweet scent of Mother pervaded the inmost halls" (Cherryh 1980, 20) of the hive. Communication among the ant-like aliens occurs through the chemistry of touch, taste, and smell, "locked . . . into the Mother's chemistry, suffering the reactions of Her body as the messages swirled through Her fluids" (129). The Mother, for example, when she first meets Raen, communicates with her not only through speech but also by tasting her tears (27): "You are beautiful," Raen answers (27). The correspondence to the Mother of infancy is reinforced by relative size. Compared to the human Raen, the Mother is immense: she is "a great pale form," a "great body"; "the walls echoed with her breathing" and "Her voice . . . vibrated in the earth" (266).

34. Cf. Jane Davison on the mother as insect queen: "The notion of some mystical role assigned by nature to be played by women in the home nonetheless still maintains its hold on the imagination. Woman has long been idealized, in Doris Lessing's words, as 'the supplier of some kind of invisible fluid, or emanation, like a queen termite whose spirit (or some such word — electricity) filled the nest, making a whole of individuals who could have no other connection.' This particular insect queen reacted to the swirl of options confronting her as any sensible termite would. I dug my teeth into my succulent wooden house and for a number of years munched on contentedly" (1980, 179–80). A. M. Lightner in *The Day of the Drones* (1969) uses the insect mother to explore fears of the mother as tyrant.

The text renders heroic rather than monstrous this huge and physical mother: she is alien, immense, wise, and safe, in a world where humans are small and treacherous or stupid.

Cherryh employs her portrayal of woman as animal, however, not to reinforce a domestic stereotype, but to examine motherhood as public and institutionalized rather than private and individualized. The Majat, for example, and the Mother as centralized intelligence in particular, are naturally good not only at biology, producing hundreds of eggs an hour, but also at Biology, manipulating chemistry and genes organically. Without machines, the hive is yet a "biologic computer" (Cherryh 1980, 33); the Majat supply humans with a chemical substance that overcomes aging and makes them virtually immortal (vulnerable only to violence); and without technology the Majat heal Raen, Jim, and the Beta people after other humans have deserted their chaotic world (282).

Indeed, motherhood is deeply implicated in politics in this novel, signaled by the name of the despot in charge of human affairs in the Reach, Moth (a shortened form of "Mother"). Moth serves as a distant mother to Raen, protecting her as Raen tries to prevent further human interference in the Reach ecology (Cherryh 1980, 75). In the initial episode of the novel, the Majat Mother analyzes the politics of reproduction as cause of the human political treachery that has killed off Raen's family: "is it possible that our two species have overbred?" (29) She seems, at first, totally wrong, since we know that family rivalries plotted by individuals have caused the murders. But she proves right, since the political aim of the factions who briefly take over (but whose plans are delayed by Moth), is to force an expansion in human and Majat population so as to break out of the Reach and invade other human space. The Ant Queen Mother thus becomes an emblem of the problem of overpopulation and Cherryh's solution of institutionalized public self-control.

The goal of reproduction, the alternative life-forms of the Majat tell us, is not simply individual reproduction, personal immortality, but rather cultural synthesis and symbiosis, communal immortality. Cherryh implies that if we humans do not listen to our biology and learn that, we shall perish as a race from overbreeding. The Majat cannot help but listen. When they have achieved a certain level of expansion, and interactions between the four hives on a planet escalate to violent rivalries because of overbreeding, then instinctual nature forces the queens to confront one another in battle, from which only one emerges. Cherryh is not advocating the simple answer of warfare to solve population crises but warning that such a solution is dangerously "natural." The Majat, though, do not die individually. Because they communicate by taste, the surviving queen, who eats the other queens, emerges as a composite being, a new cultural synthesis possessing the memories of all the queens — red, blue, green, and gold. Cherryh is offering synthesis, shared knowledge, as a solution to the problem of human overbreeding touching (Ore 1988, 64), greeting others by body slams and sideways hugs (1988, 124, 203), sniffing as greeting (1988, 42), sleeping together in heaps (1988, 38, 62 and 222). Gwyng are "lethally empathetic" (1988, 41, 51). Compared to Gwyng, humans are too privatized, substituting trade and story-telling for social grooming, and oversexualizing the bed (1988, 222, 264).

Like other animal-mothers, Black Amber represents the messy carnality of sex and reproduction: she embodies what the French feminist Françoise Parturier calls "the scandal of female flesh" (Marks and de Courtivron 1980, 62). When Tom first sees her as sexual, her sexuality seems exaggerated to him: "Black Amber's heat went on and on. After five days, my groin ached and I spent most of my time on the beach" (1988, 174). Fearing such sexual-ity, Tom constructs Black Amber's sexuality as alien to distance his fears— "Her hormone-dazed eyes" seem "huge and alien" (1988, 173)—and Tom considers Gwyng sex lives "disgusting. . . . They go into season —. . . like cats or dogs" (1988, 137). Even worse for Tom, however, is the idea of the pleasure that the females feel. Tom tells us, "And the females like being pregnant as much as they can get, because for a Gwyng, delivery is like coming" (1988, 137). Black Amber, thus representing the mother who has "jouissance," plea-sure in her sexuality (Kristeva in Marks and de Courtivron 1980, 36), is portrayed as almost continually pregnant (Ore 1988, 240; 1989, 244; 1990, 21–22).

Since Gwyng females are dominant, this negative feminized image of sexuality is attached in the trilogy to the species as a whole. Rather than anxiously hiding sex, Gwyng society publishes it. Gwyng sex is an occasion for socializing (Ore 1988, 235), when adult males gather at the house of a female in heat, and preadult relatives stay to protect the female and feed the guests. After heat, the Gwyng female throws a huge party to minimize the social friction that results because some males were successful in copulations and others not (1989, 152, 191–92). Gwyngs who pair-bond are scandalous (1989, 6–7, 15 and 138).[36] Even though Gwyng females have season, repro-duction is a continual process, more intertwined in their social system, less privatized, and therefore more obviously political. Because Gwyng children struggle more to live, crawling first to the mother's pouch, then to a host pouch, Gwyng treat their young as currency (1989, 259).[37]

Black Amber serves one purpose as cornerstone in the family romance

36. As dominant female, Black Amber is in control of her sexuality, but still trades on it: she scandalizes other Gwyng by pairing with Wy'um, a high-ranking politician on the History Committee that controls the Federation; as acting rector, she gives him a son (Ore 1988, 247–48; 1989, 117). Her "body bribe" gains her her position as sub-Rector (Ore 1988, 255).

37. While Black Amber serves as symbolic representation of the otherness of women because of their connection to reproduction, Ore parallels this portrait of alien woman to Tom's feelings about his pregnant human wife: "I felt like I was the alien and they were all of a species —pregnant females, a single word, not two, in [the language] Karst One" (1989, 241–42).

as well (1980, 276–79). In *Serpent's Reach*, humans are tragically in capable of achieving cooperation—even symbiosis—with the Majat, the with each other.

The trilogy by United States writer Rebecca Ore—*Becoming Al* (1988), *Being Alien* (1989), and *Human to Human* (1990)—also uses figure of mother as animal to symbolize carnality, exploring the mothe physicality as representing our relationship to death, change, and differenc Moreover, Ore reconstitutes the woman as animal as mother to update t classic science fiction plot of adolescent boy winning adulthood. In Or trilogy, Tom Gentry, a boy from Virginia on parole, tries to save an alien sh by Tom's drug-dealing brother; the aliens offer Tom the chance of restitutio taking the alien Mica's place in the multispecies Federation, as Black Amber adopted son, Red Clay, a Federation cadet. Here Ore revises the scienc fiction plot of winning adulthood through conquest by requiring that Tor overcome his xenophobia and accept diversity. Black Amber, sub-Rector an member of a bat-like species called Gwyng, acts as Tom's mentor-mother.[35]

As with other portraits of the mother as animal, Ore's portrait explores the physicality of the mother's body. Black Amber is associated with the messy fluids of the mother's body: like all Gwyngs—"Tropical islanders with blood-pump tongues" (Ore 1988, 81)—her diet is primarily blood and milk. Of the "wrinkles deeply grooved from her nose and eye corners," Tom observes, "*Slots for air when she presses her face against a blood animal*" (Ore 1988, 60). Like other alien animal-mothers in science fiction by women, Black Amber's means of communication are especially physical. For example, when Black Amber greets her returning son, Rhydolite, she "slingshotted herself out of a padded tube with both hands, koo'ing, weaving her body back and forth as soon as she stood up. . . . She tucked him up against her side and brushed her muzzle along his lip corners and eyelids. . . . Black Amber cradled him and nibbled his hands" (Ore 1988, 89). In the convention of animal-mother in science fiction by women, Black Amber speaks a complicated body language, especially when angry: she nibbles her palms, makes fists, smears anger juice from a fist gland on furniture or Tom's face (Ore 1988, 90 and 91; 1989, 13, 153, 155 and 245; 1990, 21). As a housewife, Black Amber is pictured as physically hostile: "Black Amber took the teakettle off a burner and nodded tensely at me. I knew Gwyng nods were hostile" (Ore 1988, 40).

This emphasis on the body is extended in Ore's trilogy to the portrayal of the entire species of Gwyng, a species where females are dominant, and literally larger than males (Ore 1988, 55, 58 and 60; 1989, 8). As a species, Gwyng are thus feminized, sharing a communal physicality—constantly

35. In the final volume of the trilogy, Tom claims Black Amber as surrogate parent: "She's my sponsor. I don't have any living genetic relations except Karl" (Ore 1990, 195).

on an alien planet: Tom must come to terms with mentor-mother Black
Amber and mentor-father Karriaagzh, and their rivalry (1989, 157; 1990, 25).
Here the "father" represents the dream of unity and transcendence, willing
to sacrifice children to that dream; the "mother" represents the dream of
immortality through descendants, education, the passing on, protecting and
socializing of the young. Reinforcing the family romance, Yangchenla, Tom's
first lover on Karst, accuses Tom of having cross-species sex with Black Amber
(1989, 240; 1990, 19); Marianne, Tom's wife, does have cross-species sex
with Karriaagzh (1990, 24 and 192). Black Amber's death and Karriaagzh's
retirement from position of Rector signify Tom's growth. He has managed to
reconcile and internalize both goals — he is himself a father, in love with his
own mother, not Black Amber or his own dead mother, but as represented
in the mother of his child, his wife Marianne.

Black Amber's death, which ends the trilogy, links woman as animal, the
Mother, with death and change. Black Amber as animal-mother also represents men's culturally constructed needs to separate from mortality, and to
overcome physical dependence on the mother. As Dorothy Dinnerstein
points out, Our "male-female compact" is "a neurosis, . . . a costly strategy for
maintaining mutually incompatible feelings, which we lack the strength to
reconcile, in a provisionally stable state of equilibrium" (1976, 245): "this
compact helps us maintain *our ambivalence toward our own carnal mortality*
. . . through [taking] the sweet, threatening bodily edge off sex feeling . . . and
. . . [providing] set channels within which the feeling, tamed and constricted,
can flow." By designating women as the repository for these fears, men may
thus hold "at bay, and at the same time nearby, the acute knowledge of
fleshly transience, without which aliveness itself cannot be fully felt" (Dinnerstein 1976, 246). We may see our fear of mortality recorded in our fear of
old women: while our cultural values insist that men do not age, or are still
valuable with age, these same values exaggerate the effects of aging in
women. In Ore's trilogy, this cultural disparity is defamiliarized, transposed
to other species, in order to be examined: Karriaagzh, the father-mentor,
comes from a long-lived species and is rumored to live to be 150 years old;
Black Amber, the mother-mentor, comes from a short-lived species, who
generally die of a genetic brain malfunction at about sixty.

As with her reproductive functions, and her feelings, Black Amber's
mortality is depicted as inscribed on her body. In the last volume of the
trilogy, Black Amber's "wrinkles [are] sagging slightly" (1990, 13). She seems
"defeated" (23): "She looked old now, stooped, the webs more wrinkled. One
eye pupil was slightly greyed. A cataract? . . . [Her] nails were thick, crum-
bling like an old woman's toenails" (114). Black Amber knows she's becoming
senile, that she's dying (193, 195), and her mortality is explicitly connected
with her maternity for Tom: "Black Amber embraced me, rocked me side to
side, then said, "My mind/my aging (agony)" (192).

As with the physicality of the mother extended to a feminized species, the association of Black Amber with death is also extended to the Gwyng in general. Gwyng live only sixty years (1989, 138), either dying of a species' brain malfunction or choosing suicide as they enter senility (1988, 175). Thus Gwyng have a special fear of death that is expressed as denial (1988, 255). Death is an "embarrassment" for Gwyng (1988, 214).

The death of Black Amber associates maternity, death, and change in one figure in Ore's trilogy, and the structure of the last book allows Tom to work out his own fear of death and change within his relationship to Black Amber and the Gwyng. As Dinnerstein points out, this association is traditional in our culture: maternity and mortality are linked because both are change (1976, 132). Woman's body incarnates and represents "Alien, dangerous nature, conveniently concentrated near at hand" (Dinnerstein 1976, 125). In this way, "woman helps man cope with . . . brute nature . . . as it exists inside him, in his own mute unfathomable body" (Dinnerstein 1976, 125–26). She helps man live with the "opposition . . . between what is humanly noble, durable, strenuous, and the insistent rule of flesh, flesh which is going to die and which even when death is remote makes humbling demands: we must feed it, we must let it sleep, we must get rid of its smelly wastes" (Dinnerstein 1976, 126). In her trilogy, Ore uses the stereotypical cultural association of woman, the body, and death to examine Tom's own fears of death and difference; eventually these fears return from the animal woman and alien species to their rightful owner, the privileged male.

Ore accomplishes this task by putting the male in the place of the female nurturer: Tom becomes the "daughter" who nurses Black Amber, mentor-mother, through her death. Tom thus confronts death, battles the Gwyng (i.e. Tom's) denial of death and reaches maturity by mothering the mother. Black Amber's death is a reversal — not only a reversal of power and roles between the mother and the adopted son, but also a return to the womb (1990, 195). As Black Amber becomes senile, she returns, as all Gwyng desire, to the pouch. She sleeps in a black tube, equipped with a nipple for nutrients; Tom bathes her and removes her wastes from the tube (1990, 198 and 202). "Artificial womb," explains a friend of Tom's (1990, 201). In the Gwyng origin story about Time and Death told by Black Amber at a party, death is pictured as a return to the beginning of a Gwyng's life: "searching for the black inside of space again" (1988, 127). Thus Ore uses the generic requirement of science fiction culture-building to create a space where Tom may learn what his culture will not teach him.

Black Amber's death ends the trilogy (1990, 211–12). Her death thus becomes the occasion for Tom's final acceptance not only of difference but also of change. In acknowledging his connection to Black Amber, Tom acknowledges his connection to all species, overcoming his xenophobia. In taking care of Black Amber, Tom also acknowledges his connection to all women, symbolized by his reconciliation with his wife from whom he had separated. Tom's story is feminized, a story of assimilation. Like a woman brought as bride to another family, Tom is brought as adopted son to an alien world where no one is "like" him: his achievement is to find connection in difference. In this trilogy promoting tolerance, the refrain recurs, "We are all aliens together" (1989, 165).[38]

Aliens among Us: Female Anger, Racial Other

If not literally aliens, the heroes of women's science fiction are often women of color, their alien estate in our society magnified by comparison with a more equitable future or an alternative world. The figure of the alien woman of color is common among white as well as black women writers of science fiction. Consuelo, the Chicana hero in Marge Piercy's *Woman on the Edge of Time* (1976), declared crazy by her brother, is operated on by doctors experimenting with neurological control. "These men believed feeling itself a disease," she realizes, "something to be cut out like a rotten appendix. Cold, calculating, ambitious, believing themselves rational and superior, they chased the crouching female animal through the brain with a scalpel" (1976, 282). Alienated from her family, from her society, Connie feels herself prey for the powerful men around her.[39] Writing to women about women, Anne Wilson Schaef explains: "No wonder we feel different! No wonder we feel estranged from ourselves and other women. From childhood we are told that we do not belong, that we can never be included in the 'in' group. We are always on the outside looking in." (1985, 40). In science fictions by women centering on the woman of color as alien, however, this estrangement takes the form of anger: "The anger of the weak never goes away," asserts Connie;

38. Other science fictions that draw on the convention of the woman as animal but not discussed in this chapter include C. L. Moore's "Shambleau" (1933) in *The Best of C. L. Moore* (1975, 7–32); Leigh Brackett's "Hafling" (1943) in *The Hafling and Other Stories* (7–38); Andre Norton's *Uncharted Stars* (1969); James Tiptree Jr.'s (Alice Sheldon's) "Love is the Plan, the Plan is Death" (1973) in *Warm Worlds and Otherwise* 1975, 173–93); Cynthia Felice's *Godsfire* (1978); Doris Piserchia's *Spaceling* (1978); C. J. Cherryh's *The Pride of Chanur* (1980; see 1982a) and the rest of the Chanur series; Phyllis Gotlieb's *A Judgment of Dragons* (1980) and the rest of the starcat series; Marcia J. Bennett's *Shadow Singer* (1984); and Eleanor Arnason's *Daughter of the Bear King* (1987), *A Woman of the Iron People* (1991), and *Ring of Swords* (1993).

39. Sybil in *Woman on the Edge of Time*, a black woman, is also represented as alien; see Piercy 1976, 84–85; Connie meets her in the state mental hospital, where she, too, is committed for madness. In her forward, Marge Piercy thanks Phyllis Chesler, who wrote *Women and Madness*; Piercy drew heavily on Chesler's research about women's treatment at state mental hospitals and from Chesler's interviews for her portrait of Connie (see Chesler 1972, esp. 226 and 232). For an extremely thoughtful reading of Piercy's novel in the light of materialist utopian thought, see Tom Moylan 1986, 121–55.

"The poor and the weak die with all their anger intact and probably those angers go on growing in the dark of the grave like the hair and the nails" (Piercy 1976, 50–51). Here Connie is "talking back" to the white Anglo professor who exploited and sexually harrassed her years before, imagining a just punishment for him and revenge for herself. *Woman on the Edge of Time* highlights Connie's alienation by contrasting her life with a utopian future culture, where sex and race are not limitations to but expressions of self, and where madness is not treated punitively.

Piercy's narrative of the mad brown woman is taught as a feminist classic. It is not generally recognized that this complex of themes in Piercy's novel — heroic woman of color, alienation, enacted anger against socially sanctioned injustice, collaborative resistance, and madness — occurs in a set of science fiction novels historically positioned in the first decade after the regeneration of the feminist movement in the 1960s. In this section I will look at science fictions by Cecelia Holland, Octavia Butler, Joanna Russ, and Ursula K. Le Guin that share with Piercy's fiction the appropriation of the woman as alien to resist oppression at the intersection of gender and race and to explore women's anger as a tool for change.

"Every woman has a well-stocked arsenal of anger," wrote the feminist poet, activist, and theorist Audre Lorde, "potentially useful against those oppressions, personal and institutional, which brought that anger into being. Focused with precision it can become a powerful source of energy serving progress and change. And when I speak of change, I do not mean a simple switch of positions or a temporary lessening of tensions, nor the ability to smile or feel good. I am speaking of a basic and radical alteration in those assumptions underlining our lives" (Lorde 1984, 127).[40] In Cecelia Holland's *Floating Worlds* (1975), the brown anarchist hero Paula Mendoza lives on her anger, using it as her political guide. In this massive volume, Holland offers a portrait of a woman who has politicized her anger to survive, to maneuver among violent people without herself using violence, and to change worlds. Initially an anarchist on an earth that is an ambiguous utopia of the future — free of government (including patriarchy), with material goods for all, but ecologically a wasteland except under domes — Paula takes a job as diplomat, a go-between to the patriarchal Styth empire.

In exchange for power, however, Paula loses freedom. As a patriarchy, organized through competitive male aggression into a military hierarchy, the

---

40. Lorde further distinguishes between hatred and anger: "Hatred is the fury of those who do not share our goals, and its object is death and destruction. Anger is a grief of distortions between peers, and its object is change. . . ." (Lorde 1984, 129). One of the women whom Phyllis Chesler interviewed for *Women and Madness* reflected, "I do wonder, though, what the world could be like if she (and my mother) agreed with such anger, or had some kind of feminist vision: what would it be like?" (1972, 261).

Styth empire severely oppresses women: women, men's property, may not possess money (Holland 1975, 155 and 196); Styth culture enforces rigid gender roles (54) through veils and long dresses for women (69, 151 and 200) and through restriction of women to women's houses; and the culture endorses male enforcement of restrictions on women through misogyny, beatings, and rape (85, 176, 183, 274 and 420). When Paula leaves the protection of her own planet, she becomes the property of Saba, the man with whom she was supposed to negotiate a treaty, and now also her lover. As a patriarchy, the Styth empire enslaves not only women but also many men, especially those of other races. Holland draws on the history of several cultures to depict Styth slavery, portraying the sale of slaves in a market (182), the gelding of male slaves for use in women's households (175), and the designation of "nigger" not for the black Styths but for brown and white Martians and Terrans who become Styth slaves (190).

"Women of Color in america have grown up within a symphony of anger, at being silenced, at being unchosen, at knowing that when we survive, it is in spite of a world that takes for granted our lack of humanness," wrote Audre Lorde; "We have to learn to orchestrate those furies so that they do not tear us apart" (Lorde 1984, 129). Holland introduces Paula, feminist and child of anarchy, into Styth patriarchy as an observer whose symphony of anger will not be silenced by social training. In her new home Paula is constantly angry: at the requirement of the veil (Holland 1975, 151), at the disappearance of her autonomous self under the demands on her by others (185), at Saba's dominance (229), at the casual Styth use of her affection for the people they own—the slave Pedasen, whom they kill (300), Paula's lesbian lover Illy (299–316), and Paula's half-breed son David (317)—all to restrain Paula's actions. Paula orchestrates her anger for survival and to resist constraints of the Styth system on her own freedoms. Frequently she refuses to veil herself in public (200); she refuses marriage to Saba despite the potential legal protection thus afforded to their child; she establishes a lesbian relation with Illy, one of Saba's wives, as resistance to his cruelty (215–21);[41] she treats the slave assigned to her as friend, not servant (179); and she refuses to herself use violence, although she manipulates it in others.

Returning to Mars and Earth on a diplomatic mission, Paula escapes from the Styths when the Martians attack Earth and the Styths retaliate against the Martians. During her stay as an anarchist revolutionary on Earth, which is occupied by fascist Martians, she learns a new form of anger from her lover and compatriot, Dick Bunker, and other defeated anarchists: anger not only as survival and resistance, but also as witness. With the Earth a

41. On lesbianism as resistance to patriarchy, see Adrienne Rich's classic essay on "Compulsory Heterosexuality and Lesbian Existence" (1980).

wasteland and its peoples killed by Martians or deported as slaves by Styths, Paula tells her enemies, "I'm their witness. . . . I'm the last witness to what happened down there, what you [Martians] want to forget, and the Styths want to forget" (Holland 1975, 446).

This novel ends, as an ambiguous utopia, with either hope or death — we are not sure which. Paula has revenge, through simply letting the fascist Martians and the militant Styths act out their cultural roles: Paula spends months helping resisters on Earth sabotage the Martian takeover, but the Martians who destroyed Earth are conquered and enslaved by the Styths; Paula refuses Saba's desires and successfully thwarts his friend Tanuojin's attempt to take over her mind after Saba's death; Paula helps Ketac, one of Saba's sons, to achieve power in the Styth Empire over Dakkar, who had killed her friend-slave Pedasen; and she forces Tanuojin to give her the Earth under the guise of exiling her. Since Dick Bunker has earlier escaped on Earth, there is the small hope that she will not be alone in her Eden, a small piece of seashore on the Earth where the air is breathable. She may face only death, yet still the piece of land where she ends is itself hope, for an Earth that can renew itself after the depredation of men.

In these science fictions by women, the fantasy of black or brown women as aliens among us is not a racist fantasy of excluding the other but, instead, a dream of heroic women who have suffered so much that they no longer internalize social regulatory mechanisms, reversing a pattern of female victimization.[42] In *Mind of My Mind* (1977) by the black writer Octavia Butler, the black hero Mary is a mutant with special mental powers, bred along with other telepaths in a racial experiment by her four-thousand-year-old father. Doro, able to take over another person's body, is a hyperbolic example of the patriarch, literally fathering thousands of children, but continuing a breeding program because he cannot reproduce himself — although telepathic, his children do not have his powers. As patriarch, Doro thinks of his people as his "family," controls their marriages and who has children, and frequently enforces his desires by beating his unwilling subjects or threatening their death (Butler 1977, 12, 31, 39, 113–14 and 205). Doro dreams of building a race like himself (129 and 204), thinks of his people as a breeding experiment (13, 55 and 97), but brings mainly suffering, since his telepathic victims receive pain from their gifts, picking up others' painful emotions and insane ideas. Mary explicitly compares Doro to Nazi scientists, accusing him of not caring that his people are "so far gone they look like they've been through Dachau" (195). Doro's ability to take over another person's body can occur only with that person's death, and moving to a new body is a

---

42. See Chodorow 1978, 43 on the process of children internalizing parental values so as to regulate themselves.

compulsion for Doro, who feeds off the victim's energy. He is a cannibal, treating other people as "food" (97), as "cattle" (209); he is a "parasite" (217), living off others' lives, not only by taking their bodies but also by his racial experiment.

When Mary comes of age, Doro, who has long had an incestuous relation with her, marries her off (Butler 1977, 30). The white man Doro puts her with, Karl, also forced into the marriage, is himself an accomplished patriarch, using his telepathic powers to program other people as servants and to control women as sexual "pets" (56–57, 103–4, 216). Vivian, the woman Karl would like to marry, seems to Mary a robot, controlled to serve men (41). Although the character of Mary is ambiguous, not simply a hero, she is rendered heroic by contrast with Doro's and Karl's unthinking abuse of their powers and by her resistance to them, even when she cannot win. When half way through the novel Mary goes through transition and becomes a mature telepath, the first master she overthrows is Karl: Mary is a new being, closer to Doro, who cannot help attaching herself symbiotically to other telepaths, whom she then controls, in a "pattern." After transition Mary, then, controls an unwilling Karl.

Mary's maturity thus puts her in "control" of several other telepaths. The second half of the novel tells of Mary's ethical journey toward learning how to be this kind of leader or head of a "family." At first, her politics are limited. Before transition she longs with bitterness to be one of the "owners," not one of the owned (Butler 1977, 49 and 102). Shortly after transition, she feels proprietary about the other telepaths she is linked with and has control over (61 and 64). When the first powerful telepath resists her physically, she beats him and his partner and drains his strength (114) — in short, she acts like her models, Doro and Karl. Although Mary realizes that she will kill to survive (122), she has already been shown as heroic for this strength — the scene in which we meet Mary shows her bashing in the skull of a man who tries to rape her (24). What differentiates Mary from Doro is her political growth, although only from bad to good master. Mary fears that she will be like Doro, a cannibal (123), but realizes that her pattern, her network of links to a large and growing group of telepaths, allows her to draw a little energy from all rather than draining and destroying one person — she is a vampire, a symbiont, not a parasite (133–35, 145–46 and 217). Mary's pattern provides her with another strength: intimate knowledge of many other people. As she comes to know the telepaths she is linked to, she realizes that she provides them, biologically and naturally, a protection against the overload of emotions. Thus she can rescue her people from lives of abuse and insanity, binding them into a community that can do good to one another, if not to outsiders. Near the end of the novel as she prepares to face Doro, she realizes, "I'm not the vampire he is. I give in return for my taking. . . . I've got ethics all of a sudden" (210). However ambitious, Mary is not power hungry but, instead, desirous of connections to others like her.

Still, Butler, by complicating matters, uses Doro's patriarchal mode of operation and Mary's new patternist society to explore racism. Butler introduces the new race, telepaths, who render the old races — black and white — inferior as "mutes," in order to defamiliarize the terrain of racism as a way to better examine it. At intersections of gender, race, and alien oppression, her characters act out old biased reactions: Karl and Jan initially hate Mary because she is black, even though they are all telepaths (Butler 1977, 44, 88 and 113), while the telepaths recreate slavery by taking over "mutes" for production, service, and sexuality. Emma, an old wise woman at odds with Mary, sees what Mary does not: "I know what ['mute'] means. . . . I knew the first time I heard Mary use it. It means nigger!" (161) Thus Mary's triumph, the triumph of a young black woman, formerly abused by her parents and her society, is at best only partial; Mary's biology has led her to reestablish a plantation society and a racist hierarchy — for everyone's own good, of course.

Despite Mary's partial political growth, Butler still lets her act the hero, and it is Mary's anger that motivates her, while it is the community she has built that empowers her. Audre Lorde explains that "Every Black woman in America lives her life somewhere along a wide curve of ancient and unexpressed angers" (1984, 145). Certainly Mary has lived along that curve, angry at Doro for his patriarchal control and the racial breeding program that causes her people pain (Butler 1977, 39, 197 and 205), angry at racism (113, 121 and 188), angry at Karl for his sexist and racist assumptions (144). Doro, Mary's father-lover, able to enlarge his own telepathic mental powers by feeding on the energy of others, and able to take over another's body, fearing Mary's growing mental strength, attacks her.[43] Mary kills Doro by drawing on the strength of all the telepaths in her network, and Butler does not undo that anger by assigning Mary guilt: "Now she took her revenge. She consumed him slowly, drinking in his terror and his life, drawing out her own pleasure, and laughing through his soundless screams" (220). Somehow Mary has managed not to internalize the social regulatory mechanisms that would make her submissive and feminine, easy prey to Doro. The novel presents as heroic Mary's reversal of the pattern of female victimization that readers had seen in her alcoholic mother, cowed by Doro.[44]

The price of outwitting or rejecting the feminine role, however, is often death, a price the alienated women of these novels are willing to pay. That is what Mary expects when Doro attacks her. Similarly, when Piercy's Connie

43. On Butler's black female heroes, see Frances Smith Foster 1982.
44. For an alternative reading of *Mind of My Mind*, see Roberts 1993, 106–7, who reads Mary as descending from a line of science fiction goddess myths.

in *Woman on the Edge of Time* poisons the doctors, she exchanges her own life for this one chance to enact her anger and change the future, since the result is Connie's lifelong internment in state institutions. This relationship between anger and death is also central to Joanna Russ's dystopic novel, *We Who Are About To . . .* (1975–77). Russ's hero lives at the intersection of several persecuted sects. A descendant of Sephardic Jews (Russ 1975–77, 14) and member of a persecuted religious sect, The Nobodies or "Tremblers" (29–31),[45] the unnamed female hero is also a former communist revolutionary (32–33, 114, 118), and suspected to be a lesbian ("left-handed" 58). As a member of any of these groups, she is an alien.[46] In her dying meditations she reflects, "When you were born, there was no real place for you, no one was fond of you, not really, not of that real self only you knew" (146). But from her point outside society, at the intersection of many unprivileged groups, the hero can see truths those accepted inside cannot.

The main truth that Russ's hero sees is that all of the characters are condemned to die. Lost in space, the five women and three men are ejected with six months' supplies onto a planet with appropriate atmosphere and water, plantlife about which they know nothing, and no animal life. Russ uses the familiar scenario not to begin the banal plot[47] of justified emergency colonizing, but to satirize humanity's illusions of grandeur; her hero is the voice of this critique. Rather than the dream of self-sufficiency that Western imperialists have entertained since before *Robinson Crusoe*,[48] Russ presents the impossibility and nightmares of such a venture: the planet may exist in endless summer (Russ 1975–77, 18 and 104); the plant life may contain poisons or simply incompatibilities (23); having babies can kill you (85–86); erupting wisdom teeth can kill you (22); even if there are babies, humans each carry five to eight lethal genes (23). Russ's message expands to remind us that we are all dying, always, that nature is often hostile, that even "Earth. Kind old home" offered "smallpox," "plague," "earthquakes," "vipers," "bliz-

45. See Russ 1975–77, 33: "And I'd prefer it if you called me what we call ourselves: Nobodies — I'm Nobody, who are you? Are you Nobody, too?" The questions are an allusion to the beginning of a poem by Emily Dickinson. I think, from Russ's context and the poem, that we are meant to take "Nobodies" to stand for women in general, an often persecuted sect (sex).

46. Russ reflects in an interview, "For women, there's simply no easy way of finding some kind of fulfillment. The whole idea of going from your own world to an alien world makes sense only if you're not an alien in your own world. It's very hard to feel at home here when you're not" (McCaffery 1990, 207).

47. In an interview, Russ observes, "My work is haunted by the banal plots that are not there. People get upset because they recognize the cues and think they're going to get a nice old adventure story. When that doesn't happen, they wonder what the hell is going on. I do this metafictional commentary a lot" (McCaffery 1990, 199–200).

48. Russ, *We Who Are About To Die . . .* (1975–77) refers to desert island literature on p. 62.

zards," "tsunamis," and "liver flukes" (20).[49] "We're nowhere," announces the narrator on the first page of the novel, but that nowhere is not the utopian "no-place" promised by the lost-in-space-so-colonize plot.

The narrator refuses to give up her reproductive freedom to join the impossible colonizing venture of her fellow passengers after their spaceship crashes, making this an antipatriarchal, as well as antiutopian and anti-imperialist novel. In a "great womb robbery" (Russ 1975–77, 49), the men attempt to set up a colony, aiming to subjugate all the women to childbearing (of the five women, two are probably past childbearing and one is twelve). They enforce male dominance with violence. Alan Bobby first tries more seductive sadomasochistic erotics on Nathalie — "I could take you over my knee and spank you" (39). When that fails to work, he knocks her down (39), covering over his guilt later with elaborate gestures of chivalry (43). This behavior is not simply "Cultural reversion" (36), as the narrator at first claims, or even a "mass-delusional system" (150), as she later describes it but, more fundamentally, patriarchy as we have known it: even in the future, "Relations with men are still apt to be patterned on a few rather dull models" (10). The narrator is a hero who, seeing the truth of the patriarchal system, opts out: "They were going to force me to have babies. I was going to be tied to a tree and raped, for goodness' sake" (150).

Refusing to be part of the recreation of colonialism and patriarchy, Russ's hero runs away, instead, to die, and to learn what dying has to teach. When the others stranded on the planet come to force her back among them, she kills them. Her act is a measure of her just anger. "Anger is a necessity. It's part of all radicalism," says Russ in an interview; "You need this anger to resist looking at the structure and saying, 'It's us, it's our fault' " (Larry McCafferey 1990, 209).[50] "But I don't feel like forgiving anyone, you see," explains Russ's hero in We Who Are About To . . . — "I'm nasty. . . . The headiness of anger.

49. In a recent interview, Russ admits her parody of the science fiction novel of colonization: "I was poking fun at that tradition, sure. . . . The whole Robinson-Crusoe-and-the-desert-island business is, at bottom, an imperialist myth: you find a place 'out there' and you make it yours. . . . This goes on in SF all the time — you can see it in Marion Zimmer Bradley's Darkover series, for instance" (McCaffery 1990, 190). Indeed, I think that Russ is satirizing one specific novel, as well as the tradition of the desert island/stranded on a planet colonial fiction: Marion Zimmer Bradley's Darkover Landfall (1972), published three years before Russ's We Who Are About To . . . Like We Who Are About To . . . , Darkover Landfall is the story of a group (much larger) who crash on a planet far from known space, and attempt colonizing — successfully. As in We Who Are About To . . . , in Darkover Landfall patriarchy is reinstituted because of the link between women and reproduction (Bradley 1972, 107). The novels even share a character name: daughters in both novels are named Lori (1972, 159).

50. Russ continues, "If you lose touch with this outrage, you wind up forgetting what you were mad about in the first place; you start feeling that you'd really rather not get involved, that you can't change things, that it's no use. Oppression is always mystifying and confusing. Lying, really" (McCafferey 1990, 209).

Perhaps I'm an addict. An anger addict" (Russ 1975–77, 68). In the novel, Russ imagines the self constructed out of a myriad of details: "details plucked unhesitatingly from the real, unstable times and places and put together into a meaning, a mosaic, a symbol, an icon, because that's what mattered and that's how it mattered" (139–40). Anger, then, sustains the self through the socially inflicted details of self-doubt. In the fragmented meditative sequence[51] that is the last third of the novel while the narrator dies, we follow the growth of self out of a mozaic of memories, to the sequence when she overcomes her self-doubt with anger. When a vision of her former male lover, L.B., returns to accuse her of murder — "Out of spite. . . . Anger. The chance to do what you'd always really wanted to do" (151) — her anger gives her the strength to reply, "You fake! . . . You never loved me, never, never, you only pretended . . . to destroy me! . . . Then you're the killer!" (152) The vision calmly acknowledges the truth of her insight, and in the remainder of the novel she reconstitutes herself through further visits from hallucinations, who collaboratively help her understand anew the radical politics of her past, as well as the memories of her self that are herself.

After learning what *ars moriendi*, the art of dying, has to teach, the narrator kills herself. Despite the learning, her death recalls Phyllis Chesler's finding in her psychological study, *Women and Madness*, that "Women who *succeed* at suicide are, tragically, outwitting or rejecting their 'feminine' roles, and at the only price possible: their death" (1972, 48). Russ reinforces this connection by the narrator's hallucinated accusation from Cassie: "You're schizoid" (1975–77, 136). Russ further underlines this tragic connection during the narrator's final joke on her audience, imagining a last minute rescue, with her response an echo from Sylvia Plath's "Lady Lazarus": "What a damned nuisance, I will have to be alive again" (1975–77, 169). The novel asks whether the price of a woman's knowing herself must always be madness or death, since a patriarchal culture cannot allow a woman who knows herself to live in it.

51. Russ suggests that women can't write because there are no structures for them to write in: men's conventions portray only men, and women have been restricted to writing about love and marriage. She suggests science fiction as one option, but also, as another, lyricism: "the organization of discrete elements (images, events, scenes, passages, words, what-have-you) around an unspoken thematic or emotional center. The lyric mode exists without chronology or causation; its principle of connection is associative" (1972b, 12). *We Who Are About To . . .* is, I think, Russ's experiment in lyricism as a form of women's writing. Since there are no conventions that allow us to tell women's death as heroic (only as just punishment or tragic), Russ uses the lyric form, which she explains "is setting various images, events, scenes, or memories to circling round an unspoken, invisible center. The invisible center is what the novel . . . is about; it is also unsayable in available dramatic or narrative terms. That is, there is no action possible to the central character and no series of events which will embody in clear, unequivocal, immediately graspable terms what the artist means. . . . Unable to use the myths of male culture . . . [the writer] uses a structure that is basically non-narrative" (1972b, 13).

Revolution and mass murder in these novels are presented as empowering fantasies about enacting anger against socially sanctioned injustice, as revenge is presented in the contemporary masculine detective novel. "I rather enjoyed killing them off," admits the narrator (surely also the author of her characters here) in Russ's *We Who Are About To* . . . (1975–77, 155). Near the end of Russ's *The Female Man*, the narrator confesses that of the four characters living alternative model lives of resistance, she prefers the militant one, Jael (also known as Alice Reasoner): "I think . . . that I like Jael the best of us all, that I would like to be Jael, twisted as she is on the rack of her own hard logic, triumphant in her extremity. . . . Alice Reasoner, who says tragedy makes her sick, who says never give in but always go down fighting, who says take them with you, who says die if you must but loop your own intestines around the neck of your strangling enemy" (1975, 212). Since violent women are punished not only in society but also in novels, this privileging of the violent woman is authorial effrontery — Russ's own attempt to kill off the Angel in the House that Virginia Woolf recommends for all women writers. Killing off the angel means facing and claiming one's own anger as a tool for change.[52]

In their double oppression as women and also as blacks or Chicanas or Jews, the heroes of these fictions by Cecelia Holland, Joanna Russ, Marge Piercy, and the black writer Octavia Butler represent in hyperbolic form female as well as racial and often class oppression. These fictions end violently, with the hero's assertion of her anger at male oppression. These women refuse their socially prescribed roles as victims and rebel: the stories all include mass murder or revolution. Le Guin's Odo creates a revolution. Consuelo poisons four of the doctors who experiment on human brains, in order to preserve the freedoms of a future she has time-traveled to. Cecelia Holland's Paula Mendoza orchestrates Styth conquest of the Martians who destroyed Earth and forces Tanuojin (by resisting his mental takeover) to give her what she wants, exile on Earth. Octavia Butler's Mary kills her father-lover and mentally eats him. Russ's hero kills all the other survivors when they try to force her to rejoin their group and have babies. Combining the current status of minority women with the science fiction convention of

---

52. When I teach Russ's *The Female Man* to my college undergraduates, the class always divides along lines of gender, and politics become very personal when we discuss the cocktail party scene, where Janet, the woman from the future, breaks a man's arm for harrassing her (Russ 1975, 33–47): I ask how many of the students have been sexually harrassed at a party, and all the women raise their hands, while only one or two men do; then the heterosexual men in the class listen with growing horror, and the women with growing jubilation, to personal stories of what women did to revenge themselves on men who oppress them sexually — I do not ask for these stories, but they are always told; having read about Janet's resistance, they feel authorized to tell of their own. This is a moment of great guilt and solidarity among the women in the class, when they talk out loud about their anger.

violence in defense of individual freedom, these women ask, "If we look at the women-as-other through the lens of the science fiction hero, what would we see her do?" What women in our culture do (which Chesler points out) is generally self-destructive.[53] But these novelists empower their women, in the same way that the Western or detective fiction empowers ordinary men, to enact their anger at socially sanctioned injustice.

In her short story, "The Day Before the Revolution" (1974), Ursula K. Le Guin adds a coda to this story of the angry alien woman of color. Le Guin pictures the old woman, as well as the black and lower class woman, as alien — "None of it [clothing, cosmetics] would make the slightest difference. The old woman would look a little less, or a little more, grotesque" (Le Guin 1975, 268–69). Odo, the famous revolutionary whose revolution is hundreds of years in the past in *The Dispossessed*, in "The Day Before the Revolution" is an old black woman recovering from a stroke: her "toes, compressed by a lifetime of cheap shoes, were almost square where they touched each other, and bulged out above in corns; the nails were discolored and shapeless. . . . the skin was the color of mud, and knotted veins crossed the instep. Disgusting. Sad, depressing. Mean. Pitiful. She tried on all the words, and they all fit" (Le Guin 1975, 262). The color of mud, though, in Le Guin's story, is the color of fundamental human heroism: "But will you drag civilization down into the mud? cried the shocked decent people," Odo remembers, "and she had tried for years to explain to them that if all you had was mud, then if you were God you made it into human beings, and if you were human you tried to make it into houses where human beings could live. But nobody who thought he was better than mud would understand" (274). Confronting all the inadequacies of her stricken, aging body, and her sentimental memories of her past, Odo prepares to die; coincidentally, the Revolution she has worked all her life to bring about prepares to begin — it is "The Day Before the Revolution."

Le Guin encapsulates a theory of the revolutionary self in her short story, or at least the revolutionary self as old woman. The self comes in layers, added on as one grows up: Odo peels back the public revolutionary, "the tireless worker and thinker," destroyed by a stroke, and the private "lover, the swimmer in the midst of life," destroyed by the death of her partner Taviri. Facing death, one returns to the fundamental, to the girl who was free, so one can look at death as freedom, too. Le Guin's theory, then, is a romantic one of childhood: the child, the daughter, is free. Women are constrained to

53. Chesler suggests that depression is a characteristically feminine response to loss, since women can't lose what they never had (1972, 44); depression, then, is keeping faith with the feminine role, even in deadly fashion, since it feels safer to women to be depressed than to express discontent in physical violence (45). That women more often attempt but don't complete suicide, Chesler sees as a female "signal of ritual readiness for self-sacrifice" (49).

be who they are—either deformed, like the A-Io women with shaven heads (Le Guin 1975, 268), or burdened, like the Odonian revolutionaries who choose the burdens of the public work of reform. Only in the daughters can Odo see the freedom she pursued as an ideal: "Amai had grown up in Odonian Houses, born to the Revolution, a true daughter of anarchy. And so quiet and free and beautiful a child, enough to make you cry when you thought: this is what we worked for, this is what we meant, this is it, here she is, alive, the kindly, lovely future" (268). Only in the daughters and in her own death can Odo see the freedom she pursued. While the day before the revolution everyone else is excited by the strikes, the secessions, the impending revolt of soldiers, Odo sees that the revolution must already have occurred, in the lovely, unconstrained daughters, in order for the strikes and secessions and revolts to occur. The day before the revolution, Odo sees that the revolution is done, and so lets herself give up her burden and go freely, seeing death as freedom. This is a long way from anger.

But this final freedom that Le Guin imagines is achieved only by passing through anger, as one of the layers of self. At first, on this last day before her revolution, Odo is angry at herself and others for the loss of her anger, the anger that fueled her revolutionary goals: "They just came to look, as if she were the Great Tower in Rodarred. . . . A phenomenon, a monument. . . . She who had mined the shipyards, . . . cursed Premier Inoilte to his face, . . . and pissed in public on the big brass plaque in Capitol Square" (Le Guin 1975, 271). As her day wears on, however, she acknowledges that she has through necessity given up her anger in favor of endurance: "After a lifetime of living on hope because there is nothing but hope, one loses the taste for victory. A real sense of triumph must be preceded by real despair. She had unlearned despair a long time ago. There were no more triumphs. One went on" (270). Odo had unlearned anger in order to learn going on. Le Guin suggests that the woman who is a revolutionary must transform her anger, the anger that produces despair and revolution, into going on, the anarchical process of continual change to keep oneself and one's society free. Le Guin's story, then, Odo's story, might just as well be titled, "The Days After the Revolution." In order to be won, the Revolution must already be won in each woman, in each daughter, the day before the revolution, and over and over after it. "True Journey is return" (266), an Odonian would say.[54]

And so, in these novels, the very existence of the alien changes the norm. In *Black Feminist Criticism* Barbara Christian points out, "In every society where there is the denigrated *Other* whether that is designated by sex, race, class, or ethnic background, the *Other* struggles to declare the truth and therefore create the truth in forms that exist for her or him. The creation of

---

54. And so Le Guin may count writing as revolutionary work, as well: Odo muses, "she could still write, and that was her work" (1975a, 271).

that truth also changes the perception of all those who believe they are the norm" (1985, 160). These science fictions by Piercy, Holland, Butler, Russ, and Le Guin depict revolution as the right to murder under intolerable social conditions; they also present fantasies about women's resistance of socially sanctioned injustice through enacting their anger.[55]

Joan Slonczewski's A Door Into Ocean and Carol Emshwiller's Carmen Dog: Complicating the Paradigms

In writing alien women, women reclaim misogynistic cultural stereotypes, give them a local habitation and a name, and remodel them so they can live within them. In her essay "What Can a Heroine Do? or Why Women Can't Write," Joanna Russ asks how women writers can use male myths (1972b, 5). In her novel, The Female Man, Russ answers. She claims for Jael, the woman warrior who has killed the general of Manland, several of the misogynistic stereotypes for the dangerous female:

> even the Crazy Womb, the Ball-breaking Bitch, the Fanged Killer Lady.
> "I don't give a damn whether it was necessary or not," I said.
> "I liked it." (Russ 1975, 184)

Russ claims these stereotypes, gives them a place to live in the character Jael, and remodels them as a complex response to the question of militant resistance. In her essay on "Slavery, Race and Ideology in the United States of America," Barbara Jeanne Fields proposes that ideology requires continued creation, that it cannot be inherited, and that therefore the rewriting of stories is necessary to trouble the smooth transmission to the next generation, or even to interrupt its creation in this generation (1991). But women writers may negotiate what generic conventions they draw from science fiction not only with the masculine tradition but also with other women writers. In this final section, then, I will offer close readings of two novels, Joan Slonczewski's A Door Into Ocean and Carol Emshwiller's Carmen Dog, that use the convention of the woman as alien to negotiate with previous women writers' texts. Neither text offers a "pure" woman as animal or woman as machine. Slonczewski mixes the symbols of animal women with the conventions of the lesbian utopia to explore the issue of mothering, and relegates the woman-as-machine

---

55. Other science fictions that follow the conventions of aliens among us include Ursula K. Le Guin's Eye of the Heron (1978), and Octavia Butler's Wild Seed (1980); although the female heroes are white, James Tiptree, Jr.'s (Alice-Sheldon's) "The Women Men Don't See" (1973), from Warm Worlds and Otherwise 131–72, to some degree falls into this category. A. M. Lightner's The Day of the Drones (1969) is a race-reversal and gender-reversal novel featuring a black female hero who enters a white postholocaust society as explorer, and returns with such changed ideas that she is jailed for fear of political unrest.

to equal-rights capitalistic Valedon. Emshwiller offers a story of fluid change between animal mother and masochistic humanoid alien women that allows her to orchestrate her critique of feminist movement with sympathetic comedy.

Joan Slonczewski's *A Door Into Ocean* (1986) presents woman as alien to the second power, since Shorans, inhabitants of the newly discovered culture on the moon of the planet Valedon, are animal-like women with purple skin and webbed fingers and toes, living in an alien lesbian pacifist culture. Slonczewski's novel mediates debates between 1970s utopias by Jo-anna Russ, Sally Miller Gearhart and others, and the mid-1980s gender-reversed dystopias by Pamela Sargent, Sherri Tepper and others.

Let me digress a moment to sketch the genre of the lesbian feminist utopia and these debates that Slonczewski is entering. Two main kinds of feminist utopias emerged during the 1970s, aligning themselves with different schools of feminist politics: the separatist lesbian utopia, such as Joanna Russ's Whileaway in *The Female Man* (1975), Sally Miller Gearhart's Hillwomen in *The Wanderground* (1979), and Katherine V. Forrest's Maternas in *Daughters of a Coral Dawn* (1984); and the feminist utopia that accommodates a range of sexualities but generally takes as norm bisexuality, such as Marge Piercy's *Woman on the Edge of Time* (1976) and Marion Zimmer Bradley's Amazons in *The Shattered Chain* (1976), *Thendara House* (1983), and *City of Sorcery* (1984). Although they are often thrown together in the same category in criticism, these two kinds of feminist utopias — lesbian and bisexual — have different purposes. The lesbian utopia grows out of the sense of exile from the dominant culture of lesbian subculture, as well as essentialist politics, and imaginatively creates a place where lesbian pleasure can be real (healthy, normal, central, out in the open). The bisexual utopia extends equal-rights feminism to sexuality and assumes that reformed society would also reform sexuality to be more inclusive, not just at the social level, but even at the individual level — the bisexual utopia imaginatively creates a place where each person is socially constructed to desire both sexes. The lesbian utopia has been frequently condemned by critics for its essentialism, while it has not been recognized that its purpose is not to exclude men, but simply to establish a safe place for lesbian pleasure.[56] Feminists have entered the

---

56. On these lesbian utopias as feminist utopias, see Carol Pearson 1977; Angelika Bammer 1991, 67–118; and Robin Roberts 1993, 66–89; on these novels as separatist utopias, see Peter Fitting 1987 and 1992 (and Pamela Sargent's 1992 reponse to Fitting); and Jenny Wolmark 1994, 82–107; on these novels as lesbian utopias, see Bonnie Zimmerman 1990, 143–57. Bonnie Zimmerman suggests that the purpose of all lesbian fiction is "to create lesbian identity and culture" (1990, 20) but cautions that there is no single truth of lesbian identity (25). For an excellent summary of the history of theories of lesbian identity, see Zimmerman 1990, 50. On separatist politics, see Faderman 1991, 210–12, 218, 220 and 238; and Zimmerman 1990, 126–28. In her critique of essentialism in "Lesbian Identity," Biddy Martin suggests that "The ultimate formation of a politics of nostalgia, of a return to that state of innocence free of conflict

conversation about the lesbian utopia, not only in criticism, but also in the genre of science fiction. A series of "utopias" in the 1970s and 1980s "misread" the earlier lesbian utopias and use the genre of gender-reversal science fiction to attack the treatment of men in novels portraying all-women utopias: Marion Zimmer Bradley's *The Ruins of Isis* (1978), Cynthia Felice's *Double Nocturne* (1986), Pamela Sargent's *The Shore of Women* (1986), and Sherri Tepper's *The Gate to Women's Country* (1988). These novels are *not* lesbian utopias, although Bradley's, Felice's, and Sargent's represent lesbian encounters sympathetically; all three establish heterosexuality as the norm, making a fictional argument that heterosexuality alone is inclusive, and so "fair" to men.

To put in conversation the radical separatist politics of 1970s lesbian utopias and the conservative equity-only politics of 1980s gender-reversal science fiction, Slonczewski borrows the technique of double but ambiguous utopias from Ursula K. Le Guin's *Dispossessed* (1974). Le Guin's novel pictures both the capitalist culture of A-Io (which protects the ecology) and the anarchist culture of Annares as better places to live than the early 1970s USA. Similarly, Slonczewski's *A Door Into Ocean* contrasts two future civilizations, one on the planet Valedon, one on the moon Shora — both further advanced in women's issues than Slonczewski's own United States in 1986.[57]

Valedon is a patriarchy (whose highest governing official is called the Patriarch) and an imperialist dictatorship. The economy is capitalist and the major products are stones, metals, and machines. The city-states of Valedon, in loose federation, are always at war, and the economies of the world depend on war. As we saw in chapter 1, Valedon science depends on domination of nature, has created a rich technology, but is not successful in redressing the problems of daily life, such as Seaswallowers, on Shora. This does not sound

---

conceived as women's primary emotional bonds with one another, enacts its own violence, as all dreams of perfect union do" (1988, 87). Gender conceived as essential or socially constructed is not just a political position held in a vacuum, but also a strategy for survival. Social construction has been much more consistently useful to heterosexuals, who can argue that the roles of women are constructed and so can be changed for the sake of equity between men and women in education or careers or housework. Essentialism has been seen as useful to lesbians at times (especially during the 1970s), who argued that what is natural can't be changed and so we must be allowed to live with it. Essentialism, now that scientists are claiming to have found a "homosexual gene," seems much less useful, even dangerous — who wants to be operated on to have the gay gene removed, the way doctors in the 1930s removed one adrenalin gland from lesbians to correct their disease (see Faderman 1991, 100)?

57. In an e-mail message to me, 14 May 1996. Joan Slonczewski, in response to my comment here wrote, "I did not think I was showing Valedon as 'superior' to our own society; although women are in the army, the government structure is highly hierarchical and undemocratic, with no social welfare system."

like a utopia, but in two senses, ambiguously, it is: Valedon is a rich planet with vast natural resources still not ruined; and Valedon permits equality for women, who have every career open to them — even the military. In fact, Jade, General Realgar's second in command and intelligence officer, even fiercer than he, is a woman. In contrast, Shora, the moon entirely covered by water, whose inhabitants all are female and so also all lesbian, is a pure democracy that acts collectively by full consensus. The Shorans, pacifists, have not seen a war in a thousand years but have developed a variety of psychological strategies to handle conflict, including "witnessing" in groups against someone (a sit-in), and "unspeaking" between individuals. One visiting Valedonian suggests that only people who have weapons too terrible to use can have developed nonviolent methods of retaliation, and that Shorans have these weapons in their biological science, which includes the ability to create viruses and enzymes for any purpose. Shoran economy is communalistic, so that all share all resources (they call themselves "Sharers"), and their primary products are medicines and sea silk raw or woven into cloth. As we saw in chapter 1, their science depends on immense knowledge of the ecology and fitting humans into it with the least disturbance; for example, they handle Seaswallowers by learning to live with them rather than trying to destroy them. There are no gender roles on Shora, because there are no sexes, only women, yet as a utopia it remains ambiguous, partly because whether it can protect itself by nonviolent means from a violent culture remains an unanswered question at the novel's end, and partly because the society still experiences severe political divisions and conflicts between individuals; additionally, at the moment of the story, the culture is threatened by the coming of men.

Although Slonczewski presents both planets as "better" than ours, her novel also makes it clear that Shora is superior: equal rights for women and inclusion in the military are not enough to make Valedon a livable place, with its patriarchal, hierarchical, militaristic values. On Valedon, reproduction is still controlled by the state (through limits on the number of children, rather than through outlawing abortion), women still do the "second shift" except among the upper classes, where robots are used, nor are basic necessities of life equitably distributed, while women's husbands and sons and now sisters are still killed in wars. The lack of viability of Valedonian culture is represented by Slonczewski's representation of the woman as machine. On this equal-rights planet, the problem of who does the childcare is not solved by communal responsibility, as it is on Shora, but by facsimile mothers. Realgar's children have been raised by "nanny servo" (Slonczewski 1987, 43), "of broad maternal build wrapped in a cheerfully embroidered peasant skirt" (190). Slonczewski's woman as machine, however, does not escape her role and find herself in this society, since she symbolizes the alienation of parents from their children. When Berenice tries to take leave of the children she may soon "mother" (since she is engaged to their father), one child cries, "You can't go already. . . . Then there's just the old nanny servo; she's ugly, and she smells like motor oil" (43). Raising children by machines, suggests Slonczewski, prepares them to live not in a community but in an alienated hierarchy.

In Slonczewski's *A Door Into Ocean*, the lesbian culture on Valedon's moon is seen as alien, Valedon as the norm. To Valedonians, Shorans are "foreign" (Slonczewski 1987, 3), "witches" (12), "rebel catfish" (208), and "subhuman" because they can no longer interbreed "naturally" with hetero-sexual Valedonian men (89–90). On Valedon, lesbianism is illegal—"immoral cohabitation" in the wording familiar from many states' laws in the United States (30).

However, Slonczewski negotiates the conventions of science fiction by conflating the convention of the alien lesbian utopia with the trope of alien animal mothers on Shora. Adult Shorans seem animal-like to Valedonians (and to readers) because of their bodies, the aquatic abilities adapting them to their ocean planet: they are strong "amethyst" (Slonczewski 1987, 4) women with webbed fingers and toes, able to swim long distances and to stay underwater for up to fifteen minutes; their purple color results from a symbiotic microbe, which other humans may acquire, that helps manufacture and store extra oxygen for long minutes underwater. These adaptations, however, are the result not only of evolution, but mainly of engineering. By their science Shorans have the power of reproduction heightened to immense degree: they reproduce themselves through genetic engineering, change the plants and animals around them, and construct a variety of useful microbes to better the life of the ocean planet—creating oil-eating bacteria, for example, when Valedonian traders and military dirty the ocean. As we saw Cherryh do in *Serpent's Reach*, Slonczewski has compressed female biology with Biology, and so magnified the powers of Mothers: Shoran mothers mother the earth as well as their children. It is this alien power that Valedonians fear. Slonczewski does not romanticize feminists' political goals by assigning those goals to Nature and masculine goals to Science; she acknowledges that an alternative society would need an alternative way of exercising power in relation to the natural world.

Slonczewski also uses the trope of alien animal mother to suggest that Sharer society is an ambiguous utopia, in need of conversation with the outside. As Jane Gallop suggests, "The psychological condition of possibility for the feminist collective is the daughter's ongoing infantile connection to the mother" (1989, 16). How does a daughter grow up in a community where individuation, moving out, is seen as either political disagreement (unspeaking) or psychosis? In *A Door Into Ocean*, Lystra's former lover Ril-wen lives apart on a small raft and is seen as psychotic in her preference for stone-wealth (collecting gemstones) over community. Especially in the stormy relationship between Merwen and her daughter Lystra, Slonczewski suggests that utopian feminist daughters have as much trouble as any other kind with their rigid mothers. While Merwen sponsors Spinel on Shora, for example, and argues that Valedonians are indeed human, when he starts dating her daughter, he becomes again a "malefreak" in her arguments with Lystra (Slonczewski 1987, 147). By including divisions between mothers and daughters, this novel does not criticize the older generation of feminists so much as suggest that feminism must continually change and be redefined with each new generation, if not more often. If growing up does not constitute individuation, and daughters still need to separate from mothers, then the collective must change to express that difference of daughters from mothers.[58]

In addition, through the trope of the animal mother that connects mother to nature, Slonczewski calls into question the power of motherhood that earlier feminist utopias idealized. Shoran mothers, despite their science and because of their pacifist values, cannot protect their daughters from rape, although they have taught their daughters to "protect" themselves. When Lystra is raped by Valedonian soldiers, an act of dominance not desire, her body has been protected with a stinging ointment that forces the soldier to withdraw (Slonczewski 1987, 163 and 268). All Shoran daughters have also been taught to use "whitetrance," a self-induced coma, to withdraw from conflict and frighten attackers away. But neither of these strategies can prevent rape itself. There is no natural power that mothers can call on — only conflict and the means to negotiate it.

At the same time as Slonczewski renders ambiguous the notion of a lesbian utopia, she also "corrects" 1980s "misreadings" (especially by Sargent and Tepper) of lesbian utopias as mainly intended to exclude men. A *Door Into Ocean* reestablishes the idea that a different reality is possible, one based on lesbian pleasure and women's way of knowing the world, a knowledge without violence because it is without penetration.[59] On Shora, there is no mining, since the world is water covered: the water prevents access to surface minerals and so to development of the technology to mine beneath the world's surface. Instead, Shorans have developed an organic technology, grown from plants, which does not require penetration of their world to use it. On Shora, there are weapons, and people occasionally kill each other on

---

58. Thus the daughters do not have to experience what Jane Gallop calls "the unbearable choice: either total merger with the mother or total loss of her" (1989, 23).

59. As the psychologist Phyllis Chesler points out, in her study of women diagnosed as mentally ill in the 1960s, almost all the lesbians she interviewed had psychiatrists who not only viewed lesbianism as a dangerous mental illness, but also denied that the women whom they were treating were lesbians (1972, 193–97). According to Chesler, these lesbians' "sense of reality, their *knowledge of pleasure*, is being treated as either non-existent, second best, or dangerous" (197).

purpose or by accident (with knife or blow), but there is no war, and animals are not hunted to death. Shellfish are used for food, but otherwise Shorans are mainly vegetarian. Shockwraiths, with octopus-like bodies, are hunted for their arms, but they are not killed to gain them: Shorans use their knives not to penetrate, to kill, but to cut off an arm, which will regrow. With such episodes, Slonczewski suggests that a lesbian society, women who find pleasure through caressing each others' bodies, will know their environment differently from a heterosexual society, men and women who find pleasure through male penetration. But Slonczewski does not see this extension to knowing the world as an innate biological difference between lesbians and heterosexuals: each could learn their worldview from the other.

Slonczewski also offers a compromise to those writers who criticized the lesbian utopias as separatist, especially Sargent and Tepper: she concedes that lesbian utopias do not need to exclude men, if men will change. Thus Slonczewski also disagrees politically with the strategy of essentialism to protect lesbian culture. In A Door Into Ocean all the characters have socially constructed sex roles; therefore men, too, may change. "For all his headfur and fingerclaws," says Usha when she first meets Spinel, "He would make a good daughter" (Slonczewski 1987, 17). In this novel by a feminist who has sons, Spinel, a boy, is welcomed into the lesbian utopia, but holds himself apart. Having journeyed to Valedon to experience firsthand the other culture, Usha and Merwen invite Spinel to return with them to Shora, so that Shorans may live with a Valedonian and discover whether they are indeed "human."

Spinel agrees to the adventure, but endures extreme culture shock; much of the novel tells of his acclimatization to Shora. Gradually he proves that Valedonians are human because one Valedonian boy can participate responsibly in Shoran society, but his own biases make difficult his growing up into Shoran values. When Spinel begins to turn purple, having become infested by the breathmicrobes that allow Shorans to store oxygen for underwater swimming, he fears that he is "metamorphosing into a moon-creature," that he is "becoming a monster" (98). When he gives up and returns home, he ponders, "Perhaps he could yet be a Sharer and himself, too" (175). But he finds that he has been changed too much to be his former self. He teaches Valedonians Shoran techniques of passive resistance and organizes sit ins and strikes; he becomes, in Valedonian terms, a "spirit-caller." When he returns to Shora, he further alienates himself from his native culture by disapproving of Valedonian military tactics, and he joins Shorans in their resistance to the war. Finally, he agrees to join Shoran society fully, taking a "self-name," a sign of Shoran adulthood, and trying to learn "white trance," the self-induced coma that Shorans use to avoid conflict (Slonczewski 1987, 342).

But the hardest task Spinel faces is love. With whom does a heterosexual have sex on Shora? Lystra, Merwen's daughter, and Spinel fall in love, and through this plot move, Slonczewski argues the constructedness of sexuality. Spinel is asked to become a truly female man, a lesbian man, by his lover Lystra, to love her by "sharing pleasure" (Slonczewski 1987, 161), rather than by penetration (162–63). Instead of the women becoming heterosexual, as in *Herland*, the man is asked to become lesbian, to learn fusion: "they both clung together as if they would merge into one" (Slonczewski 1987, 144). Thus *A Door Into Ocean* also treats the issue that many critiques of the lesbian utopia focus on: what will we do with our sons whom we love in a lesbian utopia—throw them out?[60] The answer in *A Door Into Ocean* is to teach them how to become lesbians, people without a desire to intervene violently in the world.

Although very different in other ways, Carol Emshwiller's *Carmen Dog* (1990) is very like Joan Slonczewski's *A Door Into Ocean* in its mixing of the tropes of woman as alien in a complicated politicized fiction. At the beginning of her introduction to *The Second Sex*, Simone de Beauvoir reflects on the ways that women are exhorted to remain women, real women, and playfully asks, "Are there women really? .... One wonders if women still exist, if they will always exist, whether or not it is desirable that they should" (1974, xv). In *Carmen Dog*, Carol Emshwiller answers, portraying the comically disastrous results when housewives and mothers start turning into the beasts and pets that men have long supposed them to be. Taking their places, loyal pets turn into the housewives and caretakers that society needs to replace them. Such is the hero of the novel, formerly "Pooch" who, when her master's wife turns into a snapping turtle (Emshwiller 1990, 8), assumes the role of housekeeper, takes the name "Pucci," and dreams of a career as an opera diva while babysitting her master's child.

Carol Emshwiller's novel, like Slonczewski's, is not "pure." Pooch (or

---

60. Such a critique, while sympathetic to lesbians and bisexuals, is Marion Zimmer Bradley's *The Ruins of Isis* (1978). The novel is prefaced with this men's song from the matriarchal culture:

> I am only a man
> And have no part in paradise.
> Twice have I tasted bliss
> And twice have I been driven forth;
> Once when I left my mother's womb
> And again when I was driven forth
> From my Mother's house.
>   When I am done with life
> Will the Goddess take me, perhaps
> To her loving breasts?

Sons are cast out from the matriarchal societies of Pamela Sargent's *The Shore of Women* (1986), Sheri Tepper's *The Gate to Women's Country* (1988), and Ursula K. Le Guin's "The Matter of Seggri" (1994); only LeGuin's is also a lesbian utopia.

Pucci as she renames herself) is neither animal woman nor masochistic humanoid alien, but a fluid mixture of the two, on her way from one to the other: "slender fingers where her paws once were, cheeks covered with little more than a peachy down" (Emshwiller 1990, 7). To be human, to be a masochistic feminine humanoid is, with full irony, Pooch's goal, all the while the female humans are abandoning that role in despair and triumph. When Pooch runs away in midmetamorphosis, for fear she will be blamed for the bite on the baby's arm, she adopts human romantic illusions and dreams of her true love, meanwhile masochistically hoping that her Master will take her back if she apologizes and works hard: "She hopes that after she says all this and makes her promises, he'll see that she's worth keeping—a thought not uncommon to many creatures of her sex" (17–18). While the women-animals are fleeing their oppressive roles, the animal-women are ironically hoping to take them up. As the doctor comes to take an animal for experimentation, animals offer to be the one he chooses: "They are thinking of their own desirability in contrast to his dumpy old wife and they are hoping for a meaningful relationship—almost any kind of relationship, even if it is somewhat sadistic" (48).

Emshwiller's use of sadomasochistic erotics is much more self-conscious than that of the writers we examined in the first section of this chapter, and heavily ironic. Pooch comically shares the erotically-charged innocence of many of De Sade's heroines, and Emshwiller's Chapter V, "Daunted," begins with a quotation from de Sade: "May your crimes make you as happy as your cruelties have made me suffer" (Emshwiller 1990, 41).

The men whom Pooch meets and fantasizes about—all are sadistic: the impresario, the doctor, even her Master. The impresario, whom Pooch seeks shelter with, has an apartment decorated with "pornographic candles, pornographic magnets, pornographic pillows on the sofa, pornographic lamp with pornographic shade, pornographic ash tray" (Emshwiller 1990, 71), even "a pornographic eraser (worn down just 'there')" (72). Forcing Pooch to take an aphrodisiac in exchange for supper, the impresario stages a *ménage a trois* that includes his cat Chloe and Pooch learns "the many ways that music, ribbons, belts, pepper, and guacamole could be used" (79). The doctor, equipped with "cattle prod, handcuffs, and muzzle," experiments on the animal-women, "who nearly swoon with pleasure at the treatment they receive in the laboratory as long as it didn't become *too* painful, and who enjoy being the center of attention in whatever manner and for whatever reason" (49). Even her Master, whom Pooch greets as a rescuer, greets her with "a cruel and frightening kiss" (124)—"not at all fatherly" (124).

Unlike the other novels we looked at, where the sadomasochism was offered as an eroticism to grow beyond into mutual recognition, Emshwiller offers the sadomasochism of her animal females with human males as wry commentary on the human condition. The male sadists are not invincible, but comic victims of their own guilty urges: "Perhaps it could be a time of new and strange excesses," the Master fantasizes about the dog he has "bought," "trained," and "disciplined" — "Courage would hardly be needed with such as her. If, for instance, he wanted to tie her, spread-eagled, to the bed, she would not wonder at this behavior" (Emshwiller 1990, 9). Emshwiller's view is that of a feminist Rabelais: within any ideology must be room for humanly pleasurable excess and derangement. Pooch is conflicted because she senses the demeaning quality of sadomasochistic relationships with authoritarian men, escaping from all of them, yet she feels guilty for the brief pleasures she takes with them. The narrator implicates the reader in Pooch's guilty pleasure as well: how can we help wondering what to do with guacamole when in bed with a cat, a dog, and a fat man wearing only a "black leather posing cup" (79)? If Pooch is not, the reader is implicated by this technique in her own oppression. But ideology is also called into question for denying us what pleasure is available.

Not only sex, but all the physicality associated with the trope of animal woman is presented as comic. When Pooch is invited inside by the impresario, she hesitates before accepting: "Certainly she would never consider going in except for the thought of food, especially for the baby, and though he has not mentioned inviting her to breakfast, she feels a tiny drop of drool at the corner of her mouth. In order to keep up her dignified pose, she doesn't dare lick it away. She hopes he hasn't noticed" (Emshwiller 1990, 70). Again and again Emshwiller humanizes her female characters by animalizing them. Pooch, now a young lady, dreams of chasing rabbits, and fights against her urges to bite, to bark, to howl at the moon. "A conviction that physical urges which one cannot help having are unjustified, undignified, presumptuous," explains the psychologist Dorothy Dinnerstein, "undercuts the deepest, oldest basis for a sense of worth; it contaminates the original wellspring of subjective autonomy" (1976, 73). Emshwiller uses these animal details in her characterization of Pooch not only to establish her as a sympathetic character, but also to suggest the psychological sources for her feelings of inferiority, victimization, and masochism. This is the way that the denigration of women as animals works in human women, as well, of course. Emshwiller lets us, for once, laugh at this process and so triumph over it.

But Emshwiller also uses the sadomasochistic psychology of the alien humanoid woman to comment politically on women's positioning themselves as victims. When Pooch is locked up in the pound, the narrator reflects on Pooch's response: "Pooch is used to such simple fare as this, having eaten little else all her life, though now and then she's had a tidbit from the table, which frequently she wished she hadn't had. It only whetted her appetite for things she didn't dare allow herself" (Emshwiller 1990, 14). Here, early in the novel, Pooch succumbs to the role of victim, and glories in her self-pity as a means of endurance. The anger that might help her escape is buried too far under feminine stoicism to be available for her use. Later, when Pooch joins with other women, she will find other means to resist. Now self-pity is all she has.

But Pooch is not only reaching toward the status of masochistic human-oid female; she is also growing out of herself as alien female animal. In Emshwiller's portrayal of animal women, all men's fears are realized: as the psychiatrist explains to Pooch's Master, "Some are, you know, on the way up, others the reverse. As I said: woman to beast, beast to woman, and not much point to it all it seems to me" (Emshwiller 1990, 1). That women are animals, aliens, men have long feared, and now their fears are justified. With glee Emshwiller explores men's fears as means for women's power: Central Park is now too dangerous for men to walk in at night, and women, armed with tooth and claw, have truly taken back the night (92–93). Comically men attempt control: government officials decide to outlaw all but primates from the human race (78).

The physicality of the animal mother, associated with the unjust power of mothers over infants, and with the mysterious forces of change and death, Emshwiller exploits in the figure of Rosemary, the doctor's wife who turns into an abominable snow person and organizes the animal-women into femi-nist (creaturist?) movement: "Rosemary the abominable. . . . Savage, silvery white, and abominable, but abominable in all the best ways: abominable to contemplate, abominable to meet in the mountains as well as on the streets of the city, *wonderfully* abominable and on their side!" (Emshwiller 1990, 82). In Rosemary, Emshwiller fantasizes women's power as mother converted into political power, nostalgically but comically yearning for the time of goddesses: "all creatures who come under Rosemary's spell feel that they are home at last. . . . This is motherhood at its most dangerous" (115). All crea-tures, that is, except male creatures, who feel that

> This is motherhood gone wrong! . . . in all her terrible splendor. This is motherhood just as they've always suspected it was. Great and terrible World-Mother: Big Mama. Venus of Willendorf no longer fitting in the palm of one's hand, but as she probably really was, maybe seven feet tall, and in this case with little beady eyes peering out from beneath furry brows. (Emshwiller 1990, 152)

In Emshwiller's novel, the trope of woman as machine, also present, offers a critique of men's construction of women to answer their own needs. As the women turn into animals, the men have "worried of late, wondering how to replace these highly trained but changing women" (Emshwiller 1990, 13). If women refuse to take care of men, what will men do? "It's a question of priorities, and for once motherhood and related topics seem to be at the top of the list," explains the scientist:

"though it's true they are hoping to find ways of eliminating it altogether. Already research is being done not only in *in vitro* fertilization but also in the coupling of the germ cells from the male only. The present problem would be solved, then, by simply going around it. In the future one would not need to create any humans (so-called humans, that is, for a great deal of doubt has been cast on the status of women as human beings all through the ages of course, but now in particular) . . . at any rate, one would no longer need to create beings with two X chromosomes at all" (78).

If women are unreliable, goes the comic logic of the men in *Carmen Dog*, then it is not up to men to take over childcare, but up to scientists to invent a mechanical replacement for women. The men's "utopian" alternatives, presented as farcically inadequate in the novel, are test tubes and laboratories. They will create babies in test tubes so that they can reproduce only males (Emshwiller 1990, 78), and will use "only the best genes in the nation, those belonging to governors, generals (three star or above), atomic scientists, as well as those of the directors of nuclear reactors, presidents of the largest corporations, oil magnates, and so forth" (119). Moreover, scientists and government officials envision children from one to three growing up in a "Responsive Early-Life Playpen," which provides food rewards for learning behavior, painted eyes for eye contact, and "a Mother's-Arms device from which to get lots of hugging" (100).

The inadequacy of this program is comically demonstrated when the female animals take over the Academy of Motherhood and place the three most important Vice Presidents in the playpens. The transforming females hope that "these most important members of the Academy can be reprogrammed to behave in a way that is more sensitive to the needs of all creatures," and pick a program "for particularly recalcitrant children, good for either the terrible twos or the frustrating fives" (Emshwiller 1990, 128). But after a day in the playpens they have helped design, "All three men are beginning to feel that mothering itself may be a more powerful weapon than they had thought," that it should be kept "in the hands of men who can deal with it" (149), and that it "should be dealt out, even to infants, in small, insignificant doses so that it can always be held within reasonable bounds" (150). Emshwiller thus employs the trope of woman as machine to expose masculine demands for service from women. Rather than coming alive and claiming autonomy, however, Emshwiller's mothering machines turn into monsters; for the scientists, unable to see real mothers as capable, create the machines as their fantasy of the perfect mother. The perfect mother, attentive only to one's every need, turns out to be their worst nightmare: "the vice presidents have no choice but to sink into the great pink breasts and be done to as the machine-mother wishes" (150).

The comic subject of metamorphosis, with its long tradition from Ovid to Woolf and Kafka, is also Emshwiller's subject in *Carmen Dog*: a quotation from Marcus Aurelius — "Change is nature's delight" — begins Chapter XVIII (Emshwiller 1990, 140). The comedy is further complicated by the politics of gender: rather than only from human to animal, whichever direction these females change, they still end up aliens, dangerous animals from men's point of view. Emshwiller "unmetaphors" the trope of woman as animal, deconstructing the misogyny by claiming the stereotype for women's own use. For example, when Pooch reflects early in the novel on "her rapidly changing friends" and the narrator inserts a commentary, who is being commented on — wives or pets?: they "have suffered just such a fate (whatever it is), having become too hard to handle at home in all sorts of ways. However one may enjoy the possession of an intelligent animal, too much intelligence, too many pertinent and impertinent questions, and too much independence are always hard to put up with in others, and especially in a creature one keeps partly for the enhancement of one's own self-image" (6).

Through setting in motion the trope of woman as alien through metamorphosis, Emshwiller offers us the possibility of transforming the misogynistic stereotype in a metaphor for radical change. When Isabel was a "Beautiful people," in "heels, three inches high," she wanted to die; as a wolverine she wants to *be*: "I wanted to die. Not really, though. Now live on. Be. Be! I only just realize" (Emshwiller 1990, 19). When the men take over the Pound for incarceration of outlandish females, the women take over the SPCA, transforming it into the SPCAC: "the Society for the Prevention of Cruelty to All Creatures" (81). Females in *Carmen Dog*, who so easily cross the borders of human and animal, reality and fantasy, are thus portrayed as beings of power. The scientific, prosaic men of *Carmen Dog*, who can only be one thing, should be afraid of these women!

In this context, of radical metamorphosis, we must understand Emshwiller's exposition of misogyny. Emshwiller, again in comic fashion, catalogues all the myriad ways in which women are other, "these creatures" (Emshwiller 1990, 1). The Master's wife, whose habitual snapping (3) makes her transformation into a snapping turtle inevitable, gets dropped off at the Aquarium by her husband, who wonders if his gift will count as a tax write-off (8). Slinky, sinuous Phillip the snake is seen that way by men so that she may be available for gang rape (28–29); she advises Pooch that she should learn to use her body to get what she wants from men (15). Loyal earnest Rosemary is rejected by her husband as his first experimental subject for torture only because he needs her as typist (26). Not only the men, but also the females suffer from some variety of misogyny: Pooch has internalized it and realizes that she will never become fully "*Homo sapiens*, knowledgeable man," no matter how she tries (99). Part of the comic technique of *Carmen Dog*, the myriad ways that men try to negate women, testify to women's vitality. *Carmen Dog* tells of women claiming the stereotypes as their own: the cows, the cats, the hens, the snakes, the dogs—all the misogynistic terms for women as alien animals come alive in Emshwiller's language to speak for human strengths. They become metaphors for power, rendering heroic if still comic the feminist movement that is generated.

By this means, *Carmen Dog* offers a comic vision, a sympathetic parody, and a loving critique of contemporary feminism. Emshwiller unmasks all the idols of the tribe of feminists. She makes sympathetic fun of chauvinistic essentialism and the credo of sisterhood: when animal-women and women-animals come together to organize politically at the rally, "they are all sisters. They are in this together and here it clearly doesn't matter what sort of beast you are, or came from, or will one day be. How wonderful, Pooch thinks, to be whatever one really is, even if half dog and even if something of the savage wolf, as has proven to be the case with her" (Emshwiller 1990, 83). By the device of following the feminist yearning for freedom—to be what one is—with the comic bathos of half dog, half wolf, Emshwiller allows us to question the whole goal of essentialist identity politics. But at the same time, Emshwiller also asks us to take full, exaggerated delight in the difference between our feminine constructed selves and the animal lurking beneath.

Carmen Dog especially criticizes academic theorizing as pretentious. Pooch naively presents her pen as phallus, when she mourns her lost yellow ballpoint—"the pain of not having the pen is more bearable than the other pains" (Emshwiller 1990, 92), she emotes. The practice of recovering great women of history is satirized by the feminist attic hideaway, papered with posters of famous animals that celebrate these animal-women's heritage (105–6). The goal of reforming our misogynistic language is seen in comic light as Pooch reflects that, "while she *is* a bitch, she does not want the word used in a way that is demeaning to herself and to other bitches like her and . . . the same goes for the word *girl*" (69–70). Emshwiller mercilessly and lovingly parodies our love of community and talk and touch: at the SPCAC rally, "they all get up and dance around in their various ways, changing places and kissing and hugging each other. Pooch holds, in turn, the coarse haired, the soft haired, dry scales, stiff back feathers, down front ones, warm bare skin. . . . It feels good" (84–85). And the charismatic feminist leader Rosemary, housewife turned revolutionary abominable snowperson, offers a utopian vision as idyllic and silly as many we have heard at feminist gatherings or read in our feminist newsletters: Rosemary's future would include not one partner but two for childcare, for one creature should never have to stand in the place of two; women must not fear success because they don't need it—smoke can't rise without air, and humans need both; and the earth is mother of us all, so we should hug a tree (85–88). Clearly this is not enough to change our human condition. Most of all, with enormous love and concern, but with impatience at the high-minded seriousness of feminism, *Carmen Dog* points out that feminism is not going anywhere—"If only there really was a conspiracy!" (66), longs Pooch. Rosemary's last words are

"Not win." "For if we do 'win,' " Rosemary cautions, "We will surely lose everything" (122).

The main reason, of course, for feminism not going anywhere is what also ends the book, stops the story from going on: romance. Pooch loves "doggedly," and will "save herself until her true love comes along," even though when she decides this, she hasn't yet met such a man: "For a few moments she falls into a deep and satisfying daydream common to female creatures of her age and experience, or rather inexperience" (Emshwiller 1990, 17). Later in the novel, after she has recognized a man she can long for, she fails even to recognize or look at him when they bump into each other, because she was "looking, . . . so intently for someone else . . . for the imaginary man, larger than life" (64). If women's dreams are impossibly rose-colored, men's dreams of the ideal woman are pathetic: she is a dog— "she's his. He picked her out, bought her, trained her, taught her everything she knows. . . . And what a good hard worker! . . . How sweet and uncomplaining!" (9). When Pooch's Master comes to claim her, they put on her dog collar, and she reflects, "At least she now knows where she really lives and who she belongs to, and everyone else will know it too, at a glance. She feels almost as though she had slipped on a wedding ring" (120). Cruelly, Emshwiller lets Pooch reject her Master's brand of sadism, only to accept a younger version. Pooch marries the tenor Bert and adopts the baby, later having a litter of three male setters of her own. Phillip marries the sadistic doctor, and Chloe the sybaritic impresario. Ruefully, the narrator remarks, Pooch "will never again allow herself to sleep on a doormat, unless of course it might benefit some other creature for her to do so" (160). So much for feminist independence. Pooch is completely contained, and no ending is written beyond in this novel. Except that Pooch writes an opera in memory of Rosemary, and the universe, the narrator reminds us, "is recreating itself every fraction of a second" (160). Perhaps sometime it will change?

To end this chapter we may borrow Molly Hite's formulation for women's mainstream fiction, to describe the effects of this convention in science fiction by women: the representation of the woman as alien especially allows "telling the other side of the story" — making "visible the association of alterity — otherness — with woman as a social, cultural, and linguistic construction" (Hite 1989, 4). Stories of alien women in science fiction by women thus take on, unmetaphor, and live out the cultural stereotypes of women.[61] In each

---

61. These science fictions are also nostalgic in the sense of providing compensations for the loss of the mother, and in this way they "correct" the classic romance, where the mother is almost always absent and events are controlled by relation to the father: the humanoid alien woman builds a home with a stranger; the woman as machine, made by men to serve them, becomes self-nurturing and autonomous; the woman as animal internalizes the mother and mothers others; the minority woman hero revenges her dead mother by killing the father; and the lesbian utopia provides constant mothering as the highest priority for all grown women.

case, the narratives confront and transform the stereotypes. In more recent novels, women writers argue politics by negotiating with their science fiction traditions the meanings of tropes of alien women. And perhaps they thus change the meaning of the stereotypes, little by little.

3

Cross-Dressing as a Male Narrator

What if Sleeping Beauty woke behind
the briers alone, in the dark, to
the knowledge that the curse was not
sleep but waking, and that family,
childhood, fairy godmothers and all
were dreams spun to amuse a virgin
mind in mothballs?
      She/he/it would have no choice
but to make something of the awakening.
I do, as best I can.

             —Emma Bull,
             Bone Dance

" 'I'd rather wear what I have on.' "
             —Lee Killough,
             A Voice Out of Ramah

The reflections from Emma Bull's *Bone Dance* belong to the narrator, revealed eventually as an androgyne, constructed to be someone else's "horse"
or body, conscious only by some accident. The metaphor of Sleeping Beauty
also aptly describes the position of a woman writing science fiction using the
convention of the male narrator: immersed in the fiction as a male, "waking"
to her life as a female. The quotation from Lee Killough's *A Voice Out of
Ramah* is spoken by the male character, Jared, from whose point of view
most of the story is told. Having cross-dressed as a female in what for our
culture would be male clothes — pants — he has decided to stay with what is
comfortable, whether or not it acceptably signifies his gender. This quotation
can also be read as a commentary on the woman writer's position, transgressing on the masculine voice, but wearing what is necessary for the writer's
authority. In these and many other ways, women writers of science fiction
frequently encode their double identity in their fictions.

    The male narrator is so ubiquitous in science fiction as a genre that we need to term it a generic convention.[1] Several forces made male first person narration (or a personalized third person point of view strongly defined as masculine) a convention in science fiction: the popularity of space opera naive realism (making the distant omniscient narrator difficult to incorporate), and the cultural taboos on women being scientists or explorers (the two kinds of characters most important to plotting a science fiction).[2] Indeed, in Golden Age science fiction, authorial voice or heterodiegetic narration often turns out to be personal voice or homodiegetic — even autodiegetic — narration, when the story is revealed after a page or two, or near the end, to have been told by one of the participants, usually a scientist.[3] Thus authorial voice reinforces objectivity, the trustworthiness of the narrator, and provides characterization of the narrator as an objective scientist. That the ur-science fiction by a woman, Mary Shelley's *Frankenstein* (1818), employs three male narrators means that the chief model for women writers is male narration.[4] As Mary Shelley explains in her "Author's Introduction," "I did not make myself the heroine of my tales. Life appeared to me too common-place an

1. On gender as a formal category of narration, like person, see Brian Richardson 1994, 321–22.
2. On the development of the scientist as hero in American science fiction, see Clareson, chap. 3 (1985, 81–102); on the explorer as hero, see Clareson, chaps. 6 and 7 (1985, 157–224). Christine Brooke-Rose, in A *Rhetoric of the Unreal: Studies in Narrative and Structure, Especially of the Fantastic*, argues that "One of the most striking features of much science fiction until fairly recently has been its lack of imagination with regard to narrative technique, as opposed to its imagination with regard to ideas. It took over wholesale the techniques of the realistic novel" (1981, 82; see also 100). I would go even further than Brooke-Rose and argue that science fiction is deliberately reactionary with regard to realistic techniques, overusing them in order to buttress the readers' acceptance of nonexistent scientific devices, natural forces, or alternate worlds.
3. For definitions and elaboration of heterodiegetic narration (an absent narrator telling the story of others), homodiegetic narration (a narrator present as participating character), and autodiegetic narration (narrator as hero) see Brooke-Rose 1991, 335. Also applicable to Golden Age science fiction is the distinction between "focalisation zero" (the narrator knows more than the character) and "internal focalisation" (the narrator knows the same as a character); when we later in this chapter discuss the naive male narrator, often parodied, we will be dealing with "external focalisation" (the narrator knows less than the character); see Brooke-Rose 1991, 324–25. Brian Richardson calls the narration that starts as third person but in which the narrator reveals himself or herself as a character in the story by the end a "pseudo-third person narrative" (1994, 315).
4. But see Susan Sniader Lanser's insightful reading of *Frankenstein*'s narration as a way "to write out male Romanticism and to move on in her next novel to a female-centered narrative" (1992, 164–72, esp. 165). The early experiments with female voice or point of view in science fiction by women were mostly interesting failures, domestic realism that leaves the main female characters little room to act but lacking consciousness of that restraint; female voices were infrequent until more equitable recent times, after about 1970. For early examples of female narration or point of view, see Clare Winger Harris, "The Fifth Dimension" (1928); or Judith Merril, *Shadow on the Hearth* (1950).

affair as regarded myself. . . . But I was not confined to my own identity, and I could people the hours with creations far more interesting to me . . ." (1981, xxii). Shelley, like many science fiction writers and readers after her, assumed that male adventures were simply more interesting than female ones. In her essay, "Hitch Your Dragon to a Star: Romance and Glamour in Science Fiction," Anne McCaffrey recalls the male fans who nicknamed Judith Merril's science fictions from a female point of view "diaper stories," and argues that 1950s women, "forced to write more from the viewpoint of the opposite sex," became "more adept in their characterization and portrayals" (1974, 280–81).

But using the voice of a male as a generic convention is then especially a problem for women writers.[5] As Joanna Russ puts it, "A woman writer may . . . stick to male myths with male protagonists, [and, I would add, male narrators,] but in so doing she falsifies herself and much of her own experience. . . . She is an artist creating a world in which persons of her kind cannot be artists, a consciousness central to itself creating a world in which women have no consciousness, a successful person creating a world in which persons like herself cannot be successes. She is a Self trying to pretend that she is a different Self, one for whom her own self is Other" (1972b, 10). On the other hand, a woman who cross-dresses as a male narrator is also refusing her cultural role as a woman, a rebellious act. In addition, as Russ points out later in her essay, science fiction may be the one place where women writers escape these limitations, to build a world where gender is not the same kind of constraint that it is in realistic fiction.

Nevertheless, the male narrator is such a central convention that almost all women science fiction writers, unlike women who currently write mainstream fiction, use a male narrator in at least some of their works—Russ being an exception. To give a rough estimate of the frequency, I have counted my own library of science fiction by women: out of 353 science fiction novels by women, 230 employ male narration or point of view at least part of the time—roughly two-thirds.[6] If I had counted short stories, the percentage of

5. Cf. Elaine Showalter, on women novelists born after 1800, who began to publish after 1840: "One of the many indications that this generation saw the will to write as a vocation in direct conflict with their status as women is the appearance of the male pseudonym. Like Eve's fig leaf, the male pseudonym signals the loss of innocence. In its radical understanding of the role-playing required by women's effort to participate in the mainstream of literary culture, the pseudonym is a strong marker of the historical shift" (1977, 19). Robin Roberts explains the male narrator of science fiction as women writers using a male character coded feminine as cover (1993, 16; see also 38n. 4).

6. The argument that women's writing is different from men's in style or voice—either because women are essentially different, or because women experience a different material reality owing to gender (see, for example, Temma Berg, "Suppressing the Language of Wo(Man): The Dream of a Common Language")—does not seem to hold up across the genre of science fiction. There are instances of what has been identified as feminine style: Sally Miller Gearhart's

male narrators and points of view would be considerably higher, since almost no women before 1960 used female point of view, and because the short story was the major science fiction form before 1950. Historically, women who adopted the male voice of science fiction, who cross-dressed as the male narrator, gained a kind of freedom: to accomplish in imagination the feats of science or exploration denied to women in their time. But women writers of science fiction continue to use the male voice, now that these forbidden territories have been opened to them, at least in science fiction. Why? What do they gain?

In this chapter I shall explore the ways in which women writers gain more than they lose through their strategies for negotiating the convention of male narration: cross-dressing as the male narrator, submerging their female identities as authors in the male identities of their narrators, but punishing the male narrators or converting them to feminist viewpoints; piecing together multiple narrators, male, female, and alien; and constructing transvestite and androgynous narrators who expose these authors' own struggles with double genders. Often, of course, writers use more than one of these strategies in the same novel. I shall draw on feminist literary criticism, especially those studies that discuss narration, but I shall also draw on recent feminist and cultural studies of cross-dressing as a theoretical basis for my discussion.

Because of my task, to explore the use of the male narrator by women writers, I will be categorizing narrative not mainly by the traditional first and third person, limited or omniscient point of view, not even by the extremely useful categories for women's fictions developed by Susan Sniader Lanser in *Fictions of Authority: Women Writers and Narrative Voice* — authorial voice, personal voice, communal voice.[7] Instead, I analyze three categories based

---

lyric realism and fragmented voice in *Wanderground*; the sharply fragmented associational tirades of Joanna Russ in *We Who Are about To . . .* or *The Female Man*; the squares, carefully stitched together, of utopian vision, story, and poetry of Ursula K. Le Guin's *Always Coming Home*. These are wonderful books. But these instances are not frequent enough in science fiction by women to call them characteristic. The problem of the science fiction convention of the male narrator, however, has generated special negotiations that are repeated often enough that we can call them a structural (or sometimes stylistic) characteristic of women's science fiction.

7. Lanser thus defines her categories: "authorial voice" refers to "narrative situations that are heterodiegetic, public, and self-referential"(1992, 15) — "the narrator is not a participant in the fictional world and exists on a separate ontological plane from the characters" (16); "personal voice" refers to "narrators who are self-consciously telling their own histories" (18), only those which are "autodiegetic," the "I" being also the protagonist (19); "communal voice" refers to "a practice in which narrative authority is invested in a definable community and textually inscribed either through multiple, mutually authorizing voices or through the voice of a single individual who is manifestly authorized by a community" (21). Lanser's categories overlap with my gendered categories in this way: "communal" fully maps onto my "multiple narrators"; but the woman writer assuming male voice or androgynous voice can do so either through authorial or personal narrative strategies.

on gender: 1) women writers assuming male gender to author the story; 2) women writers constructing male and female (and alien) collaborators who multiply or communally author the story; and 3) women writers assuming androgynous or alternative forms of gender to author the story, projecting their own problems with science fiction onto their narrator or protagonist. After establishing these paradigms of male narration in science fiction by women, I shall look at two individual novels — Cherry Wilder's *Second Nature* and Emma Bull's *Bone Dance* — to examine the ways that each text negotiates these generic possibilities.

Cross-Dressing as the Male Narrator

As Judith Butler has pointed out, in literature gender is always performative (1990, 25 and 136) — "a kind of persistent impersonation that passes as the real" (viii).[8] But the gender performed does not have to be purely male or female. "Fundamental to recent feminist theory," Kathleen Weiler argues, "is a questioning of the concept of a coherent subject moving through history with a single essential identity. Instead, feminist theorists are developing a concept of the constant creation and negotiation of selves within structures of ideology and material constraints" (1991, 469). In *Vested Interests: Cross-Dressing & Cultural Anxiety*, Marjorie Garber suggests that cross-dressing offers the power of "blurred gender," "an enabling fantasy" (1992, 6). According to Garber, cross-dressing signals women's break with traditional social and erotic terrain: women position themselves most against the patriarchy when they most look like men (141). Garber's theory applies especially well to science fiction. The male narrator or point of view is one of the defining characteristics of the genre, and women writers' positioning themselves as male narrators — creating a male "narrative alibi," to use Christine Brooke-Rose's term (1981, 88 and 92) — signals a break with the traditions of science fiction that women writers are quite conscious of.

Let me describe two cross-dressed narrators to illustrate my point, one "real" from fan lore, one fictional — both concerning Golden Age science fiction writers. In his *Encyclopedia of Science Fiction and Fantasy through 1968*, Donald Tuck reports a story about the early science fiction writer, Louise Taylor Hansen, who published several short stories in *Wonder Stories* and *Amazing Stories* in the 1920s and 1930s under the name "L. Taylor Hansen": according to F. J. Ackerman, Hansen "appeared at a meeting of the Los Angeles Science Fiction Society in 1939" and said "she had placed these stories for her brother, a world traveler, who had written them" (Tuck 1974, 1:205). Tuck does not believe the story of the brother. Indeed, Hansen went on to publish other stories and a book, *The Ancient Atlantic* (1969), under

---

8. Marjorie Garber points out that, although the existence outside fiction of gender only as representation is still debated, it is incontestably true in fiction (1992, 374).

her own name, even after claiming she was not the author. I think that Hansen was caught in a paradox of authorship and gender: owing to social norms and generic convention, she felt it unacceptable for a woman to author a science fiction, and so published under initials.[9] When she was identified by her fans, she constructed another narrator, her adventurous brother, to serve as alibi, but she continued to write. The detail of world travel for the brother is especially telling, for it suggests that Hansen was undergoing a crisis of writerly authority, as well as a probable social crisis: she did not want to violate the generic convention of the male narrator in science fiction, and she did not want to lose her authority as a science fiction writer by revealing her feminine gender. By inventing the brother, authorized not only by his gender, but also by his experience as traveler, she could regain that authority and protect herself from social disapproval. She tries to solve the problem of the male narrator in science fiction by cross-dressing first as L. Taylor Hansen, then as Louise Hansen's brother.

Lilith Lorraine offers a similar but fictional example in her early science fiction utopia, "Into the 28th Century," published in 1930 in *Science Wonder Quarterly*. Lorraine, really Mary Maude Wright (née Dunn), published this story under a pseudonym, but a female one. Her narrator, however, is male. Recently discharged from the Navy, sailing on the Gulf of Mexico, the young male narrator is transported to the future, to a socialist, feminist utopia several centuries ahead of his Texas. He is accidentally returned to his own time and leaves his record, but finds a way to go forward again to rejoin the woman with whom he has fallen in love. He mails his story to his aunt because "She had always been a wanderer, writing when the mood swayed her. There was always a sort of unspoken understanding between us and because of this, I have chosen her to give my story to the world. When it reaches her I shall be — elsewhere" (Lorraine 1930, 251). Clearly Lorraine also thinks that it is socially unacceptable for women to author science fiction and that the male narrator is a required convention of the genre. Lorraine, however, claims her own gender through the device of cross-dressing as the male narrator, then having that narrator certify a woman as transmitter of his message to the world. That a woman does publish the story then further strengthens the reliability of the narrator, in that delicious play with the "reality" of the story that has always characterized the Western novel. Both Hansen and Lorraine directly address the problem of the female writer writing the male narrator, but do so by cross-dressing, by creating fictional male identities for themselves, whose stories they pretend to transmit rather than author.

But anxiety about authority is not the whole story, or women writers

---

9. Of Joanna Russ's novel, Hilary Rose comments, "Her title *The Female Man*, evokes all those women writers of SF from C. L. Moore to James Tiptree who wrote as female men" (1994, 224).

would gradually have given up the male narrator in recent decades. Rather than giving up the role, the *frisson*, of cross-dressing, women science fiction writers have developed ways to use the role to their own ends. In the remainder of this section, we will look at three ways that women writers subvert the male narrator or point of view to their own ends, crossing, passing, blurring the boundaries of gender that define science fiction as a genre: the male narrator converted to a woman's point of view; the male narrator as dumb man (a parody of masculine authority); and the male narrator forced to undergo feminine suffering.

Twentieth-century women writers of science fiction inherited one strategy for using a male narrator from the feminist technological utopia: the conversion story.[10] In Charlotte Perkins Gilman's *Herland* (1915), for example, the male narrator, Vandyck Jennings, at first finds preposterous the idea that women could govern and organize a country on their own. He is gradually converted to the idea that women in Herland have done as good a job as the men in his United States, and so to the idea that women are equal to men. The narration of *Herland* is first person, but a great deal of dialogue intrudes into this authoritative male voice once Van begins to learn from the other culture and to change. Gilman uses the authoritative pronouncements of masculine objectivity to underscore the superiority of her utopian vision in Herland. According to Van, for example, Herlandian children "grew up in a wide friendly world, and knew it for theirs," and "their child-literature was a wonderful thing" (Gilman 1979, 101). And according to Van, Herlandians "had worked out a chemistry, a botany, a physics, with all the blends where a science touches an art . . . to such a fullness of knowledge as made us feel like schoolchildren" (64). But Gilman also uses dialogue to show Van's perspective as limited and Van as changing. For example, Ellador explains to Van that frequent sex without the purpose of reproduction is unnatural (animals have sex only in season)(138); and gradually, through dialogue, Van comes to agree — "Ellador's friendship, Ellador's comradeship, Ellador's sisterly affection, Ellador's perfectly sincere love . . . were enough to live on very happily" (141). Thus in Gilman's feminist technological utopia, the tradition of the traveler converted to the new land's ways of knowing and doing is adapted to feminist purposes: the male narrator is used to authorize new feminist practices, while dialogue intrudes increasingly on the male voice to indicate his change and the breakdown of his authority.

Similarly, in the contemporary utopia by Dorothy Bryant, *The Kin of Ata Are Waiting For You* (1971), the misogynist male narrator, after murdering a woman, wakes in a utopian culture where men and women are truly equal.

---

10. The conversion of the narrator is a standard technique in utopian fiction in general, extending back at least as far as More's *Utopia*, where the fictional More is gradually converted by Raphael Hythlodaye's arguments in favor of Utopia's superiority to Europe.

He later returns to his earth to plead guilty to the murder, converted to a new way of looking at his former self, as well as at women. As in Gilman's utopia, in Bryant's the first person male narration is interrupted by dialogue with utopian inhabitants who gradually change the narrator. The change itself is signaled by a dream, dreams being of central importance to this contemplative culture: "After eons there were two of me left, facing each other across the fire pit. One of me was a woman, a hundred women, all the women, hurt, enraged and furious, that I had ever known. One of me was a man, myself, every rotten, opportunistic, cruel, avaricious and vain self I had ever been" (Bryant 1980, 129). Once the narrator sees himself from the perspective of the other and incorporates that perspective into himself through the dream, he is changed. But that change has come about only because of a long dialogue with members of the utopian culture. For example, Augustine, the narrator's black female lover in the land of Ata, tries to convince the narrator that there are no true stories, and that there may be many right answers: "They are all true. And they are all untrue, as words are always untrue. Words are not dreams. Dreams are not reality. They are only dreams" (168). In the episode where Augustine persuades the narrator of this perspective on reality, the dialogue continues for three pages before the narrator's "I" takes control again. As Gilman does, Bryant appropriates the male narrator to certify the superiority of the culture where men and women are equal, where rape and abuse of women do not exist, while she employs dialogue to signify the narrator's change and to subvert his narrative authority.

At the end of the novel, Bryant uses her cross-dressing role of male narrator to make a special plea to the men of her audience: "And think that if I, a murderer whose murders were the least of his crimes, if a man like me could find himself in Ata and could . . . glimpse for a moment the reality behind the dream . . . then how much easier it might be for you" (Bryant 1980, 220). By passing as a man who learns to stop abusing women, Bryant can invite the men in her audience to identify with her narrator and convert to this new way of life.

As we can see from the description of Bryant's novel, where the earthman falls in love with an alien woman and learns from her culture a new way of living, the converted male narrator often appears in the plot of the humanoid alien woman that we explored in chapter 2. F'lar in Anne McCaffrey's *Dragonflight* (1968), Bard and Paul in Marion Zimmer Bradley's *Two to Conquer* (1980), Tom in Rebecca Ore's trilogy, *Becoming Alien* (1988), *Being Alien* (1989), and *Human to Human* (1990) — all offer male points of view and are converted to more equitable treatment of women — which is often translated to more equitable treatment of all other beings — during the course of their fictions. In each case the authority of the male narrator underlines the message against abusive treatment of women, while the increasing dialogue with the alien woman interrupts and subverts the male narrator's patriarchal authority.

Female science fiction writers thus use the convention of the male narrator to reconstruct the adolescent male science fiction hero growing into adulthood: they convert their male narrators, having them unlearn misogyny and learn equitable relations with women.[11] For example, in Andre Norton's *Horn Crown* (1981), Elron, from whose point of view the fiction is told, eventually recognizes that the "meek, timid girl who abided by the customs of our people" was actually "a cloak which [Iynne] had thrown off readily when she found a new freedom in the Dales" (Norton 1981b, 56). And he later acknowledges that rather than his defending her, "she had borne the brunt of action" (86). As a consequence, converting from the misogynist male narrator into a reformed equitable man, Elron can appreciate as an achievement when "her 'I' had become 'we' " (151).[12]

In *A Voice Out of Ramah* (1979), Lee Killough, like many women science fiction writers wearing an androgynous name, deploys the converted male narrator to underline her own writerly position. Her male narrator also cross-dresses. *A Voice Out of Ramah* is set on a Terran colonial planet, Marah, where a plague in the early years wiped out all but 10 percent of the male colonists. Rather than a simple switch to female culture or female dominance, Killough posits an alternative, estranged development of gender roles, with men still on top, but constrained by their roles. Like earth men, the

11. Similarly, in Octavia Butler's *Patternmaster* (1976), the male point of view reinforces the importance of men's learning to treat women as equals. Narrated by Teray, a strong male telepath exiting school as an apprentice, taken over as a slave, the novel tells of his escape with the help of Amber, a telepathic healer. But Teray must learn not only not to be a slave, but also not to be a master. Part of his growth must come from learning to be truly a partner of the woman Amber, who then helps him to defeat Coransee, who cannot merge successfully. Teray's conversion is gradual: first Amber wins an argument (94–95); then when Teray asks Amber to be his lead wife, she counters with an offer for Teray to be her lead husband (109); at first angry at Amber's superior knowledge of how to survive while traveling, Teray eventually recognizes her as an ally (154); finally they plan to be not spouses with one superior to the other, but heads of dual houses close to each other where both will have power. Butler interrupts and subverts the authority of science fiction's traditional male narrator with a sequence from Teray's father's point of view (where the patriarch is defeated), and with episodes where Teray links telepathically with another character and so becomes a "we."

12. Even in the early novel, J. Hunter Holly's *The Mind Traders* (1967), the main recognition of the narrator-hero Morgan Sellers, by which Sellers overcomes his prejudice to participate with an alien Rigan in a partnership to solve an interplanetary mystery, is buttressed by a parallel recognition, by which Sellers overcomes his biases against women. Although early in the novel the men treat the women condescendingly, comforting and dismissing their worries (for example 34–35), at the end of the novel, the women rescue the men at a crucial moment, lending their mental strength in a Rigan psychic battle (133–34, 138–40). The cross-dressing of the female author as male narrator and her insertion of female heroes is signaled by the androgynous names of both author and characters: J. Hunter Holly, the author, and Morgan Sellers, the narrator-hero, are both names that may be worn by either sex, while Morgan's male partner, the Rigan investigator Jael Forty of Zant, is named not only for the female biblical hero Jael, but also perhaps for Andre Norton's earlier female science fiction hero, Jaelithe of *Web of the Witch World* (1964).

men on Marah are heads of families, have sole voice in religion and final say in governmental matters. But Maran men are also in some ways feminized: constrained to the household or the temple because of their vulnerability, clothed in dress-like tunics that constrict movement, with long hair and other symbols of our culture's feminine gender. While they must never show disagreement in public to men on Marah, women wear pants, move freely over the country, do all the work and do it well (only women are ranchhands), and make many of the actual day-to-day decisions of government. Lesbianism, while publically forbidden by men, is privately tolerated, and most women are bisexual, living in extended families with many women and one man by whom they have children.

A *Voice Out of Ramah* is narrated mainly by Jared, a temple Shepherd, who has learned the terrible secret of male superiority on Marah: the population has grown immune to the virus, and Keepers maintain the 10 percent minority that keeps men's gender position secure by ritually poisoning adolescent boys. Deciding that such a practice is unjust, Jared converts. At first he tries to blackmail his religious superior into stopping the poisoning. Later Jared decides to reveal the secret to all the women of his culture, and thus effect radical change, a decision brought about by his cross-dressing as a woman. Jared had been raised to see women through the lens of his masculine privilege, believing that women are "merely man's helpmate" (Killough 1979, 117). Cross-dressed as a woman, however, in order to escape the men who try to stop his revelations, he learns that women seem "to diminish in size" around men (146), that men seem "officious," "arrogant and pompous," that they "dominate the conversation" (148). As a result, Jared reevaluates his own behavior, "remembering his encounters with women over the years and wondering how he had appeared to them" (151). When she recognizes Jared as a man in women's clothes, a woman in the group Jared has traveled with acknowledges his success: " 'You're beginning to sound like a woman' " (163). At the end of the journey (both physical and spiritual), Jared looks in the mirror and sees a different person: "The face looked familiar, though. It looked like his mother's" (165). Jared signals his final conversion with the words I used for the headnote to this chapter. He has outgrown the limitations of masculine dominance, and indicates it by wearing women's clothes (ironically pants) to his trial: " 'I'd rather wear what I have on' " (209).

Thus Killough converts Jared in order to use his authority as male point of view to authorize her own conclusions on women's equality. But Killough also continually undercuts Jared's point of view by the intrusion of two other points of view, those of Alesdra, an off-planet explorer, and Levi, a fellow Deacon. The first section (1–11) of Jared's point of view, where he reveals his initial perceptions of women, is undercut by Alesdra's conflicting observations: Jared's comment that "Women were charming, delightful for banter, but not for serious conversation" (Killough 1979, 6) is followed by Alesdra's explanation that Jared's culture is "semifundamentalist" and "male-dominated" (15), suggesting that her own future Terran culture is not. In addition, Alesdra reminds us that "natural" gender roles are actually different from planet to planet and, so, not natural at all: whereas on Marah "It's the natural order of the universe for man to rule" (15), on Hippolyte "women aborted all but a necessary few male pregnancies and kept their men in purdah" (16).

If in many novels women writers subvert the authority of the masculine narrative voice by converting their narrator and by dialogue and the occasional intrusion of other points of view, in many other novels women writers "overperform" the gender of their male narrator, creating a parody, the male narrator as dumb man.[13] A classic example is Virginia Woolf's *Orlando*, which parodies the unflappable omniscient (male) narrator of realistic fiction through her narrator's idiosyncratic commentary on her androgynous hero. But science fiction tends to localize the authoritative voice in particular characters; thus women's science fiction parodies the genre's more specialized masculine narrator. As Judith Butler points out in *Gender Trouble: Feminism and the Subversion of Identity*, political opposition to gender is often offered in parody, through hyperbole, dissonance, internal confusion, and a proliferation of heterosexual gender performances, each slightly different (1990, 31).

Unlike the purpose of the converted male narrator, the purpose of the naive male narrator who overperforms his gender is not to invite the reader to identify with him. Instead, the naive narrator reinforces recognition of discrimination by offering the reader a feeling of superiority over the dumb narrator as reward.[14] Misogyny and race hatred depend not just on anger and difference, but also on the incapacity to recognize such hatred inside ourselves. Feeling superior to the dumb narrator's biases rewards the sightful reader, the reader who can recognize and name misogyny, race hatred, and other biases, even in herself or himself.

A good example of the naive narrator to whose misogynistic and racial biases readers feel superior is Ursula K. Le Guin's Captain Davidson in *The Word for World is Forest* (1972). Beginning the novel and telling more of the story than any other narrator,[15] Captain Davidson displays arrogance as narra-

---

13. I thank Carol Kolmerten for the insight into the use of the "dumb man" as narrator of nineteenth-century feminist utopias — "I am a real sucker for a dumb male main character who is constantly outwitted by a smart woman," she wrote about the narrator of *Unveiling a Parallel* (Jones and Merchant 1991, "Introduction" by Kolmerten, xxxiv). She also more politely calls this narrator "a gullible innocent" "a bit slow on the uptake" (xvii), "the naive narrator," and "this silly man" (xviii).

14. See Christine Brooke-Rose's discussion of strategies for putting the reader in a position superior to the narrator (1981, 105–27).

15. In Le Guin 1972, Capt. Davidson narrates 1–23, 75–86, and 139–62 (total 57 pages); the anthropologist Raj Lyubov narrates 51–74, and 87–111 (total 47 pages); and the alien Athsheean narrates 25–49, 113–37, and 163–69 (total 54 pages), but Selver's narration is frequently interrupted by other aliens' viewpoints, dialogue, and communal narration.

tor through his continuous assumption that all humans share his contemptuous views of women, other races, and other species. To Captain Davidson, women are "breeding females," "prime human stock" (Le Guin 1972, 1) or "Collie Girls," "fruity beauties" (15). To Captain Davidson, "deer and trees and fibreweed" are in competition with humanity, and "this world's going to go our way" (5). To the captain, the indigenous peoples of the planet named "Forest" are "Creechies," "dumb," (3), lazy (9), and not human: "like snakes or rats, just smart enough to turn around and bite you as soon as you let 'em out of the cage" (80). "When you raise cows, you call that slavery?" (10), asks Davidson, assuming as narrator that we will agree with him and laugh at his joke. Le Guin carefully displays Davidson's biases in the first few pages of the novel, alerting her readers that, even though he is the first narrator, yet we are expected to question his views. Owing to his bias against the native Athsheans, Davidson cannot correctly infer who has destroyed his logging camp, since he thinks "Creechies" too dumb and passive to accomplish such violence (18–19). With the example of gorillas, Le Guin forces even the most conservative reader into what Christine Brooke-Rose calls "non-cooperation with the text" (125): "We'll get on better without creechies here," asserts Capt. Davidson, "just like we get on better without gorillas in Africa. They're in our way . . ." (12). Jolting the reader by this prediction of the gorilla's extinction, Le Guin calls up the cultural romanticization of humans' nearest primates to make her narrator dislikable.

Constructing Davidson as a naive narrator, a dumb man, Le Guin depicts him as overperforming his manhood. Davidson uses misogyny to reinforce his own sense of masculinity: of another officer's fear of the native peoples, Davidson observes, "he was so afraid the creechies were going to attack the camp that he acted like some woman afraid of getting raped" (Le Guin 1972, 84). As part of this overperformance, Davidson is homophobic: of the specialist on native life, Davidson reassures himself, "It was really funny the way Lyubov hated him. Probably the guy was effeminate like a lot of intellectuals, and resented Davidson's virility" (15). Since Davidson centers his definition of masculinity on aggression, violence becomes proof of his own manhood: "The fact is, the only time a man is really and entirely a man is when he's just had a woman or just killed another man" (81). This overperforming of manhood, linking it not to social competition but to rape and murder, marks Davidson as a grim parody of the conventional male narrator of science fiction, and also of our popular cultural conception of masculinity.

Capt. Davidson's hyperperformance of masculinity serves also as a warning against patriotism as cloak for violence. Davidson uses patriotism to justify his fear of others: "they'd realise that getting rid of the creechies was going to be the only way to make this world safe for the Terran way of life" (Le Guin 1972, 83). Ironically, it is human violence that has "taught" Athsheeans organized cultural violence in the form of war, since their culture had developed alternative strategies of individual challenge behavior (singing over an enemy) and universal signals for ceasing violence as part of manhood codes. Written out of the decade's experience of the Vietnam War, Le Guin's *The Word for World is Forest* uses the device of the dumb male narrator to resist United States involvement in the war.[16] Not only through encouraging her readers to dissent from Capt. Davidson, but also through critical depictions of the use of chemical warfare (like napalm)(81), through terrifying depictions of warfare against civilians (85), and through explicit reference to Vietnam (133), Le Guin asks her readers to see her story of planetary colonization and vengeful natives as a warning against a United States military takeover of Vietnam. In a particularly telling passage, Colonel Dongh, a descendant from the Vietnamese (133), explains, "If necessary we are enabled to maintain a defensive police action to prevent all-out war" (131). As in the "police action" of Vietnam, on "Forest," the "police action" is simply war, not prevention of it. In addition, through the hypermasculinity of Capt. Davidson, Le Guin suggests that rigid gender roles and their attendant biased irrationality, rather than reasoned goals, were causes of the Vietnam War.

Le Guin undermines the authority of the conventional masculine science fiction narrator in two other ways. First she multiplies types of Terran masculinity, showing that masculine behavior is constructed, not "natural," and that there are many alternatives. A second narrator, the anthropologist studying native Athsheans, Raj Lyubov, protests Terran exploitation of the Athsheeans and sympathetically tries to understand Athsheean language and culture. But Lyubov is also naive (although not dumb), since he thinks things can be fixed once they're broken, that Athsheeans can unlearn war once humans have taught it to them (Le Guin 1972, 108–9). Second, Le Guin introduces the alien viewpoint of Selver, the rebel, whose narration keeps wandering off into communal voice, as Sue Lanser defines it (see note 7). Thus, although the story seems to be told from Selver's point of view throughout chapter 2, as it is from Terran points of view in other chapters, Selver's narration is in fact discontinuous — interrupted by the points of view of Coro Mena the Dreamer (28), Ebor Dendep the Headwoman (35, 39–40), an omniscient narrator (36–37), and communal dialogue (33–35, and 40–46). In these ways Le Guin develops the authoritative male narrator to parody masculine authority, and also demonstrates the advantages of undermining and resisting that authority as a means of developing a nonviolent community.

In *Native Tongue* (1984) Suzette Haden Elgin also employs naive male

16. A very interesting treatment of Le Guin's *The Word for World is Forest* in the context of the Vietnam War is Carol Hovanec 1989; Hovanec does not discuss narrative techniques in any detail.

narrators, but not as major storytellers. Narrating primarily from women's points of view, Elgin uses naive male points of view to deflate the power of the men over the women. In exaggerated comic episodes misogynistic men reveal their lack of knowledge of women and their inhuman lack of compassion. For example, in an early episode in *Native Tongue*, Aaron Adiness speaks in a men's meeting of the Linguist Household against Nazareth Chornyak's breast reconstruction after cancer surgery, devaluing her contribution to the Household (nine children): "It isn't the woman . . . who adds the Alien languages to the Household assets. It is the MAN. The *man* goes to the trouble of impregnating the woman. . . . To attribute any credit to the woman who plays the role of a receptacle is primitive romanticism" (Elgin 1984, 11). Elgin bases her comedy on our understanding of biology, but she also guides the reader's perception of this misogynistic passage by having one man defend Nazareth, and by juxtaposing with a scene where Nazareth hears her doom: "Nazareth's hand moved, one to each of her breasts, and she covered them tenderly, as a lover might have covered them against a chill wind" (19). As her plot telling the story of women constructing a secret language demonstrates, Elgin is interested in the ways that language constructs reality. Both men and women in her Native Tongue series change reality through language. Once she sets up the power of language to change reality — the President declaring women inferior, legally minors (Elgin 1984, 7), the men's repetition of misogynistic accounts of female biology as cause of "natural" feminine inferiority — Elgin needs the comic scenes to provide readers reassurance that the misogynistic men will not ultimately be successful in debarring women from social power. She does so by putting the reader in a position of superiority to the men.

As in the case of Le Guin's Capt. Davidson, the reader's positioning as superior to the "dumb" male narrator also helps Elgin guide political reactions. The women of the Linguist Household have developed a secret project to create a language for women to express feminine reality; they hope that such a language will be able to change the world, to empower women's points of view. They cloak their real conspiracy in a fraudulent language project that the men can feel contempt for. They teach all their girl children the women's language and eventually succeed in spreading it beyond the earth to space colonies. Elgin uses the naive male point of view, whose misogynistic belief in women's inferiority will not allow him to believe accomplished female linguists could construct a language — "the time the women wasted in their silly 'Encoding Project' " (Elgin 1984, 15) — to render believable the success of the women's conspiracy. The men continually misread the women, assuming that women accept their inferior treatment as just and are too passive to be angry.

In *Native Tongue* Elgin keeps the naive male point of view comic to indicate the possibility of change but, as in the tradition of modern black humor, the comedy is used to render more horrific the crimes of patriachal men against women. For example, Elgin tells the story of Michaela, whose husband Ned sells their baby for government experiments from the viewpoint of the comically and horrifically naive husband. Elgin's exploitation of male narration heightens the horror of the crime by showing the husband's lack of guilty feelings, and at the same time places the reader in a position of superiority to the "dumb man" by allowing the reader to recognize the wife's anger that the husband cannot see. First, Elgin comically critiques masculine dependence on women's service of listening: "It was careful attention, it was intense, it was total; it was not slavish. And it fed him. When he got through talking to Michaela, . . . he was in a state of satisfaction that wiped away the rebuffs he got from others as if they'd never happened" (Elgin 1984, 38). When the baby interrupts Michaela's attention, the husband matter-of-factly decides to sell him: "Michaela's full attention was a major factor in his wellbeing, and he was bygod going to have it. . . . The fact that he could pick up a ten thousand credit fee for the kid when he volunteered it . . . that was a pleasant little extra. . . . He could afford to put a chunk of it into something pretty for Michaela, since in a way it was her kid too" (39). Because of his arrogance, his confidence in his superiority and the rightness of masculine self-centeredness, Ned cannot see the extent of the wrong he has committed, or of Michaela's anger: "And he was proud of her, because she took it like the true lady he knew her to be. He'd been prepared for a scene, and . . . a lot of female hysterics and nonsense, considering. She didn't say a word. . . . Her eyes had gotten big; and he'd seen her give a kind of jerk, like she'd been punched and the wind knocked out of her" (41). Protected by her husband's insensitivity, Michaela murders her husband without his ever growing suspicious. The naive male narrator thus buttresses Elgin's critique of our society's perception of masculinity. For Elgin, teaching men to be men leads to hierarchy, violence against women and children, and stupidity, since privilege deafens men to others' realities — they stop hearing language other than their own.

Twentieth-century women science fiction writers found models for this critique of masculinity through the strategy of the dumb narrator in early feminist technological utopias and the very beginnings of popular science fiction. For example, in Alice Jones and Ella Merchant's *Unveiling a Parallel, A Romance* (1893), the narrator, as Carol Kolmerten points out, is "a dumb male main character who is constantly outwitted by a smart woman" (Jones and Merchant 1991, xxxiv). This traveler to a utopian Mars does not display the hypermasculinity of later science fiction dumb males, but he does consistently overargue his side of the Woman Question, despite proof to the contrary in the cultures he visits on Mars. In Thursia, he argues that humans need men as heads of schools "to keep the faculty in order" (Jones and Merchant 1991, 26), despite the fact that Elodia, whom he worships, is head of the Board of Education. Moreover, he disapproves of a rich woman teaching in Caskia, not because she is not a good teacher, but because she is a woman who takes a place from another woman who might need it (129–30) —forgetting that Thursia has solved the problem of distribution of labor by having everyone work shorter hours and by redistribution of wealth (118–20). The naive male narrator of *Unveiling a Parallel* defends United States denial of suffrage to women, "the masculine instinct of superiority swelling within" him (27), asserting that "we do not hold that women are our political equals" (28). His interrogator, a Thursian male, asks, "you tax property, to whatever amount, and for whatever purpose, you choose, without allowing the owner her fractional right to decide about either the one or the other?" (28). The narrator further argues that women are "inconsequent" (30) and have no "ideas" (63), and that only men have sexual needs (77). Jones and Merchant cleverly require the readers to resist these arguments because the woman the narrator comes to love in Thursia, Elodia, is both attractive to the narrator because of her intelligent conversation, and also the mother of a six-year-old illegitimate child (103). While the dumb male narrator is never converted, he eventually admits that Marsians have built a reasonable sex/gender system, while his own seems "too thoroughly ingrained in my nature" to give up despite reason (93). The reader thus earns the favored position of rational human by resisting the narrator's ideas and judgments, by feeling superior to this dumb male narrator.

As in the case of Louise Taylor Hansen's cross-dressing as a male author, we also have an example of the naive male narrator who overperforms his gender in science fiction fan lore. In an introduction to the second volume of short stories, *Warm Worlds and Otherwise,* by James Tiptree Jr. (actually Alice Sheldon), Robert Silverberg (a contemporary male science fiction writer) sympathetically assessed Tiptree's writing career, making a forceful argument for seeing Tiptree as a male writer, despite rumors that the pseudonym was disguising a woman. Because of the parody of masculinity that Tiptree had constructed, not only in her narrators, but also in biographies of herself as adventurer and science fiction writer, Silverberg fell into the trap of her fictional cross-dressed voice.

"It has been suggested that Tiptree is female," wrote Silverberg in his introduction, "a theory that I find absurd, for there is to me something ineluctably masculine about Tiptree's writing. I don't think the novels of Jane Austen could have been written by a man nor the stories of Ernest Hemingway by a woman, and in the same way I believe the author of the James Tiptree stories is male" (Tiptree 1975, xii). Silverberg does not see that Tiptree's male narrators are often parodies of masculinity; he takes the larger-than-life masculinity as heroism, and so himself becomes the naive narrator who cannot recognize women as equal to men. Silverberg cites the world travel, the hint that Tiptree is a government agent, and the author's knowledge of "airports and bureaucrats," and "the world of hunters and fishermen" as proof that s/he is male. To Silverberg, Tiptree is "analogous to Hemingway, in that Hemingway preferred to be simple, direct, and straight-forward," and Tiptree's stories "are lean, muscular, supple, relying heavily on dialog broken by bursts of stripped-down exposition," with an air of "prevail-ing masculinity . . . a preoccupation with questions of courage, with absolute values, with the mysteries and passions of life and death as revealed by extreme physical tests" (Tiptree 1975, xv). These stories, Silverberg claims, a woman couldn't have written, and he cites especially "The Women Men Don't See" as "a profoundly feminist story told in entirely masculine manner" (Tiptree 1975, xvi).

What happens if we take up Silverberg's suggestion, and analyze the narrator, Don Fenton, of Tiptree's "The Women Men Don't See," as a parody of Hemingway's masculine adventurer-narrator?[17] In this short story, told from the viewpoint of a sportfisherman, two women run away from earth with aliens. Silverberg takes Tiptree's parody of the Hemingway narrator as straightforward laudatory imitation, reading the narrator sympathetically as a romantic hero trying to cope in a modern world where women may also be unrecognized adventurers. Certainly Tiptree's narrator is carefully con-structed in imitation of Hemingway's: this narrator sticks to the "facts," de-lights in simple diction and short sentences, admires stoicism while suppressing his own emotions, sneaks in evaluative adjectives, and fetishizes the masculine sport of fishing. This narrator, in imitation of Hemingway's, brandishes the technical language of fishing, and "get[s] to work with a bait-casting rod and some treble hooks and manage[s] to foul-hook four small mullets" (Tiptree 1975, 136–37).

Hemingway urges us to identify with his narrators. We dissent from Tiptree's parodic narrator because Tiptree leaves out Hemingway's chivalry about women, substituting an intrusive sexual interest. "As we clamber into the Bonanza, I see the girl has what could be an attractive body if there was any spark at all" (Tiptree 1975, 132), Fenton comments when he meets the mother and daughter. "Out of sheer reflex my arms go around my compan-ion's shoulder—but Mrs. Parsons isn't there," Fenton admits. And he ex-presses his resentment that she does not provide him with her services— "The muddy little woman, what does she think?" (141) Fenton further fanta-

17. For readings of Tiptree's "The Women Men Don't See" from other perspectives, see Sarah Lefanu 1988, 122–27; Julie Luedtke Seal 1990; and Veronica Hollinger 1989a, esp. 125. I was most influenced by Anne Cranny-Francis 1990, 29–38; while she examines the way in which Fenton's voice was constructed "as a parody of objectification" (37) "from a number of sexist discourses which are so effectively naturalized that even the editor, Silverberg, did not suspect that the narrative voice was a part of, not simply the authoritative medium for, the 'feminist story' " (31), she does not discuss Hemingway as model, and she treats the mechanics of reader response differently.

sizes Mrs. Parsons fantasizing sex between her daughter and the Mayan pilot, left alone while they search for water: "Captain Estéban's mahogany arms clasping Miss Althea Parsons' pearly body. . . . Captain Estéban's copper buttocks pumping into Althea's creamy upturned bottom" (150). This narrator is not only a sleazy man, quite willing to seize any opportunity, but also a dishonest man, even to himself, projecting his own desires onto Mrs. Parsons and Captain Estéban.

Tiptree's Don Fenton also shares with Hemingway's narrators a fervent racism, but unlike Hemingway, Tiptree does not ask the reader to sympathize with the racism as part of tough-minded masculinity. Of the Mayan airplane pilot, Fenton observes, "forehead sloping back from predatory nose, lips and jaw stepping back below it. If his slant eyes had been any more crossed, he couldn't have made his license" (Tiptree 1975, 133). Trashing two races at once, Fenton comments about Mayans, "Nothing like the oriental doll thing; these people have stone bones. Captain Estéban's old grandmother could probably tow the Bonanza" (133). Preparing us for the narrator's seeing aliens as enemies (160), Tiptree puts a spin on Hemingway's sexism and racism; heightens them and leans sympathy away from them.

Tiptree's Don Fenton is thus a parody specifically of Hemingway's narrators, but also of science fiction's generic masculine narrator. As opposed to Hemingway's narrators who achieve grace under pressure, or his weak male characters who never get straight the rules of masculinity, Fenton overperforms his masculinity. We can see this overperformance in the macho-technical detail of using his own "Wirkalla knife" (Tiptree 1975, 140). We can also see it in Fenton's extreme sensitivity to female rejection: "Bang, I'm dead" (151), Fenton says to himself, when Mrs. Parsons explains that she grew up very happily without a father, as did her daughter. Fenton overperforms when he calls his swollen injured leg, "a giant misplaced erection bulging out of my shorts" (145). And Fenton comically overperforms when he shoots Ruth by mistake, frantically aiming at the aliens from another planet (157).[18] Fenton sees men as dangerous (138), as predators (137) and, like Le Guin's Captain Davidson, rape as a sign of virility (Tiptree 1975, 142).

So the reader may clearly see and dissent from this Hemingwayesque narrator's view of gender, Tiptree has Ruth Parsons explain quite explicitly the problems caused by such a definition of masculinity: "Women have no rights, Don, except what men allow us. Men are more aggressive and powerful, and they run the world. When the next real crisis upsets them, our so-called rights will vanish like—like that smoke. We'll be back where we always were: property" (Tiptree 1975, 153). The narrator's earlier sexist and

---

18. Fenton shoots at the aliens after he tells Ruth that men hate war, too (Tiptree 1975, 154).

racist biases have prepared the reader to see Mrs. Parsons as reasonable here, not paranoid. Like Le Guin, Tiptree links masculine aggression to the political context of her 1970s story. When Fenton urges, " 'Men and women aren't different species, Ruth. Women do everything men do,' " Parsons replies, " 'My Lai. . . . Men live to struggle against each other; we're just part of the battlefields' " (154). The reader remains superior to the narrator until the end because the narrator never quite gets it: "She'd meant every word. Insane. How could a woman choose to live among unknown monsters, to say good-bye to her home, her world?" (164).

"The Women Men Don't See" (1973), reprinted in *Warm Worlds and Otherwise*, employs techniques similar to the postmodern ones Christine Brooke-Rose describes: "If the parody (or the stylisation) so fuses with the model parodied as to become the model, the parody ceases" (1981, 370). By the end of the novel, the enduring ignorance of the male narrator is no longer comic, but instead grim. Rather than dramatizing "the theme of the world's non-interpretability" (Brooke-Rose 1981, 364), as Brooke-Rose says for the postmodern in general, Tiptree uses these techniques toward the goal of political awareness. The chauvinist narrator sees his world as unpredictable, if women can inexplicably prefer aliens to him and men like him, but the reader is pushed into a position where she or he sees what the narrator does not, that the women are realists. Thus what Brooke-Rose calls the "tipping over into realism" (1981, 371) of postmodern fiction works politically in Tiptree, as the parody of the masculine science fiction narrator (based on realistic techniques) tips over into a grim account of the many real indignities that women survive and resent.

So far in this section, we have explored two ways that science fiction subverts male narrators: converting the male narrator to a feminine or feminist point of view; and parody, creating a "dumb" male narrator over whom the reader feels superior. A third way is to take revenge on the male narrator by making him suffer a feminine story. Unlike Elaine Showalter, who argued in her early book that nineteenth-century women writers projected their own forbidden qualities on "The Woman's Man," the main male character in their novels (1977, 133–52), I suggest that women writers of science fiction often punish their male characters with culturally feminine experiences of degradation. Because of the alternative realities of science fiction, women writers have particularly effective ways to force male characters to undergo what real women of all ages have undergone: rape, the physical dangers of reproduction, sexual harrassment, and gender discrimination. Thus, as Patricia Yaeger describes for mainstream feminist fiction, in science fiction, in particularly telling ways "male bodies and texts can be made to circulate through women's texts — breaking that circuit of meaning in which women have been the objects of circulation" (Yaeger 1988, 161).

In the introduction to this book, we discussed Mary Shelley's *Franken-*

stein as a story in which Victor Frankenstein, the main male narrator, undergoes the feminine experience of giving birth to an illegitimate child. We have further seen how, in Rebecca Ore's trilogy (*Becoming Alien, Being Alien,* and *Human to Human*), the character Tom, from whose point of view the story is told, is forced to undergo the traditionally feminine experience of translation to a new family (as in bride barter).

Octavia Butler's "Bloodchild" (1984) also falls into this category. In this award-winning short story which we examined in the first chapter for its portrayal of science, the male narrator watches a man undergo a dangerous caesarean birth and resigns himself to being raped, impregnated, and restricted to the "home." Butler accomplishes this imposition of female experience on her male narrator by building not a gender-reversed dystopia, but a doubly oppressed system, where both male and female Terrans are colonized within the family. Indeed, these future Terran colonists are brown, not white (Butler 1985, 201). This replication speaks in complex ways to minority experience, where both men and women are oppressed, especially under slavery: Terrans are kept on a "Preserve" (194, 206) to "protect" them (195); their reproduction is controlled, women forced to bear many human children, men forced to carry Tlic eggs in their abdomens until the offspring are removed by Caesarean or chew their way out; and this reproductive system is protected by Tlic arrangement of themselves with humans in "symbiotic" families. This situation is liberation compared to earlier Tlic-Terran arrangements, when humans were kept in pens and fed hallucinogens to make them eat and reproduce, when families were separated, and when adolescent boys and girls were impregnated by Tlic they did not know.

The narrator Gan, a young boy facing adolescence and promised to the Tlic T'Gatoi, undergoes a complex experience of imprisonment within a "family" that mixes love and oppression as means to institutionalize ideology — as do current families. Gan's mother enforces this exploitation: "It was an honor, my mother said, that such a person [T'Gatoi] had chosen to come into the family. My mother was at her most formal and severe when she was lying" (Butler 1985, 194). In fact, the mother recognizes that Gan's bearing of T'Gatoi's offspring is tantamount to selling her son (196). While Gan was thus raised to see as "natural" his bearing of offspring for T'Gatoi, T'Gatoi lying with her arms around Lien or the boy Gan (195) also suggests incest and child abuse. The reader is thus encouraged to feel the horror that Gan the narrator suppresses.

The material experience of watching a dangerous birth, T'Gatoi cutting the newly-hatched Tlic grubs out of the abdomen of the man hosting them, causes Gan suddenly to perceive his own exploitation: "I felt as though I was helping her torture him, helping her consume him" (Butler 1985, 202). For a brief moment, Gan allows his consciousness of the reproductive politics at work to surface: "I had been told all my life that this was a good and necessary thing Tlic and Terran did together—a kind of birth. I had believed it until now. . . . But this was something else, something worse" (203). When Gan confronts T'Gatoi, she gives him a chance to say "no," but manipulates him with pleas "for my children's lives" (208) and with threats to his sister. "Would it be easier to know that red worms were growing in her flesh instead of mine?" (210), considers Gan. Out of a complicated sense of love and family, coupled with acceptance of his dependence on his oppressors, Gan resigns himself to his role to save his sister and for "love" of T'Gatoi.[19] T'Gatoi romanticizes the relationship: "I chose you. I believed you had grown to choose me" (211). In this short story, then, the conventional adolescent male narrator/hero is punished by rape, incest, reproductive exploitation by the dominant race, and anticipation of a painful caesarean birth—and he is expected to like it, as women in many cultures have been expected to comply with their oppression. More specifically, like black women slaves in the United States, this male narrator is forced to carry the offspring of an alien race.

"Bloodchild" is narrated in the first person, but moves from internalized narration and reported past events, to conversation observed between T'Gatoi and the mother, to distancing conversation between T'Gatoi and Gan during the birth, to more disruptive dialogue between Gan and his brother Qui, and is finally resolved in conversation and implantation between T'Gatoi and Gan at the end. The first person male narration does not supply authority, since the boy is questioning all his own cultural values (and through the science fictional device of estrangement, also our own culture's family and reproductive values). The resolution of the story, where Gan resigns himself to his reproductive role, complicates the first person narrative, since the reader responds with sympathy to Gan's acceptance of his situation, but dissents from the lies about family he tells to get himself through it. Butler thus undermines the authority of the male narrator through dialogue and reader dissent.

In *Double Nocturne* (1986), Cynthia Felice imposes an experience of sexual harrassment on her main male narrator, Tom Hark. Felice accomplishes this imposition of the story of one gender on the other through the science fiction technique of a gender-reversed dystopia. On a mission to repair the central computer (AI, or Artifical Intelligence) of the planet Islands, Terran Pilot Tom Hark is captured by hostile local colonists who have their own plans for gaining power through the AI. Their hostility is based not only on a past Homeworlds war, after which they have been out of touch with Earth, but also on Tom's gender. On Islands, men are considered inferior.

---

19. During the book signing after her talk at the University of Maryland at College Park, 9 March 1995, Octavia Butler cautioned, "You do know that this story is a love story? . . . 'Bloodchild' is not about slavery."

A distinct minority, men are limited in education, may not participate in government or priesthood, and require female guardians. Men are expected to service women sexually and do all the childcare: "Who's playing with the children while they're here?" (Felice 1986, 225) asks one female government official when men are admitted to watch a court procedure. Cultural gender bias constitutes this social situation as "natural" because men are more aggressive and less rational than women — a man's courage, observes the female hero Sellia, is "all in his nutsack" (140). Men have only their "natural" rights — "the right to fight, the right to fuck" (181).

Having built a fictional society where women possess more power than men, Felice poses Hark's story as male sexual harrassment. Hark is offered the life of his captain in return for sex with Dame Adione (Felice 1986, 64) — an ethical dilemma similar to that of Isabella in Shakespeare's *Measure for Measure*. But Felice also makes Hark suffer the more subtle and continuous forms of harrassment: sexist humor (150), intrusive attention to his physical attributes by a roomful of women (150), and other personal attributes discounted in favor of physical attractiveness (his "blond curls" 35). Women on Islands do not see a competent pilot when they see Hark, but instead, his sex first: "He was tall, fair hair in a stunning bush that his travels had left in a tangle of appealing curls around his sunburned face" (126). Felice as author seems to take special care to display her male characters in phrases that many stock popular novels have visited only on their female characters. The author seems herself to be taking revenge on all those cant phrases about female attractiveness in the science fiction romance through her parodic application of them to her male characters. In addition, Felice takes great delight in inventing sexist language for men — "sweetchucks" (36), "nutsack" (140), "dangler" (150), and "muscle" (207) — making up for all those "colorful" terms our society imposes on women.

Felice marks her gender-reversed plot as punishment for her male narrator by having Hark realize that he had been guilty of a similar offense. When Dame Adione uses sexual innuendo to try to persuade Hark, he recalls his similar attempt on Captain Dace and imitates her strategy in handling the situation: "Was it her tone or the words that irritated him so much? The combination, he decided, because he recognized it as one he had tried himself on Captain Dace. . . . He would remain in control if, like Captain Dace had, he kept to business" (Felice 1986, 90). When Hark falls in love, Felice mischievously parallels her plot of sexual harrassment for Hark with a plot of conversion to men's equality for his lover: "I must be mad to stand here and talk to a muscle like he was . . . like my sister" (207).

Not only does Felice subvert the purpose of the conventional masculine narrator of science fiction through imposing on him an experience of "feminine" degradation. Felice also subtly undercuts the authority of the masculine narrator in several ways: the gender-reversal plot itself calls into question the naturalness of masculine authority, while this male narrator proves himself untrustworthy by flunking a lie detector test and by fequently making the wrong strategic decision because of his culturally limited viewpoint. Moreover, the reader feels superior to Hark through one long section where the twins, Sellia and Mala, are switched, and Hark does not realize it (Felice 1986, 288–327). In addition, Felice employs frequent extended dialogue and offers multiple narrators — not only Hark, but also Jeremy, Orrin, and Sellia/Mala — although Hark's viewpoint controls a majority of the text. Especially interesting is Felice's technique in one scene including Jeremy, Orrin, and Hark, where the point of view does not remain with a single male narrator but, instead, dissolves from one masculine point of view to another (41–52, again 66–67). Felice uses the revolving dissolution of point of view to indicate the communal nature of consciousness-raising, as the two men from Islands see their cultural assumptions challenged and their feelings of self-worth buttressed by the possibilities of an egalitarian system that Hark offers.

Gender is itself a formal constraint on narrating. Women science fiction writers who cross-dress as male narrators generally turn their disadvantage into an advantage by their subversion of ideology, through converting the narrator, through assigning the narrator unconvincing justifications of masculinity, through multiplying versions of masculinity, and through imagining masculine versions of feminine realities. Almost all of these women writing male narrators also subvert the authority of the generic science fiction male narrator — through dialogue, through making the readers superior to the narrator, through alternative points of view. In the next section, we will concentrate further on this breakdown of authority through multiple points of view.

Multiple Narrators: He, She, It, and We

In addition to cross-dressing as male narrators and subverting the traditional science fiction convention of masculine narrator, women writers of science fiction frequently construct multiple voices that challenge the power of a single (traditionally in science fiction, male) point of view. With multiple voices in a narrative, no one voice has as much power, and storytelling becomes less hierarchical. This strategy is not the same as replacing a single male voice with a single female voice, for multiple narrators fragment and redistribute the power of storytelling.[20] As Patricia Yaeger observes of the novel in general, "The novel is a form women choose because its multi-voicedness allows the interruption and interrogation of the dominant culture" (Yaeger 1988, 31).[21]

---

20. It is tempting to be psychoanalytic here and contrast a phallic concentration of power with a polymorphous perverse dispersal of power in pleasure.

21. See also Yaeger 1988, 59; Robin Roberts 1993, 19.

The multiple narrators in science fiction by women contribute to creating what Rachel Blau DuPlessis in "For the Etruscans" describes as a "female aesthetic," although I do not see these characteristics as essentially feminine. Women writers, DuPlessis argues, "know their text as a form of intimacy," "a structural expression of mutuality" (DuPlessis 1985a, 275), and they use several strategies to create this intimacy in their writing: the model of "intimate conversation" (275), the equal-rights narrator who is "open to the reader, not better than the reader" (275), "both/and" or "encyclopedic" vision, or "double consciousness" rather than duality (276–78, 285–86), and "a didactic element, related to the project of cultural transformation" (286). These strategies work particularly well for women in the genre of science fiction, because of science fiction's use of multiple points of view since World War II in an otherwise nonexperimental narrative, and because of its traditionally didactic element often constituted as world building. In this section, we will look at three different forms of women writers' use of multiple narration to undermine the generic male narrator: he and she (the heterosexual romance); he, she, and it (human and alien narration); and communal voice.

The heterosexual romance plot gave to women writers the first major impetus to narrative reform in science fiction through allowing them to give both genders a voice in the outcome of the story, by alternating points of view. Many of the generation of women writers who began in the 1950s or 1960s used this technique: Judith Merril, Andre Norton, Marion Zimmer Bradley, Anne McCaffrey, and Ursula K. Le Guin. Many of the novels that we discussed in the last chapter on the woman as alien employ this technique of distributing the power of point of view between earth men and alien women.

In a 1947 story, "That Only a Mother," reprinted in *Out of Bounds*, Judith Merril pioneered this technique of alternating gendered points of view. In this short story, a wife and husband share point of view, although the wife has the major share. This story written at the end of World War II is one of the earliest to explore the dangers of mutation from radiation. In a future war where atomic weapons are again used, we follow a woman through a pregnancy and birth. From her point of view, we see the details of her wartime work, her separation from her husband, the birth of her daughter, and her radiant love for her: "she favored her mother with a smile that inevitably made Margaret think of the first golden edge of the sun bursting into a rosy pre-dawn" (Merril 1963, 17). We know that the baby has been somehow changed by radiation mutation because of her precocity.

Although Margaret actually shares narration with her husband, that male point of view is nearly buried until the last paragraph, limited to brief telegrams and letters from the husband, Hank. In the final paragraph of the story, the husband, having at last returned to see his daughter for the first time, discovers that she lacks arms and legs, and that his wife has concealed this lack from him, perhaps from herself: *"She didn't know.* His hands, beyond control, ran up and down the soft-skinned baby body, the sinuous, limbless body. *Oh God dear God* — his head shook and his muscles contracted, in a bitter spasm of hysteria. His fingers tightened on his child — *Oh God, she didn't know"* (Merril 1963, 21). Because of clues that Merril has planted earlier in the story, describing news accounts of fathers destroying their "deformed" children (14 and 18), the reader has a basis for assuming that we join Hank's viewpoint just as he strangles his daughter, seeing his wife as mad. Thus the story offers different realities, alternating female and male points of view. Hank, the father, responsible for the mutations because of the war the men are engaged in (and Hank is specifically involved in atomic research), sees his child as damaged goods and destroys her in revulsion. Margaret, the mother, responsible for the child, refuses to see her daughter other than beautiful, loses touch with social reality in order to make another reality that accepts her child, but then is not prepared to protect her from the father. Through alternation of points of view that depend on different conceptions of reality, Merril asks the time-honored Shelleyan question of who is mad, who is the monster? Is the mother mad because she sees her child as perfect? Is the child the monster, because deformed? Or is Hank the monster, changed by war? In addition, the alternating points of view demonstrate the estrangement that gender roles work on men and women during war: they live in different realities.

Andre Norton is another writer who employed alternating male and female points of view to feminist purposes. We can examine this strategy in her novel *Web of the Witch World* (1964). At a time in science fiction when female narration was extremely rare, Norton centers her novel on Simon Tregarth's point of view, but shares narrative power with Loyse, Jaelithe, and briefly with the Sulcar captain, Stymir. The relation of narrative viewpoint between Simon and Jaelithe, newly married, marks their growth in understanding of each other. At first, we have only Simon's point of view on their partnership (interspersed with other narrative viewpoints — Norton 1964, 5–25, 35–54, 64–82, and 84–113). In this section, during the course of other adventures, Simon comes to realize that Jaelithe has regrets about their marriage. When Jaelithe realizes that she yet retains her telepathic powers despite the loss of her virginity in marriage, her joy strikes Simon as reproach:

> So — it had meant that much to her? That she felt herself maimed, lessened by what had been between them. And another part of Simon, less troubled by emotion, arose to defend her. Witchdom had been her life. As all her sisterhood she had had pride of accomplishment, joy in that usage; yet she had willingly set aside, so she thought, all that. . . . And his second thought was so much the better one! (Norton 1964, 8–9)

In this section, Jaelithe's reactions are filtered through Simon's view, and we see Simon as self-centered, although struggling with granting independence and recognition of selfhood to his wife. In the context of middle-class 1960s feminist issues, the didactic element favoring Jaelithe's witchcraft translates not as valuing women's essential differences, but as allowing Jaelithe a career after marriage. By her final comment on Simon's conflicted responses, Norton directs the reader toward acceptance of married women in the workplace.

In the middle section of the novel, we alternate Simon and Jaelithe's points of view, and the two, while separated by distance, realize that their intimacy remains (Norton 1964: Jaelithe 117–23, Simon 123–33, Jaelithe 133–42). It is such a daring challenge to science fiction convention to have a female narrator (and a married one at that!) that Norton uses a transition through the Sulcar Captain's point of view when she begins Jaelithe's separate story (113–17). It is as if Norton tries to write Jaelithe's adventures while separated from Simon from other characters' viewpoints first to show the necessity for granting Jaelithe subjectivity and her own voice. When separated from Simon, Jaelithe realizes that she still has telepathic powers and that she can use them to keep in touch with Simon — not accidentally, her returning powers thus coincide with her assuming the narrative point of view. In the context of 1960s feminist issues, Jaelithe is realizing that her independence in work reinforces rather than reduces her capability for intimacy. In her last narrative moment in the novel, she examines "this new knowledge . . . warm about her like a cloak against the chill of a winter storm. She thought that her tie with Simon had been her new skill, but it would seem there was another — and there could be more to discover. Jaelithe stretched her aching body and fell asleep, smiling" (142).

The narrative then returns to Simon in a long action sequence at the end of the novel (Norton 1964, 142–92), but his view includes recognizing Jaelithe's strength and independence: "He knew that she had those depths and silences to which she must withdraw upon occasion, that he meant none the less to her because of those withdrawals. . . . There were parts of him which would be closed to her also. But to take without question what she did have to give, and offer in return, freely and without jealousy, all he had — that was what their union meant" (184). Now, instead of filtering Jaelithe's viewpoints through Simon, Norton allows Simon to recognize Jaelithe's separate subjectivity, and to build intimacy on a balance for both of them between independence and symbiosis (to return to Jessica Benjamin's terms, which we explored in the last chapter). Norton's use of multiple points of view is thus politically charged, and yet a simple technique comfortable in the context of science fiction realism, extremely accessible to a popular audience. Norton adapts the heterosexual romance to her politics, rather than challenging it as a form.

Norton complicates her unconventional marriage plot with another story — Loyse, heir to a throne, resisting an unwanted marriage to a usurper and, threatened with rape, protecting herself. Norton further undermines the traditional science fictional male narrator by granting Loyse point of view through her action scenes (Norton 1964, 25–35 and 54–64). In addition, Loyse cross-dresses during these scenes, signaling, as Garber has pointed out, a crisis of values: "Loyse held the dagger breast high and point out, her left arm still numb from the blow against the post. If she had been hampered by skirts she could never have kept out of his hands, but in riding clothes she was limb free and as agile as any boy" (60). Norton calls up many of the themes of 1960s feminism through Loyse's point of view: freedom from marriage, self-protection from rape and violence, and resisting the confinement of feminine dress. Loyse's cross-dressing thus affirms the effrontery of Norton's granting women point of view: Norton uses her female narrators to challenge the sexism of pre-1960s science fiction and her culture's values.

As Bonnie Zimmerman notes, "Through multiple points of view or narrative voices and interwoven characters," the writer "attempts to create an egalitarian, democratic novel" (1990, 135). Within the confines of traditional realistic science fiction narrative, Norton employs many of the strategies that DuPlessis identified as characteristic of female aesthetic: intimate conversation with the reader in disclosing Simon's, Jaelithe's, and Loyse's thoughts on gender issues, an encyclopedic vision alternating gendered viewpoints, and a didactic element in Jaelithe's and Simon's conclusions on Jaelithe's powers. I do not see these strategies, however, as innately female, but instead, as narrative strategies that work as resistance because they are also similar to the conventions of "realistic" science fiction narrative.

Other women writers, especially those employing the plot of alien woman and Terran man, imitated Norton's use of double-gendered narration in heterosexual romance science fiction to make a point about equality between men and women. For example, in *Dragonflight* (1968), which we examined in Chapter 2, Anne McCaffrey uses the alternating points of view of Lessa and F'lar (ch. 1 Lessa, chs. 2–3 F'lar, ch. 4 Lessa, ch. 5 F'lar) cinematically, to indicate their initial antagonism, then their acceptance of each other as the alternation of viewpoint occurs more frequently (chs. 6 and 7 and the rest of the novel). In addition, writing half of the novel from Lessa's point of view, as well as interweaving the choric commentary of the dragons who support Lessa in her desire to fly, allows McCaffrey to portray F'lar as insensitive, in need of reformation in order to accommodate his new relationship with Lessa.

McCaffrey does not use the double narration to give equal weight to both F'lar and Lessa's desires but, instead, to weight the reader's sympathy in the direction of Lessa. For instance, in chapter 2, we wake the day after Lessa and F'lar's first sexual union with F'lar's point of view, but not so that we may sympathize with him. He is at this point, briefly, the "dumb" male narrator, his masculinity parodied: "She ought to have no complaints at all. What a flight! He chuckled softly. . . . There was no friendliness about her at all. No warmth. . . . What was the matter with the girl?" (McCaffrey 1982a, 126) F'lar cannot understand that Lessa does not see the sexual union with F'lar as consensual, since she was controlled by her telepathic link with the dragons. She sees it as rape. But the reader, who has seen through Lessa's point of view earlier and noted her feelings about F'lar's arrogance, does understand, and sympathizes with Lessa, feeling superior to F'lar's sexism. As in Norton's *Web of the Witch World*, we end the novel with the man's point of view, to underscore his new respect for women's independence. When Lessa arrives with the all-female Queen's wing to help battle Thread, F'lar "grinned with proud indulgence at the glittering sight" (McCaffrey 1982a, 285). Although F'lar's condescension may grate today, in 1968, his "indulgence" also urged male readers to give permission to women's ambitions.[22]

Although the initial experiments in the 1960s with alternating male and female point of view by women writers of science fiction are almost all feminist, by the 1970s, the technique has become unremarkable, and so is available for other possibilities. In *Flyer* (1975), Gail Kimberly uses the alternation of Mist and Jerenz's points of view without feminist content, although the careful division of the point of view into almost exactly equal parts suggests that their partnership sustains Mist and Jerenz in their adventures.[23] Kimberly's central focus, however, is racial tolerance, and Mist and Jerenz, Flyers, focus not on their own romance, where the story starts, but on the union of the three future races of Earth — Flyers, Walkers, and Swimmers — to regain lost knowledge from the days before an environmental holocaust (Kimberly 1975, 119 and 165–66). The novel ends by joining Mist and Jerenz's viewpoints to suggest the accomplishment of their goal: "They waited for the night to end . . . the three races of the world side by side, united by their shared adventures and their common goal" (163).

In *Eye of the Heron* (1978), Ursula K. Le Guin uses this technique of alternating male and female points of view, now familiar to women science fiction writers, not to demonstrate that women are like men and, so, equal,

22. If anyone doubts from reading *Dragonflight* that McCaffrey meant to challenge the conventions of science fiction romance and the male narrator, read her essay, "Hitch Your Dragon to a Star: Romance and Glamour in Science Fiction" (1974, 282), where she discusses the glee with which she parodied the exclusivist masculinity of space opera by writing from Joanna's point of view in her 1967 novel *Restoree* (McCaffrey 1982b).

23. In Kimberly 1975, the story is narrated through Mist's point of view 5–13, 16–21, 26–42, 48–62, 103–13, 117–31, 145–61, and 174, and through Jerenz's point of view 21–26, 43–48, 62–67, 69–102, 115–17, and 131–43. Mist and Jerenz share point of view 67–68, and 163–73.

but to make a point about differences, to argue that assuming a feminine point of view would change humanity. Narration alternates between Lev, from the lower class pacifist Shantih-Towners, and Luz, from the dominant-class city people, who fall in love on a distant Terran colonial planet. Lev and Luz are also from different ethnicities, Lev a descendant from European Jews, Luz from Spanish South Americans. Borrowing from oriental philosophies, Le Guin has Vera (her name means "Truth"), the wise older woman who is the author's mouthpiece, present an essentialist view of gender. Vera tells Luz,

> "I like men very much, but sometimes . . . they're so stupid, so stuffed with theories. . . . They go in straight lines only, and won't stop. It's dangerous to do that. It's dangerous to leave everything up to the men. . . . A woman has a center, is a center. But a man isn't, he's a reaching out. So he reaches out and grabs things and piles them up around him and says, I'm this, I'm that, this is me, that's me. I'll prove that I am me! And he can wreck a lot of things, trying to prove it." (Le Guin 1978, 85)

The heterosexual romance founders in Le Guin's story on this essential difference between men and women, for while Luz urges Lev and the villagers to run away, they proudly vow to fight against the City oppressors with a peaceful march. When the march erupts in violence on both sides, Lev is killed, and the romance ends. But the novel continues, and Le Guin works a sophisticated formal narrative structure around this deceptively simple center of heterosexual romance and alternating points of view.

Le Guin begins this narrative structure with a highly stylized realistic narrator, a scientific observer of every last detail, whose consciousness is shut off from the emotional nature of human beings — a technique like that of the French *roman modern* (such as the novels of Robbe-Grillet). This narrator, occupying relatively few pages of the novella (Le Guin 1978, 1–7, 8–10, 13, 34–35, 50–54, 58–59, 87–89, 91, 144–46 and 190–93) suggests, through its rigid exclusion of emotional response, a stylized critique of the traditional science fiction masculine narrator. Le Guin employs this narrator in three ways. In some descriptions, the lack of emotion indicates the inhospitable nature of the alien planet. In some scenes in the Shantih community, the absence of an individualized point of view underscores the importance of community over individuality in Shantih society. And in the climactic march scene, the clinical reportage heightens the horror of civil violence.

In addition to the alternation of Lev's and Luz's points of view and the hyperrealism of the framing narrator, Le Guin subverts the traditional masculine science fiction narrator in several other ways. Lev's and Luz's alternating viewpoints are intruded on by dialogue, a communal third person point of view, and the points of view of other individuals. Dialogue, virtually uninterrupted by narrative comment, occupies more pages than does the framing narrator (Le Guin 1978, 11–13, 13–15, 40–45, 47–49, 55–56, 65–68, 76–80, 82–86, 104–6, 134–37), much of it modeling the consensual political process of Shantih town meetings. Dialogues with Vera raise Luz's consciousness (76–80, 82–86, and 104–6) and move her into the Shantih community. The dialogue is reinforced in some scenes by a third person point of view indicating beliefs and emotions of the communal group rather than any single individual. Such a third person point of view occurs when the mediating committee wonders at the sights of the city (35–43), for example, or when Shantih-Town customs are described: "They had watched their elders arrive, sometimes by passionate debate and sometimes by almost word-less consent, at solutions to problems and disagreements. They had learned how to listen for the sense of the meeting, not the voice of the loudest" (49). (The communal "they" also occurs on 61–65, 98–99, and 160.)

Besides dismantling the authority of any single narrative point of view by frequent dialogue and a communal "they," Le Guin briefly gives her narrative over to a dumb male narrator — Capt. Eden (such a great name!) — who exposes his naiveté on issues of class and serfdom, as he ineffectually orders forced labor for Shantih-towners schooled in the politics of civil disobedience (Le Guin 1978, 92–98). "There was no sense to their behavior, but it was shameful, unmanly," Captain Eden thinks of the Shantih men; "Where was he to find his own self-respect, in this damned wilderness?" (96) When Captain Eden gives the final order to go to work, Lev chooses to interpret the order as permission to use the Shantih workplan, and the Captain goes along in order not to lose all control. In addition to Captain Eden, both Falco, Luz's father (69–75), and also Vera (138–44 and 147–50), of the older generation, are given narrative points of view: the older man of the City disgusted with the brash young men he must pass his power on to, compete with, and be replaced by; the older woman of Shantih-Town nurturing and supporting a new generation, facilitating change, and mourning the death by violence of her ideals.

Finally, Le Guin challenges the traditional science fiction male narrator most obviously by having the story go on after he dies. When Lev is killed by the need to go out and meet a challenge, which Vera tells us is to be read as a male characteristic, Luz takes over as main point of view and runs away from the challenge (a female technique!), escaping with a large group of colonists into the wilderness. A sighting of a human-like aborigine promises that this exit, however, will not be the end of cross-racial dialogue.

Premier storyteller and manipulator of the techniques of science fiction realism, C. J. Cherryh works a marvellous gender reversal in the narrative structure of a recent novel in her Chanur series, Chanur's Legacy (1992). By alternating male and female point of view and reversing gender customs of the alien species and, so, the gender of the dominant point of view, Cherryh builds an antiromance promoting her equal-rights feminism.

In her Chanur series, Cherryh developed a society modeled on Terran lion social relations, the hani, where females do the hunting and child raising in communal groups around a central male who protects territory but does little else, with other single males on the fringes watching for an opportunity to compete for a spot as head of a family. Extrapolating this social system to space travel, Cherryh has managed a wicked critique of earth women's oppression by reversing the gender biases: Chanur males are too emotionally unstable, too violent by nature, to be trusted in space, while the communal experience of family raising and hunting make hani females the ideal team to take a spaceship out for trading with other species of the Compact. In *Chanur's Legacy*, Cherryh explores the second generation of a spacemerchant family on a vessel captained by Hilfy, a niece of the original Captain Pyanfar. As in the opening of many of the previous novels, Cherryh playfully signals her gender reversal by the scene of her captain dressing, cross-dressing by human standards: "So Hilfy put on her administrative-offices best pair of black satin trousers, and (acutely aware of her youth) combed the mane until it crackled with static (and looked fuller) and the mustaches so that they somewhat covered the youthful scantness of beard" (Cherryh 1992, 2).

Having introduced first a human male and then a hani family male onto the Chanur all-female crew in earlier novels, Cherryh varies her politicized plot by sending Hilfy's crew a rival family male to beg for rescue from the spacestation where he has been abandoned by his ship. The young male hani, Hallan, shares viewpoint with Hilfy, and is exquisitely sensitive to the problems of dealing with a sexist all-female crew: he has to listen to off-color jokes that embarrass hani males (Cherryh 1992, 203), he is sexually harrassed by crewmembers (32, 186), he endures remarks about male hormones (104, 144, 147, 150), he is asked why he couldn't find a place as a husband instead of going off into space (134), and he resists the captain's worries that a male member will disrupt the close bonding of her all-female crew (252). Cherryh mischievously reverses the experiences of women in the workplace under men's power in order to catalogue the indignities that Hallan suffers. In addition, Cherryh critiques the romance ending of most gender-reversed science fictions, when Hilfy resolves Hallan's family's appeal to return him against his will, by marrying him to the entire crew.

Cherryh parallels these reverses of conventional science fiction plot and human gender customs with similar reverses in narrative structure. In this gender-reversed novel, Hilfy has the lion's share of the point of view, although she narrates with the young Hallan, who is tenderly exploring his capabilities after an upbringing that limited him (in much the same way that Norton's Jaelithe explored her capabilities in the much earlier novel *Web of the Witch*

World). With occasional short sections from crewmember Tiar's point of view, Cherryh structures her novel mainly through alternating Hilfy's and Hallan's viewpoints.[24] As we move toward the climax of the adventurous race across galaxies in this novel, Cherryh heightens the sense of excitement by the cinematic technique of switching point of view more rapidly.

Cherryh further breaks down the conventional masculine point of view of science fiction by using dialogue, by disorienting the reader during transitions to a new point of view, and by recording hyperspace dreams that distort conscious viewpoints. In *Chanur's Legacy* Cherryh uses dialogue within the ship to indicate the crew's communal organization, where no one viewpoint dominates (Cherryh 1992, 58–60, 353–54 and 383–84). Cherryh also reports verbatim series of messages from other spaceships and spacestations to represent the community of varied species that have ventured into space (130, 244–45, 283, 338, 350–54); indeed the resolution of the plots is signaled by such a message, celebrating the peace achieved between species (383). Cherryh further uses dialogue to disorient the reader in transitions to a new point of view, beginning a new section with dialogue and delaying identification of point of view until after the reader has guessed the new point of view from speech patterns (for example, 368). Such a technique disrupts the reader's identification with the point of view, reminding the reader that s/he has her own viewpoint, not necessarily one that may be identitifed with that of a character. Since Cherryh requires her readers to see beyond the sex biases of even the liberal Hilfy, and beyond the goals of even the independent Hallan, to gender equality, such disruption of sympathy is useful to her political goals. In addition, Cherryh records dreams in hyperspace where Hilfy's or Hallan's point of view turns at a subconscious angle to their conscious viewpoint. This technique unearths the fears and anxieties of male and female hani that they repress in their conscious dealings with each other (74–76, 157–59, 285–86, 346–47), revealing the underpinnings of sexism.

The gender-reversed hani customs that generate the plot and the reversed-gender science fiction narrative structure align to reinforce Cherryh's parody of romance. In the main plot Cherryh parodies the Heinleinian union of the masterful old spaceman and sweet young thing in the romance between curmudgeonly old female Chihin and sweet young male Hallan. In the subplot, Cherryh examines the Stsho, whose three sexes and ability to

24. In Cherryh 1992, Hilfy's point of view occupies 1–14, 18–33, 33–39, 42–46, 51–56, 60–64, 68–70, 72–87, 88–103, 105–12, 117–23, 125–32, 136–42, 145–66, 168–72, 176–84, 188–200, 203–27, 229–54, 256–62, 265–74, 279–85, 291–97, 300–20, 321–24, 331–33, 334–37, 338–39, 342–44, 346–47, 349–50, 354–66, 368–80, 384–86. Hallan's point of view occupies 15–18, 33–37, 56–58, 65–68, 70–72, 87–88, 103–5, 113–16, 123–25, 133–36, 142–45, 184–87, 200–2, 227–28, 254–56, 274–78, 285–90, 298–300, 325–31, 334, 337–38, 339–42, 344–46, 347–48, 367–68. Tiar's point of view occupies 39–41, 47–51, 87, 166–68, 172–76, 263–65, 290–91, 320–21, 380–82.

switch from one to another make Chanur's race across space fruitless but regenerative. Since the purpose of this quest novel is to deliver a Stsho *objet d'art* as a marriage proposal and request for political alliance, the Stsho's shifting sex renders the quest fruitless, the recipient of the gift having shifted to neuter by the time the hani catch *gtsta*. By mistake, however, the good-hearted hani have also given refuge to another Stsho exile, who has obligingly turned from *gtstisi* to *gtsto* ("something like male" Cherryh 1992, 214), to console the rejected ambassador *(gtst)* — in another reversal, the "male" being the one to pour the tea, while the "female" negotiates political business. Such an anticlimactic ending pokes fun at the world-saving endings of much cross-galaxy quest literature, and suggests the contrived nature of much science fiction romance. In addition, Cherryh further disrupts expectations because the paired points of view — Hilfy and Hallan — are not heterosexual partners but mentor and apprentice. Although technically married to Hallan along with her entire crew at the end, Hilfy is not pressing her "conjugal privileges" (367).

By the 1990s, this simple variation between male and female point of view can thus be employed without the initial justification of heterosexual partnership. In Connie Willis' *Doomsday Book* (1992), a fallible male narrator, Mr. Dunworthy, historian at a future Oxford University, alternates point of view with an heroic female narrator, Kivrin, a student doing her thesis research in medieval history by time-traveling, who accidentally ends up in a plague year. Willis uses the male/female juxtaposition not in the service of heterosexual romance, but in the interests of exploring the relationship between mentor and student. The female point of view of past experiences, however, also subtly comments not on science fiction narrative, but on textbook narrative of history. What we too often know of history are the battles, the kings, the discoveries by Great Men. What we see of history through Kivrin's feminine point of view is the action of women: as plague runs from London to Oxford and outlying villages, a castle of women heroically feed and tend the sick men, women, and children, watch them die, themselves dying one by one, their knightly male partners already dead at some distant seat of government, their only male help a priest not a knight.

Similarly, the alternation of male and female point of view in Eleanor Arnason's *Ring of Swords* (1993) documents a friendship, not a heterosexual romance. Here the point of view swings between Anna, ambassador and xenobiologist from Earth (whose sexuality remains unstated in this book, although surely there will be a sequel), and Nicholas, a traitor (eventually) to two races, who lives with the alien Hwarhath, and practices cross-species homosexuality. The exploration of difference (or similarities) between male and female that originally sparked the simple but liberating practice of alternating viewpoint in science fiction is now extended to other differences: sexual orientation and racial allegiance. Thus women writers have found subtle ways of manipulating narrative strategies in keeping with the staunch emphasis in science fiction on realism. They have experimented with great formal success while still not leaving the formally conservative realm of science fiction realism for experimental form. Women writers of science fiction thus multiply and alternate gendered narrators in ways that comment on and undermine the masculine narration of traditional science fiction, while yet maintaining the realism that makes science fiction a genre available to a large popular audience.

Indeed, women science fiction writers have built on this initial simple alternation of male and female points of view to incorporate a third, alien point of view. He, she, it — even if the alien is a creature that comes in two sexes (often it is not), the male or female of an alien is not the same as the male or female of Earth (except, of course, in that series of novels we looked at earlier, where Earth men meet and partner with alien humanoid women). In this section, however, we will explore the introduction of points of view of nonhumanoid aliens, a simple narrative trick that yet effectively destabilizes categories of race and gender. As Marjorie Garber points out, the "third sex" as a "mode of articulation," "challenges stable binary symmetry" (Garber 1992, 11–12 and 133).[25] The alien point of view indicates "excess," an overflowing of normal discursive and conceptual boundaries — not just male and female, but male, female, and something else, too.

Perhaps this strategy for overturning the male narrator originates in horror-influenced science fiction, where granting the alien a point of view distorts the realistic surface of the fiction (creating a greater feeling of horror). But the strategy also disrupts the familiar binary of male and female, further increasing readers' disorientation. An early example is Kate Wilhelm's "Stranger in the House," a novella published with another novella in *Abyss* (1967). "Stranger in the House" begins as if it is a heterosexual romance, alternating the points of view of Robert and Mandy, husband and wife. But Robert only "authorizes" the story, which is framed by his point of view for a few pages at beginning and end (Wilhelm 1973, 73–74, 136). The main narration alternates the points of view of Mandy and the Groth, an alien scientist, and so point of view includes a "he," a "she," and an "it" (88). "Stranger in the House" is a ghost story, where Wilhelm reinforces the horror by revealing the ghost as an alien, living in the house to observe humans, unwittingly killing and traumatizing them because of their untrained psi powers. The double human and alien narration, then, reinforces the horror:

25. Also see Judith Butler 1990: separating gender from sex means the possibility of multiple genders or the female body gendered as male (6). A multiplicity of sexuality gives an alternative to our binary system. Thus multiplicity disrupts heterosexual reproduction, and its medicojuridical hegemonies (19).

alien distortions of the other's reality are experienced by both Mandy and the Groth as they telepathically merge. Wilhelm cleverly represents this distortion in her narrative structure by fused points of view (98, 132). For example, we experience the Groth's disorientation through Mandy's point of view: "The bad air was weakening her. . . . One of *them* entered, and there was much noise, and suddenly blinding lights were stabbing her" (98).

This transformation of the horror of the ghost story into the horror of the alien story, giving a rational explanation for parapsychological events, underlines Wilhelm's ultimate message. Although the characters feel terror at intimate communication with the alien, the real horror is the barrier between people, especially between husband and wife, the silence where there should be communication: "The walls around other people always seemed so obvious," Mandy thought; "she had believed none existed between her and Robert. But it was there, invisible, unbreachable" (Wilhelm 1973, 114). In this novella, while having an alien reality penetrate human mental boundaries is horrifying, even more horrifying for the humans is remaining isolated from human loved ones, never able to experience with empathy another's reality. Especially horrifying is the gendered nature of this isolation. While Mandy and her daughter unknowingly communicate telepathically, Robert remains locked in his own world. We consequently see the dangers of Robert's patriarchal control over his wife: thinking her crazy, he tries to convince her of that, and considers institutionalization (114, 136).

The horror of this novella is further reinforced by undermining the traditional masculine science fiction point of view: Wilhelm employs the communal "they" (Wilhelm 1973, 112–13 and 119–20) and frequently interrupts with small passages from the points of view of characters in danger of perishing from the alien's mental communication (Wilhelm 1973: Dwight 110–12, Eric 127–29, Tippy 123–24). In addition, Wilhelm creates the Groth's point of view as a highly stylized version of the masculine scientific observer. The Groth's goal on earth is to study humans, collect data, predict their reach into space, learn how the race of Groths might eventually communicate with them. The Groth achieves these goals, but his lack of human emotions and human goals of communication (he rejects symbolic communication in favor of mental connections) convey a sense of distant alienation that Wilhelm uses to increase the horror. Ironically, the two closest minds in narrative style are Robert and the Groth, who both idealize scientific objectivity, and so thoughtlessly hurt others.

In *Cloud Cry* (1977), Sydney J. Van Scyoc also elaborates the basic alternation of male and female point of view by introducing an alien viewpoint. Rather than using racial politics to destabilize and question gender politics, however, she uses multiple points of view to reinforce racial boundaries. The main point of view in *Cloud Cry* is that of Verrons (Van Scyoc

1977, 1–7, 40–59, 70–86, 134–46, 157–73 and 181–84), a conventional explorer-scientist white male. Verrons remains the main point of view because his perspective houses the moderate rationality that is Van Scyoc's ideal. Quarantined on a planet because of blood blossom disease, Verrons draws on the scientist-explorer's central trait, the innate human need to explore (according to Van Scyoc's definition of humanity), and discovers two native humanoid species and a cure for the disease. Verrons is a highly stylized version, then, of the traditional masculine science fiction point of view. While his goal is to protect indigenous species from exploitation, he assumes the right to explore and take away any useful knowledges, by force if necessary. His view is seconded by another Terran also exiled to the planet — Sadler (102–14, 118–29).

In addition, Verrons' point of view is not questioned by the further inclusion of an alien male point of view (Van Scyoc 1977: Tiehl, 8–19, 33–39, 93–101, 130–34) and an alien female point of view (Aleida, 20–32, 60–67, 86–92, 115–18, 147–56, 174–81). Tiehl, a large bright-blue male of an ostrich-like species, offers a territorial point of view that we can understand but not identify with: real males, among the Eminheer species, do not share perch (19). Van Scyoc portrays Tiehl as "reverting" (78) to savagery under the crisis of exile — "primitive" (39), "predatory" and "savage" (168), "shed-[ding] the final restraints of civilization" (164). Tiehl K'Obrohms is thus a parody of the world-conquering masculine science fiction point of view, but not to question the value of masculinity, only to advise moderation, as in Verrons. Van Scyoc thus makes of Tiehl a third-world man, savage and predatory, and promotes the values of first-world rational imperialism against savage territoriality. Aleida, a native of the colonial planet where Verrons, Sadler, and Tiehl are exiled, is a member of a telepathic race, the Sun-Dancers, who uses her powers to fly and to subdue to her rule the "Underpeople" — others of her race who are born without the power. In Aleida, Van Scyoc's purposes conflict. We identify with Aleida's desire to fly (21) and her adolescent anger at being different and isolated among her people (22–23), but her savage misuse of her alien power pushes us back to Verrons' position again. Verrons suggests the reader-response to Aleida that Van Scyoc eventually requires of us: "there was no compassion in her soul: there was only fire" (166). Thus the other points of view in *Cloud Cry* — junior officer who looks up to senior, and savage alien male and female — reinforce our acceptance of Verrons' authority and establish his self-policed imperialism as ideal as opposed to the unrestrained territoriality of both Tiehl and Aleida.

Much more similar to Wilhelm's "Stranger in the House" than to Van Scyoc's *Cloud Cry*, Doris Piserchia's *The Spinner* (1980) uses alien point of view to manufacture horror in her story of alien intrusion on earth. The two main points of view formally represent the polarities of her story: human police officer Ekler fighting to kill the alien intruder Mordak, who is also granted point of view.[26] The emphasis on these two rival points of view centers the telling of the story on masculine competition. Ekler wants to save the earth and his family (his sister whom he cares for) and his women (first Jetta, then Nina) from the alien intruder, who spins webs over the city to imprison humans, and who counts humans as food. Having been transported unwillingly from his home planet by a human scientific experiment, Mordak wants revenge and enough territory to feed himself and reproduce. Mordak is both father and mother; his point of view is vicious, but his goal is the same as that of the humans — survival. For most of the story we readers, by default, must identify with human points of view, but by the end we can see that the goals of alien monster and human police are disturbingly similar: kill the other male so that territory and reproduction goes to one's own kind.

Piserchia helps us to criticize this basic story of masculinity run amok by using formal means to question the centrality of masculine competition. By multiplying points of view, Piserchia makes the rivalry of Ekler and Mordak less important. These points of view are all human, suggesting community, but one fighting against itself: Duff (Piserchia 1980, 53–54), a police officer who cares for Ekler's retarded sister, is set against Bailey (115–16, 117, 152–53), a renegade police officer who helps Mordak; Rumson (16–17, 38–40, 51–53, 69, 71–73, 107–11), the scientist who seeks to hide from the alien he accidentally imported through his experiments, opposes in point of view his wife Olivia (120–22), whom he loves, but whom he locks up to protect against losing her to the alien; Gusty (1–2, 3–4, 11–16, 19, 63–68, 101–5, 149–50, 153–56, 165–66, 175–81) and Hitty (113–14, 116–17), members of a group of elderly resisters who steal people from homes for the aged to give them a better life, are enemies of Jerome (35–38, 47–51, 73–77, 91–93, 94–98), a street rat who preys off the old in public housing complexes.[27] Piserchia thus multiplies the central competition between human and alien through rival human points of view, critiquing the concept of masculine rivalry rather than simply repeating the cultural stereotype in a story about good guy triumphing over bad alien. Thus the real monster is not Mordak or the offspring who escapes to hibernate, then lay more eggs who will eat more humans, but human lack of community, represented by the human soldier who shoots Ekler when he is trying to "save" humanity.

26. Piserchia 1980 is told from Ekler's point of view more than that of any other character (6–9, 19–21, 26–27, 28–31, 42–46, 55–57, 69, 77–89, 93–94, 105–7, 123–9, 130–37, 139–42, 150–52, 162–63, 169–71, 173–75, 182–83), but still not frequently enough to make Ekler a decided protagonist. The next most frequent point of view is the alien Mordak (2, 9–10, 17–18, 31–32, 59–60, 62–63, 98–100, 117–20, 142–45, 159–61, 163–65, 171–73, 183–84). Thus the story is narrated mainly from the points of view of the male protagonists locked in the deadly struggle of who gets the territory and so reproduction rights.

27. Other points of view include Tully (4–6), Hance (156–58), and Rune (23, 24–26, 137–39).

In *The Spinner* Piserchia introduces other formal techniques that help to break down the central formal dual of two competing male protagonists, one human and one alien: dialogue that interrupts any single point of view (Piserchia 1980, 18, 23–24, 27–28, 54–55, 69–71, 129–30, 161–62); a communal "they" that represents the police working in concert (32–33) and later the people fleeing the city (166–68); a communal passive that tells us what the people of the city know about the alien (60–62, 113, 181–82); dissolving from one point of view to another (53–57, for example), and abrupt changes in point of view that disorient and confuse the reader (for example, 152 in the middle of a paragraph). All together, Piserchia orchestrates her narrative structure in order to repeat the masculine story of rivalry between male human and male alien, but formally deconstructs and questions this story. No one survives this rivalry at the end of Piserchia's horror story, although younger males live to begin the rivalry over again.

In her recent trilogy, *Xenogenesis: Dawn, Adulthood Rites, Imago* (1987–1989), Octavia Butler shows how contemporary women writers of science fiction may appropriate these recent experiments with multiple narrators that destabilize gender — he, she, and it — to use in the study of the intersections of gender with race. The first novel in the trilogy, *Dawn* (1987) is narrated from the point of view of Lilith Iyapo, an African-American human woman; the second novel, *Adulthood Rites* (1988), is narrated from the point of view of Akin, a first-generation human-Oankali male; and the third novel, *Imago* (1989), is narrated from the point of view of Jodahs Iyapo Leal Kaalnikanjlo, the first human-Oankali ooloi, a third sex neither male nor female who organically controls the genetic outcome of their breeding partners. As in Plato's *Symposium* where Aristophanes imagines three sexes, Butler does away with the familiar binaries of male and female in her postholocaust future. She also does away with race as a simple category. As Donna Haraway points out in *Primate Visions: Gender, Race, and Nature in the World of Modern Science,* "At the end of *Dawn,* Butler has Lilith . . . pregnant with the child of five progenitors, who come from two species, at least three genders, two sexes, and an indeterminate number of races. . . . Butler's fiction is about miscegenation, not reproduction" (1989b, 378–79).

Butler uses her triple narrative point of view in *Xenogenesis* to break down traditional conceptions of gender and race. In *Dawn,* Butler explores through Lilith's point of view a disruption of the traditional sex/gender system: Lilith is chosen by the alien Oankali to be a leader of a group of humans, to help them to resettle the earth with the Oankali after nuclear war has destroyed it and the Oankali have rebuilt it. Butler thus starts her trilogy within the tradition of science fiction by women, portraying a new culture where women have been granted authority, even though Lilith must still fight old prejudices among her group members. But Butler also comments on the tradition of science fiction by women—written mainly by white authors, often lacking attention to issues of race—by portraying black Lilith (a new Eve) as fighting racial prejudice, and fighting within herself against an enormous fear of the alien difference of the Oankali. In addition, if we see Lilith's experiences on the Oankali ship, where humans are rescued from their holocaust and healed but also given a new culture in partnership with Oankali, as akin to the Middle Passage of slavery, Butler is also implanting racial prejudice in the Oankali. Concentrating on gender in the first book of her trilogy, Butler develops Oankali sexuality as crossing human sexual lines: the pleasure of sex in the new reproductive partnership involves a human female, a human male, and an Oankali ooloi, and the Oankali do not make it a matter of choice (1987, 184, 199 and 201). If men may be raped, who is female, who is male?

In the second novel, told from the point of view of Akin, a male human-Oankali, Butler explores the Oankali as sexual exploiters of another race, examining the intersection of gender and race oppression (Butler 1988, 294; 1989, 581). Akin's point of view is crucial, since he is a member of both races: he is the result of his human mother's sexual exploitation by the Oankali (Butler 1988, 269), and he is also a recipient of the privileges of Oankali biology. From his double perspective, Akin helps the Oankali return reproductive freedom to humans who can't overcome their xenophobia, recognizing that this solution is flawed since it institutionalizes racial difference (Butler 1988, 371).

Employing Jodahs, a human-Oankali ooloi as point of view, the final novel in the trilogy concentrates on deconstructing the category of race through imagining a people where individuals are biologically created with such differences that they cannot easily be stereotyped into groups by sex or race. What is alien, if a species itself has infinite genetic difference? (Butler 1988, 442). "We were what we were because of that organelle," Akin reflects; "It made us collectors and traders of life, always learning, always changing in every way but one—that organelle" (Butler 1989, 530). In *Primate Visions*, Donna Haraway argues that Octavia Butler's science fiction is "predicated on the natural status of adoption and the unnatural violence of kin. . . . Her fiction, especially in *Xenogenesis*, is about the monstrous fear and hope that the child will not, after all, be like the parent" (Haraway 1989b, 378).

So far in this section on multiple narrators, we have looked at the ways that women writers of science fiction employ heterosexual romance as a structure for male and female narration, and then complicate that gendered structure by introducing an alien viewpoint that calls into question "human" gender. Now let us examine a final way in which women writers use multiple narrators to undermine the science fiction convention of masculine narration: communal narrators. Susan Sniader Lanser's distinction between "sequential communal narration" (1992, 256) and "simultaneous communal narration" (256–57) is a useful one for our purposes.[28] In sequential communal narration, a series of narrators represent communal viewpoint; in simultaneous communal narration, a "we" or "they" represents a communal viewpoint. In science fiction by women, both kinds of narration include male points of view without privileging them, and so their use challenges traditional science fiction narrative practice. In their experiments with this technique of communal narration, women science fiction writers come closest to the practice of other postmodern writing without necessarily adopting the pessimistic worldview implied by fragmentation.[29]

In sequential communal narration, a series of narrators share narration to the extent that the authority of the protagonist is diffused across a group — often a family in science fiction by women, but also frequently a community. We will examine here only sequential narration by women writers that multiplies male points of view or alternates male and female points of view.[30] Such narration uses replication to deconstruct gender categories, since each repetition is slightly different, and so gradually the replication calls into question the very definitions of the category. As Walter Benjamin points out, "The technique of reproduction detaches the reproduced object from the domain of tradition. By making many reproductions it substitutes a plurality of copies for a unique existence. And in permitting the reproduction to meet the beholder or listener in his own particular situation, it reactivates the object reproduced" (quoted in Marjorie Garber 1992, 369).

In *Pilgrimage* (1952–1961), Zenna Henderson uses sequential communal narration to construct a utopian alien community modeled on the family,

28. Also see Brian Richardson's mapping of possibilities for narrative voice (1994, 323–25), and Adalaide Morris's comments on the feminist "we" (1992, 17–20).

29. In my thinking about the relation of postmodernism to science fiction by women, I am endlessly indebted to Marleen Barr's *Feminist Fabulation: Space/Postmodern Fiction* (1992) and *Lost in Space: Probing Feminist Science Fiction and Beyond* (1993), and also to Robin Roberts *A New Species: Gender and Science in Science Fiction* (1993), chap. 6; I admire their vigorous shaking of the science fiction canon. However, I have not finally agreed with them except in part (they have convinced me on some specific works), and have followed, instead, Christine Brooke-Rose in *Rhetoric of the Unreal* (1981), who argues that science fiction maintains its ties with realism, and when it experiments, does so more often in the direction of the French *modern moderne* hyperrealism, rather than the Anglo-American postmodernism.

30. Unfortunately, we cannot then examine all the wonderful experiments in multiple female narrators — Joanna Russ's *The Female Man* (1975), Faye Weldon's *The Cloning of Joanna May* (1989) — fictions that use multiple but usually related female narrators to explore identity in process. Angelika Bammer suggests that Russ's multiple narrators help readers reconceptualize the identity of woman along a range of possibilities, so that Russ's feminist projections are not totalizing (1991, 94). Bammer argues that multiple narrators in Russ also portray resistance to patriarchy, exposing how women must live in two worlds (102). Similarly, urges Bammer, Connie/Luciente in *Woman on the Edge of Time* is a multiple protagonist, suggesting that it is impossible for a woman to be whole in our current society (101).

but a family that crosses boundaries of race and class. Her novel is told by a series of first person narrators of the People, a group of aliens with psychic powers who crash-land on Earth. Narrators include two alien females (Karen and Melodye), two alien males (Peter and Bram), and two human females who join the community (Miss Carolle and the framing narrator Lea). Henderson underlines her major point of racial tolerance through a style of regional Western realism that makes the People seem like ordinary people. The People — all people — should be accepted because people are basically alike and good at bottom. Her fairly nonexperimental alternation of narrators, then, reinforces the ordinariness of these extraordinary people: Lea,[31] who weaves the stories together by means of her own story of rising out of depression because of the People's charitable welcome of her; Karen (Henderson 1963, 19–43), who tells the story of Valancy, the teacher who discovers she's one of the People when she fortuitously comes to teach their children; Peter (50–79), son of a woman of the People and a human father, who brings himself and his younger sister on a quest back to the People after his parents' death; Melodye (82–116), Karen's roommate from college, who finds a whole lost village of the People repressing their gifts when she is sent there as their teacher; Dita (122–63), a human teacher who helps children by reading their minds, persuaded to join the People by Low, the man of the People she falls in love with; Miss Carolle (167–214), a teacher who has lost the use of her legs but has the strength to rescue a boy with psychic powers and a love of music; and Bram (226–55), who falls in love with the first visitor from another planet of the People, but does not want to leave his home on Earth. These stories almost all emphasize crossing racial lines from human to People to fall in love, to adopt children, or to teach and further the growth of another person. Many of the narrators or major characters are teachers, for these stories are not adventures emphasizing conquest and technological discovery but, instead, documentaries of people facilitating other people's psychological growth and development. The People's psychic powers, then, are hyperbolic recastings of the psychological strengths that any child or healing adult has buried, yet to be uncovered.

While Henderson rigorously holds herself to realistic techniques, she yet experiments with ways she can sustain a sense of community through her narrative structure. Not only through the sequential narrators and Lea's interweavings, but also through parody of the traditional masculine science fiction narrator in Bram (who wants the People to take over earth and straighten out human problems with their new technologies), through refraining from closure (ending not with a resolution to Lea's story, but simply with the last sequential narrator), and through a spare use of the communal "we" (Henderson 1963, 24, 141, 143, 151 and 159), Henderson shapes her realistic narra-

31. Lea narrates 5–19, 44–49, 80–81, 117–22, 164–67, and 215–26.

tive into a utopian dream of community analogous to the safety of family. " 'We came from some other world,' " explains Low to Dita, "wistful pride at belonging showing in his 'we' " (141). From individual linear narratives, a series of "I"s, Henderson thus constructs her "we" to extend to society in general the family's means of facilitating growth.

Zenna Henderson adopts sequential communal narration to suggest that her humanoid aliens construct a utopian community modeled after the family, a family that potentially may cross the boundaries of race and nation that humans have bound themselves by. Similarly, in *Journey* (1978), Marta Randall employs sequential communal narration to suggest the elasticity and inclusiveness of the family as an institutional model for government.[32] Feminist critics have noticed that utopias by women frequently model government on the institution of the family, with decisions made by consensus rather than vote, children and education as central concerns, and regulations adapted to facilitate individual development. While her novels are not utopias, but instead space opera adventures, Randall yet creates a family protagonist — the Kennerin of the planet Aerie — and focuses on family as the model for government in her alternative world. Mish, the mother, reflects, "What seemed chaos was in reality an almost shapeless order" (1978, 2), marking the settlement as functioning like a family. Randall also suggests that the family may cross racial and national boundaries by featuring the Kennerin, a black family, as protagonists, and including white and alien peoples in the settlement (13–14). Randall emphasizes the extended family in her structure by using communal sequential narration by family members: the mother, Mish Kennerin; the father, Jason Kennerin; the children Hart, Quilla, Jes, and Meya; the housekeeper Laur; Tabor Grif (eventually a son-in-law married to Quilla); Manuel Hetch, the family friend and captain of the immigration ship; and Dr. Hoku, the family and settlement doctor. While the family is eventually separated and dispersed by death and Hart's unethical experimentations, the romance structure reinforces the narrative structure of family by providing reunion in the next generation in the form of Hart's son.

Ursula K. Le Guin's *Always Coming Home* (1985) employs postmodern techniques of multivocal sequential communal narration to suggest not fragmentation, but collaboration as social and narrative practice. Re-visioning the writer/reader relationship, Le Guin offers a miscellany of material, multiplying not only points of view but also genres. The multiple perspectives offer a way of decreasing the author's authority and control, and of increasing readers' options. In "A Conversation with Ursula K. Le Guin," in *Para-Doxa: Studies in World Literary Genres*, Le Guin explains that she meant the novel to be read not in linear fashion, but in varied order: "*Always Coming Home*

---

32. Marta Randall's *Dangerous Games* (1980), sequel to *Journey*, uses similar sequential communal narration.

. . . I genuinely meant for people to read in any order they felt like, to bounce around in it" (Le Guin 1995, 53). The multiple perspectives, borrowed from anthropological techniques of ethnography, also offer a way of suggesting the diversity within a culture. The multiple perspectives further provide a way for the female author to deal with the science fiction convention of male narration. Le Guin, in a practice common in the 1980s in female writers, uses predominately female narration: Pandora, the extremely self-conscious framing narrator is female, as is Stone Telling, from a different oral storytelling tradition, the equally self-conscious narrator of the novel whose voice is buried in three sections of the lengthy book. But these female narrators are surrounded by the stuff of culture, narrated by dozens of other people, male and female. For example, Part II of Stone Telling's life (Le Guin 1987, 183–214), the novel kernel of *Always Coming Home*, is followed by a note on the valley stage (215); five dramatic works (216–53) — one from the masculine viewpoint, "Chandi," a retelling of Job for another culture (241–53); a comment by Pandora on the difficulty of getting the messiness of the wilderness into a book (254–56); a description of the Dancing the Moon Festival by Thorn, a male (257–64); fragments about the Moon Dance from other speakers, male and female (265–66); poems by both men and women (267–78); and eight life stories by both men and women, one in verse (279–322). Thus the narration is distributed across gender and genre, but narrative power is also not allowed to accumulate with any one authoritative narrator, whether framing narrator or main character. All narrators are limited, circumscribed, untrustworthy, only part of the story.[33]

While Henderson and Randall use sequential communal narrative to suggest unified community despite conflict and separation — to reinforce the romance motifs of science fiction — and Le Guin turns the sequential communal narration to postmodern ends, Faye Weldon, an Australian writer, adopts the sequential form to dystopic satire. In *The Shrapnel Academy* (1986), the military-industrial complex exposes itself upstairs at a conference banquet, while the exploited masses foment rebellion below. By alternating points of view in the matrix of a parodic omniscient narrator, Weldon lends ironic futility to the goals of both groups.

Weldon deftly juxtaposes the conflicting viewpoints of eighteen people (the militarists Murray, the General, Baf, Victor, Sergei, and Joan Lumb; wives and companions Shirley, Bella, and Muffin; the reporter Mew; Ivor the white chauffeur and Edna the taxi driver; the international servants Acorn, Hilda, Inverness, Agnes, Yew, and Matilda) — even Harry the dog (Weldon 1986, 106–9). Weldon's response to the convention of male narration is thus

33. For a careful and appreciative detailed reading of Le Guin's *Always Coming Home* as text deconstructing itself, see Lee Cullen Khanna's essay, "Women's Utopias: New Worlds, New Texts," in Libby Falk Jones and Sarah Webster Goodwin, eds., 1990, 130–40.

to provide too much of it: the self-righteous military solutions of imperialists, for example, are repeated in slightly varied versions by Murray, the General, Baf, Victor, Joan Lumb, and Shirley. All the men—upstairs and downstairs—personalize their conquerors' goals by polite stalking of the females. And even the dog's point of view is masculine and violent. With the exception of Mew, a radical journalist from a feminist publication who survives the holocaust with Ivor, the feminine points of view give permission to masculine values, and even the narrator, although ironically, repeats large portions of military history with its justifications of destruction.

The fragmentation resulting from so many points of view is exactly Weldon's goal: when, after 140 pages she reintroduces Ivor the chauffeur, she asks, "Remember Ivor, the chauffeur whose task it was to drive General Leo Makeshift and Bella Morthampton down to the Shrapnel Academy?" (Weldon 1986, 155) The fragmentation further underlines the theme of her satire: a culture centered in warfare inevitably destroys itself. Thus follows the title, the setting at the Shrapnel academy, and the ending, pieces of modern military technology and body parts flying as Baf's miniature weapons of the future ignite each other while upstairs is planning the destruction of downstairs.

Weldon's plethora of points of view is interspersed with dialogue, lists, a seating chart and a timetable—the compulsive outward order creating a parodic omniscient narrator, who also inserts histories of warfare and advances in military technology. At one point the narrator offers us "the scale of emotional underprivilege":

White men
Black men
White women
Black women
Animals. (Weldon 1986, 99)

The narrator critiques the actions of both the childlike militarists, enamored more of their destructive toys than of human life, and the immigrant male servants who let a woman die in childbirth for fear of deportation and who then kill and serve Harry the dog to the upstairs as revenge and prelude to revolution. But the narrator's parodic distance and acid commentary also precludes outrage: this is the way of the world, and there is no hope of change offered. Indeed, both groups deconstruct, rather than one killing off the other, although the result is the same—this little piece of the empire perishes in a cataclysm which, Weldon suggests, will almost certainly repeat itself for the rest of British colonialism. Thus Weldon uses sequential communal narration not for nostalgia, to establish a sense of community, but instead for critique, to trace the fault lines of British colonialism. The narrative technique dissolves with the explosion, of course: "Reader," cautions the narrator at the end, "I know you do not like this ending to the story. It seems a cheat just to blow everything and everyone up. I wish there was some other possible ending, but there isn't" (185).

Having looked at examples of sequential communal narration, let us turn to simultaneous communal narration, point of view merged in a "we" or a "they." We have already examined a small instance of this technique in *Eye of the Heron*, where Ursula K. Le Guin combines a highly stylized "objective" omniscient narrator, frequent intrusions of dialogue, and a "they" communal narrative for the people of Shantih-Town — all to undermine the authority of the traditional male science fiction narrator.

The communal narrator representing family, like the heterosexual romance, was one of the earliest interventions tried by women science fiction writers to incorporate feminine viewpoint while not yet overturning the generic convention of male narration. For instance, in *Three Against the Witch World* (1965), Andre Norton tells the story of the return of the "Old Race" to the East through two points of view. The novel alternates between the point of view of Kyllan, the warrior son of Simon Tregarth and Jaelithe, and a communal "we" composed of the triplets (Kyllan, his sister Kaththea, and his brother Kemoc).[34] The "we" of the novel directly addresses the issue of gender, although along essentialist lines; the heroes are stronger together because each of them provides a particular strength: "we seemed a single person — I the arm for action, Kemoc the brain, Kaththea the heart and controlled emotion" (Norton 1965, 12). Norton accepts stereotypical gender differences, but she employs that stereotyping to justify including the feminine in her communal point of view.

Cast out of Estcarp because of their unusual powers, Kyllan, Kemoc, and Kaththea explore the forbidden East beyond the mountains, later returning to open the territory to their countrymen and to reunite the "Old Race." Norton alternates Kyllan's single point of view with a communal "we" to emphasize their success when the triplets act in unison, and the hardships they undergo when they are separated. Finally, she broadens the family "we" near the end of the novel to underscore the community then established, when the magically closed East is opened to the descendants of the "Old Race" from Estcarp to the West. For example, the triplets succeed in their journey across the mountain, when united; here the point of view is mainly

---

34. Norton 1965 is told from Kyllan's viewpoint throughout, except when he speaks communally for a group he is part of: primarily the triplets, 5, 12, 13–26, 30, 38, 51–58, 61–62, 65–98, 129–33, 142–45; but also, the Estcarp border guards, 26–29; only Kyllan and Kemoc, 30–37, 48–50; Kyllan, Dahaun, and Ethutur, 150; and the immigrants from Estcarp, 190.

communal "we" (Norton 1965, 65–98). In contrast, they are wounded and captured by different opposing forces when separated by Kyllan's misjudgment (151–90). On the final page, Norton moves from individual point of view (Kyllan's) to communal "we" to indicate that the triplets' values, especially the welcoming of social change, have been incorporated in a new, broader community: "We stand in a time of chance and change, and move into new designs we do not understand. . . . For we did thereafter indeed buy Escore with steel, raw courage, and such witchery as was not tainted" (190). In this novel, as in many of the Witch World Series, Norton's political message is based on the "mistakes" of World War II, where the United States, in Norton's and Witch World terms, did not intervene soon enough and chose to remain isolated (130).

Using a similar technique, but with different political goals, Margaret St. Clair, in *The Dolphins of Altair* (1967), contrasts the communal care of the environment of the Dolphins, whose story is told through a communal "we," with the social disorder and disregard for the environment of the humans, whose stories slip into individualized points of view (for example, dolphin "we," 12, to human Sven's point of view, 13). The narration yearns toward a utopian unity of narrative point of view between these two groups: "There is a task yet unaccomplished. The final fusion of the human and dolphin natures is yet to come. Then we sea people will walk on land, and you Splits will be free of the sweet depths of the ocean. The covenant looks *forward*. The best is yet to come" (St. Clair 1967, 188).

In *Port Eternity* (1982), C. J. Cherryh uses the communal "we" to explore class resistance in sophisticated ways. Cherryh isolates the problem of hierarchy within a single spaceship—*The Maid of Astrolat*, owned by the Lady Dela, and run by Azi, the genetically altered, artificially reproduced humans who serve as slave labor for Cherryh's future in outer space. The story of the ship's loss in hyperspace, what ships move through to go faster than light, is told, however, not through the dominant characters of Dela or her born-human lover Griffin, but through one of the Azi, Elaine. Elaine, however, employs "we" as the person of her narrative, representing either the whole ship's complement or, more frequently, the Azi: Elaine, Dela's lady's maid; Lancelot, Dela's lover; Vivien, the accountant; Mordred, Percivale, Gawain, and Lynnette, the ship's crew. Thus Elaine in her "we" incorporates male and female points of view, especially under the class-based category of Azi. As the character names indicate, Dela has constructed her ship as a fantasy world from the romance of Arthur and the knights of the round table, and when the entire crew of Azi eventually experience the "story-tape," their psych-sets are irretrievably altered.

Cherryh at first attributes the "we" of Elaine's narration to her Azi psychset, tuned by genetic alteration, then drug-enhanced tape learning, to special empathy. When Elaine suffers for Lance's feelings of abandonment from Lady Dela's affair with born-man Griffin, Elaine explains, "They psych-set me so that I can't stand to see someone suffering. Born-men feel; we react; so the difference runs" (Cherryh 1982a, 18). The narrative thus registers Elaine's empathic perspective as "we," Elaine attuning herself to others' needs. Although Elaine is especially focused on Dela's needs, her empathy allows her to see the injustice of their situation as Azi servants, if only to accept it. If Dela tires of the Camelot fantasy, Elaine reflects, she might sell the ship and all her servants—but Elaine represses her own worries in the interest of her fellow servants, commenting, "We had enough troubles, all of us" (17). Elaine cannot interpret reality only through self, but necessarily through the communal "we."

In the first half of the novel, the communal "we" also reinforces class hierarchy: the Azi are psych-set as communal, supportive of Lady Dela. Commenting on erotic relations among the Azi, Elaine tells us, "We have better sense than to cause ourselves such pains [as love], and we have better manners than to tease one another too seriously—which, besides, would be interfering with Dela's property, and rather like vandalism" (Cherryh 1982a, 19). Azi cannot fall in love but are rewarded with sex and affectionate feelings by their programmed psychological reactions. Elaine's "we" speaks for Azi as a group, who accept the status quo of class hierarchy and are loyal to the values that privilege their owner, Lady Dela.

In counterpoint to the plot, however, this conservative communal "we" changes and develops as class consciousness. As the plot progresses, the spaceship becomes lost in hyperspace, and so the crew members become aware in heightened fashion that reality is not fixed, for they were caught by "A wandering instability, a knot in time and space" (Cherryh 1982a, 47). In the between of hyperspace, where Elaine views "through" reality, she realizes that reality is constructed, a fiction: "the brain constructed its own fantasies of matter and blue skies and green grass and solidity, screening out the irrational and random" (49). Similarly, tapes construct Azi psych-sets, fashioning their identities as happy slaves. But during the emergency, Elaine accidentally allows the forbidden tape of the story of Camelot to be experienced by the other Azi, and they are "helpless in the dream that had gotten loose on the ship, that filled the *Maid* and told us what we might have been" (119). Like the wandering knot of space/time, the tape changes their reality, transforming their formerly real class hierarchy into the enabling romance of knights and ladies (rather than slaves) serving a king and queen. Elaine explains, "We're small people, pale copies, filled with tapes and erasable. But something had begun to burn in Lance that had more complicated reasons" (80). The tape is also damaging in that it assigns discordant motives to Mordred and Vivien, who then are distrusted by the others.

At the same time that the Azi imbibe forbidden but enabling fantasy, their class consciousness is raised by a shift in power as the Lady Dela defers in the crisis to Griffin, the man. At the intersection of gender and class, Elaine's "we" takes on this tinge of class consciousness, no longer representing the whole ship, or the Azi in support of Dela, but rather the Azi in disagreement with the born-man Griffin (Cherryh 1982a, 74–76, 80). From this new perspective, Elaine and her "we" begin bitterly to express the inequities of the Azi position: "But we're like the walls. Born-men can talk to us and know our opinion's nothing, so it's rather like talking to themselves. Sold on, we're erased ... no gossiping elsewhere, that was certain" (88). Understanding that all reality is constructed, Elaine and the Azi eventually come to see that the difference between Azi and born-men is not so natural after all: "They made us out of born-man material, and perhaps, the thought occurred to me, that somewhere at base they and we were not so different" (169). In response to Dela's suffering, Elaine even ventures to include herself and her mistress in a "we":

> I patted her shoulder, hating to see her that way.
> "We could go help them," I said. "We can fetch things."
> It was unthinkable, that impertinent we. (Cherryh 1982a, 138)

Eventually, under the stress of distrust of Mordred and Vivien, encounter with an alien culture, and rising consciousness of self and will, Azi community breaks down, Elaine's "we" becoming less frequent (Cherryh 1982a, 143, 149–51). Gradually her "we" reassembles with more individual freedom, becoming the storyteller's "we": "So we live, Lance and I, in a tower on that shore, a long time in the building, but of time we have no end. ... Whether we dream, still falling forever, or whether the dream has shaped itself about us, we love. ... And whenever the call goes out, echoing clear and brazen through the air, we take up our arms again and go" (191). In celebrating the enabling power of fantasy, Cherryh has moved the Azi slaves into the personae of heroes — Elaine's final "we" is the timeless "we" of questing knights. Cherryh, who herself writes in both the genres of science fiction and fantasy, thus transgresses the boundaries of both by ending her science fiction novel with this Camelot fantasy. Through this means, Cherryh makes a metafictional claim for the power of fantasy. The slaves of her "realistic" science fiction have been freed by the power of their fantasy: both men and women join in the "we" and on the battlefield, and both slave and master join in the "we" and in love that erases class lines.

Susan Sniader Lanser suggests that in mainstream fiction by women communal narration is problematic, since it is associated with nostalgic utopian ineffectuality. This problematic association seems largely avoided in science fiction, where multiply-gendered communal narration becomes an avenue of resistance to patriarchal dominion in both form and theme.[35] Women writers disrupt the conventional male narration of science fiction through communal narration by placing family or community point of view at the center of their fictions, even when that family or community is sorely troubled. Indeed, many of these fictions end in apocalypse or take place in a postholocaust future full of problems, but also new possibilities.

The Female Man: Transvestites and Androgynes

Ironically, science fiction—by definition centered on extrapolation to a future not yet here or to a "scientifically" possible alternative, what does not exist—remains firmly wedded to realism as a narrative mode. The androgynous voice, adopted by many women writers, resolves the stalemate of having to choose either a realistic male narrator or fragmented multiple narrators through the technique of building an alternative world. Many women writers escape the male narrator yet remain in realist mode by giving a "realistic" voice or point of view to the nonexistent (now-existent?) female man. As Maria Minnich Brewer argues, in feminist "postnuclear" science fiction, the woman writer's "consent to the reproduction of the patriarchal narrative is effectively questioned and withdrawn" (1987, 47).[36]

In this section I am treating together androgynous narrators with those cross-dressed narrators who conceal their sex, thus performing both male and female roles in the story. As Judith Butler and Marjorie Garber have urged, gender, socially constructed, is performance, especially in fiction. In science fiction, it doesn't matter whether that gender is performed through clothes or the body, if it is perceived as transformable. In science fiction it's all done with mirrors, anyway, since inventing worlds and alternative forms of life is by definition part of the pleasure of the genre.

At the center of the complicated narrative structure of Leslie Stone's early short story, "Out of the Void," published in *Amazing Stories* in 1929, lies the first person journal of the first man into space who turns out to be a woman—Dana Gleason. With "regular features that were almost girlish except for a masculinity developed by the full life of a globe-trotter" (Stone 1929b, Part I, 448), the first human astronaut in Leslie Stone's story "successfully passes"—in Marjorie Garber's terms—and so gives a "secret pleasure" (Garber 1992, 9). However, Dana, although the central narrator, is allowed

---

35. Nostalgic utopian fictions in science fiction by women are more often narrated from a single woman's or group of women's point of view—see Bartkowski 1989, chap. 4.

36. Marjorie Garber sees androgynes and cross-dressers as nostalgia for the time before the fall into knowledge of sexual difference, for the maternal phallus, originary wholeness (see 1992, 127). The pronounced sexuality of the androgynous narrators of women's science fiction calls into question this reading, although a few—Jane Palmer's planet mother in *The Watcher* (1986), for example—might fall into this category.

a voice only to tell the story of her falling in love with Richard Dorr, who guesses her disguise and joins her in the first rocket exploration of Mars. Even though as a "female man" Dana is the hero of Part I, as soon as she loves she becomes only a victim to be rescued, and point of view shifts away from her.

As Virginia Woolf writes in *Orlando* (1928) published the year before Stone's story, "Different though the sexes are, they intermix. In every human being a vacillation from one sex to the other takes place, and often it is only the clothes that keep the male or female likeness, while underneath the sex is the very opposite of what it is above. Of the complications and confusions which thus result every one has had experience" (Woolf 1992, 189). In Stone's story, Dana confesses in her journal, "Had the Professor only known me for what I am, he would never have come to me [to be the first astronaut], but haven't I proved myself equal to any man? . . . I, born of woman though I am, can not and will not give up the heritage my father has given me. No man shall force me to admit that I am a woman-thing even though I was born with the body of one" (Stone 1929b, Part I, 452). Following her father's prescription, Dana compensates for her inferior status as a woman by cross-dressing and learning to be a man. Only through this means does she win the Professor's confidence to become the first astronaut. When Richard Dorr punctures her disguise, Dana, "losing a world," according to Stone's story, is given "something else, something more precious" — she discovers her "womanhood" (Part I, 455). It is not a fair trade.

Stone's "Out of the Void" builds a complicated set of narrators around the androgynous figure of this first astronaut. The framing narrator parodies Hemingway's narrators, an unnamed American male who begins his story by escaping from his wife on a fishing trip and ends it with a misogynistic joke at his wife's expense. Within the male narrator's story are contained several other narrators. The first is Sa Dak, a silver male alien, who captures the narrator and promises to release him after his mission is completed, introducing us to the protagonist, whose message he brings, and offering us a vision of alternative science. Soon, however, Sa Dak's voice is left behind and the narrator's returns, but with information he could not know. We later learn that this record was compiled with the help of Elsie, the professor's daughter, who quietly loved the hero, Dana Gleason (Stone 1929b, Part I, 447 and 454). Elsie "had already passed her twenties; the bloom of her youth was gone, given without thought of self to the service of the old scientist" (Part I, 447). Her participation in the adventure story, as Dana prepares for "his" rocket ship exploration of Mars, is that of observer and caretaker, who "sat in her corner mending and embroidering" (Part I, 448), and who made sure that the ship was equipped with handkerchiefs intialed "DG" (Part I, 449). Her self-effacement is so complete that her story is told by another's voice, and we have only the barest clue that it is hers: it is a love story of admiration for Dana Gleason, traveler, explorer, wit, woman-hater. Still, as Marjorie Garber points out, the transvestite in literature marks the space of desire, that which escapes (Garber 1992, 75). Elsie's love for Dana exists in this area of virtual reality, where Dana is both man and woman.

In the very center of the story, we come to Dana Gleason's own story, the silver metal manuscript brought back by Sa Dak to the professor and his daughter. There we learn that Dana is a woman. Dana's diary, though, ends very early in Part II with the crash of her rocket not on Mars, but on an unknown planet. Even though the rest of the story ostensibly reports from Dana, Dana loses her "I" and becomes a third person in the narrative; at the same time, she also loses her place as hero in the narrative and becomes the victim — stolen by the aliens and eventually rescued by Dick. Once Dana is separated from Dick, we see that cross-dressing here quite explicitly literalizes female anxiety of phallic loss (Garber 1992, 356): when Dana loses her masculine role, she also loses Dick, if only to be regained when he proves his masculinity. Gradually we realize that our perspective for the rest of the story is that of the alien villain, and at the end Sa Dak reveals himself as that person.

Even though we lose the cross-dressed hero to femininity by the end of the story, Stone's narration is wonderfully androgynous. This story is related by a man's man on a fishing trip, by a silver alien villain, by a woman who loves a woman she thinks is a man, and by a woman disguised as a man who attempts the first trip to Mars. It is significant, I think, that the author's name, Leslie, as well as the hero's, Dana, are names that may be worn by either sex.[37]

In the light of Leslie Stone's cross-dressed hero, we can better understand Joanna Russ's female men, the female heroes who enact men's stories in Russ's novels of the late 1960s and early 1970s: Alyx (wearing an androgynous name) in *Picnic on Paradise* (1968) and *The Adventures of Alyx* (1967–1970), Janet in "When It Changed" (1972) and Janet, and Jael or Alice Reasoner in *The Female Man* (1975). As Russ explains in her 1972 essay, "What Can a Heroine Do? or Why Women Can't Write," the legacy of plots that a writer inherits is bound by gender, many of them denied to women. In the 1960s and 1970s, Russ busily rewrote this legacy of plots to make available to women writers many of these stories from the masculine literary tradition. For example, in "What Can a Heroine Do?" Russ complains that the stories "A young girl in Minnesota finds her womanhood by killing a bear" and "An

---

37. For a brief analysis of other narrative practices and the conventions of the science fiction romance in Golden Age science fiction by women, see Donawerth 1994.

English noblewoman, vacationing in Arcadia, falls in love with a beautiful, modest young shepherd" but "must return to the court of Elizabeth I to wage war on Spain" are not available to women (Russ 1972b, 3). But in Russ's "When It Changed" (1972) the daughters prove their adulthood by going off into the woods and reappearing with a dead beast, while Russ's later "What Did You Do During the Revolution, Grandma?" (1983) tells the story of a time-traveling female hero (cross-dressed!) adventuring to a medieval court, where a young girl falls in love with her, whom she must tragically leave behind. In Russ's *The Female Man* (1975) Joanna explains how to become a female man in a bitter diatribe: first, to avoid harrassment, you become "One Of The Boys" (Russ 1975, 133); then, using "the knowledge you suffer when you're an outsider. . . . the perception of all experience through two sets of eyes, two systems of value, two habits of expectation, almost two minds" (137–38), you seize power (139), and "To resolve contrarieties, unite them in your own person" (138). Thus Russ's cross-dressed female men not only rewrite men's stories for women, offering them alternative powers, but also anatomize the anxieties of twentieth-century women, who must live in two cultures at once. As Sarah Lefanu argues, "I would contend that Russ's feminism is to be found not so much in her utopian creations as in her deconstruction of gender identity, of masculine and feminine behaviour" (Lefanu 1988, 175).[38]

Many writers have followed Stone and Russ, creating cross-dressed heroes, from whose points of view their stories are told, who temporarily fool the audience. We have already mentioned the cross-dressed leonine captains, Pyanfar and Hilfy, of C. J. Cherryh's Chanur series. Marion Zimmer Bradley's Lythande (in *Lythande*, 1986) also falls into this category, and Bradley's Magda Lorne, in *The Shattered Chain* (1976) complicates the plot by cross-dressing as an Amazon—the group of women who themselves claim the right in their culture to crossdress as men. As Marjorie Garber suggests, cross-dressing makes a space of "commutable selves" that offers an unfixed identity (Garber 1992, 32). In many of these stories, just this topic is at issue — identity. Hilfy is growing into her role of captain. Magda is struggling with her double identity as Darkovan and Terran. In Octavia Butler's *Kindred*, Dana, our point of view character, is "cross-dressed" through much of the novel, since she wears her contemporary pants in the pre-Civil War Maryland she time-travels to, and is even mistaken at times for a man. In this novel Butler appropriates this concern with cross-dressing and identity to show Dana in the process of coming to terms with her slave past. Her problems with her own black woman identity crisis are highlighted by the expectations

38. See also Lefanu 1988, 35–36 on Russ's Alyx, and Lefanu's chapter on "The Reader as Subject: Joanna Russ," 1988, 173–98.

in slave-holding Maryland that slave women do the work of men,[39] a parallel to her own situation in twentieth-century Los Angeles, where Dana does blue-collar work in order to survive as a writer. Even her husband Kevin, who adapts as a white man more easily to the leisured role of master in Dana's slave past, expects service from her, in the future as well as in the past.

In *Drinking Sapphire Wine* (1977), Tanith Lee, with the science fictional technique of alternative technologies, enlarges cross-dressing to cross-bodying. In Lee's future, robots service humans, protecting them until death is impossible. Robots grow alternative organic bodies for humans, and when a human is injured or commits suicide, robots simply replace the faulty body and the person goes on. People have, then, the ability to design their own bodies for future use, in case of accident, and adolescents frequently commit suicide in order to move to a fashionable new body. As Marjorie Garber suggests, the construction of gender is literalized and essentialized by the cross-dresser — and taken into the crosser's own creative hands (Garber 1992, 47). The "I" of *Drinking Sapphire Wine* is a male at the beginning of the novel, a female at the end. Since she/he designs both bodies, s/he has taken cross-dressing very literally into her/his own hands.

But Garber's point about essentialism is also part of Lee's scenario for the future. Sex in this alternative world is relentlessly, essentially heterosexual. It is "natural" that men and women are tied to their biologically reproductive bodies in this future for their sexualities: men desire women and women men. The narrator confesses, for example, that "As a male, my paternal urge was around ten percent, very low. But when a female, though only at certain intervals, the [reproductive] yearning came strong" (Lee 1977, 71). But it is also understood that not everyone gets the right body to begin with, and that curiosity and experimentation are also "natural," as well as fashionable. " 'I wonder what sex Danor is going to be for the homecoming,' " a friend asks (12). And so, although "predominantly" (10) male or female, everyone crosses in this future. Sometimes male, sometimes female, everyone who is hetero-sexual in this future is also bisexual, since they have had sex with both males and females, who are often the same people in variously-gendered bodies. "Our sexual leanings, despite our current bodies, seem fairly fluid, so I'm not sticking any labels on anyone" (133), reports the narrator of her group. Only when a

---

39. I think in *Kindred* (1979) that Octavia Butler was especially influenced by Angela Davis' powerful early essay on "Reflections on the Black Woman's Role in the Community of Slaves" (1971). Davis is writing against the stereotype of the black woman as matriarch of the black family under slavery, reconstituting a heroic vision of black women: "It is true that [the black woman] was a victim of the myth that only the woman, with her diminished capacity for mental and physical labor, should do degrading household work. Yet the alleged benefits of the ideology of femininity did not accrue to her. She was not sheltered or protected. . . . She was also there in the field, alongside the man, toiling under the lash from sun-up to sun-down" (18).

colony of people in exile develops, does a lesbian couple emerge, since those two no longer have the capability to cross to heterosexual bodies (170).

In *Drinking Sapphire Wine*, Lee develops androgyny to define the narrator's experience of self-discovery: culturally taught to be dependent on the robots, the narrator learns that s/he is self-sufficient when exiled for her crimes to the desert. In a sympathetic parody of the Robinson Crusoe story of many science fictions, Lee guides her narrator to make a garden in her lonely desert, "green shoots blowing like fine green hair before that morning wind. . . . Some in bloom — little flowers or buds that might turn out to be anything" (Lee 1977, 82). Thus, through work on the garden and reflection on her past experiences in many bodies, s/he realizes her self-sufficiency: "Sexuality hadn't been much of a problem yet. I was too worn out. . . . Still, the reflection of the beautiful girl with the eyes of the beautiful young man I had formerly been induced in me a kind of sinuous excitement I was going to have to beware of" (91–92). In Lee's novel, the narrator, both male and female, claims sexual desire for the self in a narcissistic dream that aids the narrator's growth out of dependence on robot servants and her/his adolescent peer group.

Lee develops the androgynous nature of the narrator further to define ideal love as between two people who understand each other as if they had been in the other's shoes — literally in this case, since Hatta cross-dresses in the narrator's last male body in order to make her love him. When Hatta (in the body of the romantic male poet that the narrator had formerly worn) makes love to the narrator in her new female body (the tanned female explorer), Hatta asks, "Was I as good as you were when you were me?" (Lee 1977, 152)

In both *Drinking Sapphire Wine*, and also its prequel, *Don't Bite the Sun* (1976), featuring the same narrator, Lee undermines the science fiction convention of the male narrator through sequential androgyny: her narrator experiences both male and female existence, frequently speaking from all of her/his sexualities at once. Since Lee is experimenting with comedy in the genre of science fiction, her multiply-bodied, multiply-gendered grotesque narrator offers, instead of the singular view of the traditional narrator, a carnival of sexual experience and point of view.

Melissa Scott's *The Kindly Ones* offers an androgynous hero through a different technique, one that explores a future where the equity principle, "it doesn't matter if you're a man or a woman," truly operates. At the end of the novel, readers still don't know what biological sex the industriously sexual first person narrator, Trey Maturin, is.[40] S/he operates in an urban culture

---

40. Similarly, in Melissa Scott's *Shadow Man* (1995), the conarrator Warreven is legally a man on Hara, a colonial world that still recognizes only two sexes, but thinks of self as a "herm," one of the nine legally-recognized Concord federation sexes. The other narrator, a Concord businessman, Mhyre Tatian, belonging to our Terran future expanded into space but not our culture, disoriented by the Haran insistence on two sexes, longs for the world he left, where "people had been sane, reasonable, ordinary, had known who and what they were" (115).

where education and career are not limited by gender, and where bisexuality flourishes: Scott carefully describes in erotic detail the bodies of her/his sexual partners, but not her/his own. In the middle of the novel, nostalgic for the world of acting s/he had left behind to become a Mediator and Medium (speaker to ghosts, social outcasts on Orestes), Trey goes to bed with an Orestian actor, Rehur: "He shaved off his body hair, to make it easier for the puppeteers to add later detail. It was startling, but not unattractive, and there were lithe muscles beneath that hairless skin" (Scott 1987, 67). There are hints that Trey had also at one time slept with Leith, a female former Peacekeeper and now pilot. And Trey finds her/himself actively desiring the female heir of Electra, Signe Orillon, with her "rather long face, with a starkly defined cheek and jaw, and the Orillon slanted eyes," and her lips that "gave strength to an otherwise delicate face" (242). When Trey finds out that Signe is married, s/he feels "a moment's pang" (242).

Scott teases the reader, provoking our anxiety to categorize people by gender. She also underlines the narrator's bisexuality and invisible gender by numerous references to cross-dressing and androgyny. Hahala, an actress, is described as compelling and "virile" (Scott 1987, 51). Trey envies an actor playing a part s/he would have liked, a part that could traditionally be played by either sex. The Orestian theater includes plays for "minne" and "manne," actors who specialize in cross-dressed roles (106, 197). The computers in this future speak in "sexless" tones (240), and the soldiers in the final battle are so disfigured by their wounds, that their gender is not possible to determine: "He—no, she" (315).

The androgyny of the narrator, as well as these other numerous references to cross-dressing underscore not only the breaking of our culture's gender codes by this distant future culture, but also the breaking of other codes. Orestians live by a rigid code of honor that separates people into legitimate citizens belonging to feudal families bound to observe feud with other families when their matriarch or patriarch requires; para-anin, who ritually step outside of the family to avoid feud but also give up citizens' rights; and ghosts, who are declared outlawed, and are despised. In her study of cross-dressing in literature and popular culture, Marjorie Garber has argued that frequently the transvestite indicates a "category crisis," when a category other than gender is up for questioning. That is the case with class and social code in Scott's *The Kindly Ones*: from the beginning of the novel we experience the destruction of our own gender codes; by the end of the novel, we witness the destruction of the Orestian code, and the class of ghosts is outlawed (Scott 1987, 333–38).

In this traditionally masculine plot, where a military venture restores a wrongfully deposed heir to rule, Scott uses the pointedly ungendered narrator and Mediator to challenge science fiction practices of storytelling. This particular universe is saved by two female pilots, a fifteen-year-old male heir, a transvestite resistance leader, and a bisexual counselor with unnamed gender.

The new rulers instituted will be limited by constitutional rights and a new assembly in which all classes are represented. The convention of masculine narration, even in this rigorously realistic science fiction, is further undermined by multiple narrators: bisexual Trey, who tells most of the story, yet shares point of view with Leith and Guild, the pilots and co-plotters, who also share a lesbian partnership (Scott 1987, 147).

By narrating so much of the story from this androgynous viewpoint, from an unidentifiable gender, Scott achieves two results important for her equal rights gender politics. The increasing anxiety a reader feels to know the narrator's gender drives home how important to our current culture gender is, while the length of the novel and the central importance of Trey's numerous actions demonstrate that, indeed, we can imagine a world where sex is not stereotyped, where women can do all men can do, and where men can do all women can do.

In *Gender Trouble: Feminism and the Subversion of Identity* Judith Butler argues that "the cultural matrix through which gender identity has become intelligible requires that certain kinds of 'identities' cannot 'exist' — that is, those in which gender does not follow from sex and those in which the practices of desire do not 'follow' from either sex or gender. . . . They appear only as developmental failures or logical impossibilities from within that domain" (Butler 1990, 17). In science fiction, as Scott's *The Kindly Ones* most emphatically demonstrates, the writer can disrupt this "logical process," because she can revise social norms so that a practice our culture designates "illogical" becomes "logical." She can even create a sex from which such an "illogical" gender or practice of desire follows "by nature."

Such is the logical illogic of alien androgynes in many contemporary science fictions by women. In Jane Palmer's *The Watcher*, part of the story is told from the point of view of Opu, an alien from the species Ojalie, winged and beaked hermaphrodites, through whose exotic sexuality Palmer explores the disjunct roles of modern women: career woman and mother. Under an entirely different biological and social system, where reproductive mates "both inseminate and give birth" (Palmer 1986, 2) Opu lives apart, flies home from work, yet, like today's working mothers comically suffers a household irrevocably changed by her child: "As things would immediately be dislodged and flung about as soon as she had tidied up, she had long since stopped bothering and only invited the most broad-minded of her friends in" (3).

In *A Literature of Their Own: British Women Novelists From Bronte to Lessing*, Elaine Showalter argues that "The androgynous mind is, finally, a utopian projection of the ideal artist: calm, stable, unimpeded by consciousness of sex. . . . Androgyny . . . represents an escape from the confrontation with femaleness or maleness. Her ideal artist mystically transcends sex, or has none" (1977, 289). In contrast, the androgynous narrators of science fiction by women are industriously sexual. As Judith Butler points out, the androgyne is not outside the categories of sex, but instead, serves to confuse and redistribute the elements of sexuality, transgressing and challenging its categories (1990, 100–1). In science fiction, androgyny—the failure to repeat the socially expected performance in gender—doesn't signal getting gender "wrong"; nor does it signal an absence of the body and sexuality. Instead, it signals a move to another culture where alternative sexual possibilities can exist, or to a reality not formerly perceived although all around us. In Carol Emshwiller's short story, for example, the mother narrates "The Childhood of the Human Hero" (1973), watching her son grow up, worrying about his future. The mother as narrator suggests that here at least gender should be safe and predictable, and that surely here the woman writer may write her way beyond the convention of the male narrator. But when the son breaks another ballpoint pen doing the problem on "Farmer Brown who plows half an acre in twenty minutes and Farmer Jones who has plowed thirty-two acres in seventy-six hours," the mother reassures her son, "I was a boy once myself, mother though I have become" (Emshwiller 1974, 230). Suddenly into the comfortable stereotypes of mother and son intrude the complex interaction and identifications that human emotional relationships necessitate. After a list of the magic tricks and surprise packages the son sends away for, the stuff that makes a boy into a hero in our culture, the mother offers, "Are you willing to take a chance on a secret? Listen then, the mother has both breasts and penis sometimes. She *has* to. There's no other solution to some of those knotty little problems of sexual identification; face them every day and see who wears the blue jeans. (Everybody does)" (232). The preadolescent boy, desiring to achieve masculine gender, is countered in this story by the mother who has achieved her gender and knows that that is not the whole story. The science fiction convention of the male narrator constructed by the female writer is also a knotty little problem of sexual identification—partially solved by androgyny. As in this short story by Carol Emshwiller, androgyny generally in science fiction by women is not linked with essentialism but, instead, ironically, highlights gender as arbitrary, imposed, and merely ideal (Butler 1990, 140).

Cherry Wilder and Emma Bull: Negotiating the Paradigm

We can now turn to two novels to see how writers employ or transform the solutions that much of women's science fiction offers to the problem of the male narrator. Despite their postmodern publication dates, neither Cherry Wilder's *Second Nature* (1982) nor Emma Bull's *Bone Dance* (1991) relies on postmodern techniques to challenge science fiction realism. Rather, using the techniques of realism itself, they yet resist the convention of the male narrator, Wilder by assembling a complex of multiple narrators—male, female, and alien—and Bull by constructing an androgynous first person narrator who must uncover the secret that "his" identity is also "hers."

In *Second Nature*, Wilder offers an interrelated web of narrators—he, she, and it—who interact in social problem solving, not heterosexual romance. The complicated set of narrators buttress the text's main theme, because Wilder's novel tells the story of lost and found communication between races: as in Rebecca Ore's trilogy, Wilder's many races and species discover that "We are all aliens together." In each section of *Second Nature*, narration is limited to one point of view, but there are many such points of view. The only "I" is the alien sea monster, the Vail (Wilder 1982, 11–15 and 15–17), not an "I" for readers to hold on to or identify with, since this "I" sees a human as "a legendary creature . . . a minmer or nipper" (11). Thus the value of individualism and the authority of the narrator are disrupted. But this disruption is also posed as a problem: without individualism, without a sense of the passage of time (a point on which the Vail differ greatly from humans), why remember? One Vail reflects on just this difference between its species and humans: "I have been influenced by the minmer's preoccupation with the passing of time, the actual passage of single days and nights in the continuum. . . . 'Minmer,' I said impatiently, 'your brain is like a boru shell, full of little numbered grains of sand' " (13–14). Eventually, after migrating to escape drought, the Vail forget their annual communications with the minmer. Ironically, recontact with humans from earth restores their contact with the Vail, that and humans' ability to remember, to store in their brains facts and ideas like little grains of sand.

Besides the Vail, Wilder employs four other main points of view and two minor ones—all "human."[41] The main male narrator, Maxim Bro, is an idealist, a gentle man, a recorder and rememberer. By designing a society descended from scientist-explorers, who value remembering enough to institutionalize it, Wilder rewrites the science fiction hero as explorer but not warrior. Bro is the "Dator of Rhomary" (Wilder 1982, 19), an official appointed to record remembrances, a cultural vestige of the original scientific purpose of the expedition shipwrecked on this planet. Maxim Bro as narrator is also a highly stylized version of the conventional masculine science fiction hero: his job is gathering data, documenting geography, sorting through theories of evolution, analyzing indigenous life. For Maxim Bro, women are as alien as other species, and he observes them as objects of study rather than as partners in discovery. In one particularly telling episode, Maxim, on his way to an outpost, "trades" women with another young scientist on his way to the city (183–84).

41. In Wilder 1982, besides the alien Vail, there are two major and four minor human points of view. The story is told from Maxim Bro's male point of view, 19–58, 90–116, 166–91, 213–23, 236–54. The story is told from Gurl Hign's female point of view, 59–70, 117–32, 143–45, 191–205, and 223–27. The story is told from Los Smitwode's male point of view, 70–80, 132–43, and 205–13. The story is told from spaceship survivor Valente's male point of view, 81–90, 146–66, and 227–35. There are brief sections of points of view from early envoys to the Vail: Maire, 11, 17, and 36; and Paddy, 15.

While yet portraying Bro sympathetically, Wilder undermines Bro's heroism and, so, his point of view, by refusing him achievement of his main quest. Bro is traveling to find survivors of a ship from Earth wrecked and strewn across the planet. Bro does eventually make contacts, first with the elusive Shape-Changers, then with the legendary Vail, but these are accidental, products of a whole interwoven set of unplanned encounters, not a result of his purposeful journey. He does not make first contact with the survivors of the wreck, and thus we see that his gathering of data is always secondhand, contaminated by many tellings, not objective data at all, but already shaped into stories by other tellers and points of view. Wilder's methods of telling her story encourage us to see that even Bro's own firsthand encounters are shaped subjectively by his own point of view. "He saw them imperfectly in a haze of lights as if sunlight had flooded the cabin," we are told about Bro's perceptions of the Shape-changers; "he felt that slow lightning strike at his brain as it had done once before on the deck" (Wilder 1982, 116). This awareness of subjectivity is heightened by comments on human nature by the aliens. The Vail and the Shape Changers agree that humans are "a self-pitying race" (169). Since Maxim Bro's goal for remembering is preservation for a community, this recognition that stories are communal and subjective is not tragic. It is the reader's conception of individual heroism that is reshaped by Wilder, not Bro's expectations for himself. The people of the land of Rhomary live comfortably with the realization that science is an art of telling stories.

Not Bro, but a woman and a child out flying a kite achieve Bro's quest —making contact with two survivors from the ship from Earth. Gurl Hign and her son Ben, involved in the very domestic activities of mother looking after child and child at play, succeed as explorers.[42] Gurl Hign, female, rancher, is shadow narrator to Bro's conventional masculine narrator in the structure of Wilder's novel. As many episodes are narrated from her point of view as from Bro's, though not as many pages. She is a shadow of Bro's narration in several ways. Although there are several other points of view, all of Gurl's sections follow sections narrated from Maxim Bro's point of view. The sections narrated from Gurl's point of view thus stand as retellings, or corrections, of Bro's stories, even though they do not record the same events. For example, whereas Bro's first section ends with his being charged with his quest to find the survivors from the wrecked spaceship (Wilder 1982, 58),

---

42. Thus Wilder seems to me to be commenting on the scripts of male heroes as limiting to women writing from their own experience, in much the same way that Ursula K. Le Guin comments in "A Carrier Bag Theory of Fiction" in *Dancing at the Edge*, where she rejects "the killer story," the plot of male hero killing and conquering, in favor of the novel, "a fundamentally unheroic kind of story," a story that has not heroes but people in it, a story that may be based on women's experience: "I said it was hard to make a gripping tale of how we wrested the wild oats from their husks, I didn't say it was impossible" (1989, 168–69).

Gurl's first section begins with her dream—more accurate than Bro's hope —that humans will regain contact with the Vail (59). At the end of a later section narrated from Bro's perspective, the child Ben asks if he can come along to fly his kite and Bro declines, his mind busy with plans to row upriver to find the human survivors, and perhaps the Vail (223). In the following section narrated from Gurl's point of view, she accompanies her son Ben to the hills to fly his kite (227)—where they meet the human survivors of the wrecked spaceship climbing out of the swamp in which their lifeship has landed (234–35). And finally, as a woman, even a woman rancher on a frontier, Gurl Hign's perspective is limited even more to the secondhand nature of experience for humans, gaining knowledge from the telling. Whereas Bro directly meets the Shape-Changers, Gurl knows them only through the memory of her dead husband's reported conversation with them.

Wilder thus draws on the experiments of other women science fiction writers, pairing her main male narrator with a main female narrator, unraveling the authority of the conventional science fiction male point of view, and incorporating women's as well as disparate men's points of view. But Wilder's male and female pair do not progress into the plot of heterosexual romance, although along the way Maxim Bro marries Gurl Hign's daughter. Instead, together, and with the aid of many other members of their community, they solve the problem of the disappearance and reunion of races: comparing stories about the Shape-Changers; outfitting Bro for his trip upriver to find the shipwrecked humans where instead he finds the Vail; passing on to Gurl the guesses about shipwrecked humans that allow her to recognize the survivors when she finds them. Wilder complicates this partnership into a community by adding several other narrators: Los Smitwode, doctor at the frontier town where Gurl Hign acts informally as mayor; Valente, doctor survivor from the wrecked spaceship; and even brief tantalizing dreams of the Vail from the children Maire and Paddy who grow up (in the past) to be envoys to the Vail.

In her essay on utopias in *The Oxford Companion to Women's Writing in the United States*, Lee Cullen Khanna argues that contemporary feminist utopias offer a "deconstruction of conventional discursive categories, including the category 'human.' Indeed, such writing encourages a continuous rethinking of identity" (1995, 893). The less frequent points of view in Wilder's novel—Los Smitwode, Valente, Maire and Paddy—multiply the possible definitions of humanity, and so let us see analogies between communicating with other species and communicating across racial boundaries. In *Second Nature*, Wilder breaks down the categories of race and humanity. The inhabitants of Rhomary Land, cut off from Earth for centuries, are no longer human: they are six-fingered and are developing VESP; they are short and splayfooted because of the gravity that is heavier than Earth's; they are dark brown because of Rhomary's sun. This new race is named by the Vail "minmers" (misnamed for "human," which the Vail can't pronounce). The "humans" who find the "human" inhabitants of Rhomary again, though, are also lost, forced immigrants, and not of uniform race: one is a tall blonde Swiss doctor; one is a short dark Chinese crewwoman; one is a tall metallic android. Each subsequent narrator enters into dialogue with previous narrators, with varied belief in or valuing of the Vail and other races. This narrative technique, however, is not a debate, but rather a display of curiosity and communication (Wilder 1982, 115).

Human society, characteristically built out of curiosity and communicative abilities, consists for Wilder of the circulation of words, records, remembrances, and meanings partly shared, partly changed. As such, human society can extend its borders to encompass the alien, crossing its own boundaries. Wilder's view of human society is exemplified in *Second Nature* in the story of the circulation of the word "minmer." Originally the Vail's mispronunciation of the word "human" (Wilder 1982, 11), "minmer" describes for the Vail the humans on Rhomary, so the word is coined by the alien Vail and shared by Vail and people of Rhomary Land. Later, however, humans from the wrecked ship are helped by the Vail, who think them also "minmers" — passing on that word to Valente in a dream (230–31). Having learned the word from the Vail, Valente greets the colonists of Rhomary Land with that word when they meet, thus testifying to the survival of the Vail: "Yes!" says Gurl Hign, "Yes, we are the minmers!" (235). Meaning something different to each group, the term "minmer" circulates in ways that yet allow communication across differences. The different viewpoints of the characters do not separate into alternative realities, but together result in the conflicted mix that makes up a social world. For Wilder, we all begin as aliens apart; human remembering and recording mean that we may become aliens together.

As Marjorie Garber reminds us, cross-dressing indicates a "category crisis," a "failure of definitional distinction," and it marks a border crossing (Garber 1992, 16–17). Wilder marks the border crossings of her own cross-dressing as a male narrator, her exploration of the definition of human (minmer?) in the recontact story, and her celebration of the possibilities of communication across differences with the presence of an androgynous character whom she does not grant point of view. Jaygo, a hermaphrodite (Wilder 1982, 44–45), is a tantalizing background character, last hereditary envoy to the Vail (if there is ever a sequel to *Second Nature*, surely Jaygo will be the protagonist). Able to "hang in the balance," to play two "personae" (71–72), Jaygo as hermaphrodite unites past and future, linking remembrance to the adaptive mutations that are changing humans for their life on Rhomary (44–46). The category crises s/he signals, though, include not only the crossing of racial boundaries as humans reinvent themselves, but also the problem of the female man, the struggle for authorial voice of the female narrator in science fiction (Gurl Hign), the woman writer writing a male narrator: how does one gain "a status less equivocal" (Wilder 1982, 80)? Or is it necessary? "Equivocal" means, after all, multivoiced.

In her essay on her own life, "The Profession of Science Fiction, 43: Far Fetched," Cherry Wilder tells the story she heard as a child in New Zealand, of the "Lost Tribe of Murchison," cut off by an earlier earthquake, who wander out of their valley fastness into a modern town after a 1925 earthquake releases them (Wilder 1992, 7–8).[43] In *Second Nature*, the romance structure of Wilder's science fiction, the losing and finding, occurs not just for a single family, but for a whole species, and Wilder cleverly reflects this losing and finding in her form. The novel opens with the alien "I" of the Vail; it closes with a dialogue wherein the humans of Rhomary, changed by evolution on an alien planet, and again by recontact with humans from their home planet, speak again with the Vail, their benefactors. In addition, the humans of Rhomary reconnect another alien species, the Shape-changers, to the Vail. Humanity is thus defined by the ability to communicate, to remember and to find what is lost, to restore bonds between those who do not know how. The Vail do not biologically find memory easy, and the Shape-Changers choose not to make lasting connections. In the essay on her life, Wilder emphasizes her own descent from European Tasmanian immigrants and Maori natives, and she tells stories from both traditions: the Maori, too, have a Lost Tribe, the Te Anau (9). Wilder's characterization of humanity, then, makes the storyteller the most human of humans, for the storyteller is the rememberer, the keeper of what might be lost: "When we say 'I remember . . .', what does this mean? It involves storytelling, alternations in tone, and the beginnings of characterisation" (Wilder 1992, 5). Undermining the conventional male narrator of science fiction while employing his voice, Wilder builds a complicated network of interrelated storytellers, male, female, and alien—a society, crossing its own boundaries, that communicates, a society of beings who remember.

Emma Bull, in *Bone Dance* (1991), in contrast, constructs an androgynous narrator, a narrator who crosses boundaries continually within his/her own identity, while making an individual identity. For Bull, storytelling is the means to constructing identity, and Bull uses this poetic strategy to intervene in identity politics, creating a narrator who is neither male nor female and so must construct a new identity for the self—a process Bull is arguing we can all follow.

Like Melissa Scott, Emma Bull plays with the mystery of first person narration: while third person narrative always already genders the point of view, simply by applying the pronoun "he" or "she," an "I" does not. Since our culture treats male as norm, most readers immediately read the "I" as

43. See also Rousseau 1992, 15–25, on the connection to Australian colonial myths of Wilder's lost and found colonialism, nonviolent resolution, and interest in new races.

male, but Bull does not satisfy that immediate conclusion and, instead, makes a mystery of the identity of the narrator, complicating the conventional science fiction story of adolescent (male) self-discovery and offering an objective correlative in form for the mystification of gender in our culture. The other characters notice that Sparrow tries not to be noticed (Bull 1991, 79). And when Frances, who *does* know Sparrow's secret, arrives (94), she hints but does not immediately tell: "In the whole secretive fabric of your life, your body is the most private thread. Because it's the outward sign of all your secrets" (114). We are offered clues: the narrator is named Sparrow (19), has long hair in a braid (26, 154), and the first card at the Tarot reading during which Sherrea tells the narrator's future is Joan of Arc (27); for good measure, the last card is another androgynous card (28). Not until a hundred pages into the novel do we learn, however, that Sparrow is an androgyne, and even then, androgyny is not represented as essentially a single state, the way we involuntarily treat male and female in our culture: "When I figured out that either you were both or neither, I started watching for it," comments Sparrow's friend Sherrea; "You do a chameleon thing — maybe it's not even conscious — that makes you seem female when you're with a woman, and male when you're with a man. Like you take on the local coloring. In a mixed group you kind of shift around" (143–44). Unlike Scott in *The Kindly Ones*, rather than simply suspending our knowledge of the gender of the narrator, thereby creating a world where gender equity is possible but the essentialist construction of sexuality remains unchallenged, Bull defines her narrator as androgynous, intervening into identity politics with her third term — "I'm not a man. . . . I'm not a woman, either," says Sparrow (Bull 1991, 160).

In *Bone Dance*, the science fiction master narrative — of male adolescent achieving adulthood by rescuing the world, thus earning a place in society — is turned around. Bull's hero-narrator, not masculine (not feminine either), must first construct an identity and earn a community, and only then can s/he rescue the world. Moreover, the identity must not be too solid, for the metamorphic possibility of Sparrow is part of Sparrow's strength: a dream tells him/her, "Your left foot is in the past. Your right foot is in the present. . . . You are the dancer between the old world and the new" (Bull 1991, 266).

Legba, the Hoodoo spirit or *loa*, androgyne, trickster, symbolizing metamorphosis (Bull 1991, 137), first seems to be Sparrow's patron. But it is Oya Iansa, cross-dresser, goddess of the whirlwind, who spoke in Sparrow's dream: "You are the dancer between the old world and the new, because I made you to be so" (266). For these loa, as for Judith Butler, gender is not static, but always becoming (Butler 1990, 111–12). "Would you prefer the evening gown, or the tuxedo?" (Bull 1991, 116) asks Sparrow, wearing jeans, of Frances, who complains about Sparrow's choice of clothes. Even when s/he dresses in the morning, Sparrow must make choices about what gender to be, and s/he is limited to jeans if s/he wants to be both at once.

But Sparrow stands in two worlds in ways other than sexuality, as well. In this near future dystopia, scientists of a hundred years previous have invented a way for minds to house themselves in others' bodies, calling these altered people "horsemen," because they ride others. The horsemen were scientists, used for espionage, to interfere especially in South American politics. Unable to control their ability to take a new body, however, government soon lost control of the horsemen, and banding together, the horsemen took the United States hostage with an atomic bomb, some naively aiming to enforce peace, others to gain power. One, Tom Worecski, forced the others to detonation, creating the fallen world of this future. Frances is a horseman, complicit in this act without intending it, and hunting down the other horsemen to prevent further abuse of power.

According to Mick and Frances, Sparrow was a constructed body, a "horse" or "*cheval*," never supposed to achieve individual consciousness, designed to be ridden by either male or female horsemen in order to keep them from taking the bodies of living people (Bull 1991, 100–1). A problem that Sparrow must solve, then, is constructing an identity across boundaries of male and female, past and future. It is no easy task, since s/he came to consciousness with memories involving skills and languages, but no personal history. Mick, a horseman who befriends and then betrays Frances, fears that Sparrow is another horseman, pinning the androgyne to a possible gender: " 'What if he — she — doesn't know?' Mick said desperately. 'What if it's one of us, but messed up, so he doesn't remember?' " (101) Sparrow must learn to discard this identity and construct one of his/her own, but one still multiple. Through such multiple identifications, argues Judith Butler, comes a complex identity (67, 76).

The first step in Sparrow's quest, then, is discovering this history. But history does not supply identity. Two mysteries remain, one enforced by others, one repressed by the self. Sparrow has gaps of days in consciousness because someone has ridden him/her: s/he has been "shut out of my own mind" (Bull 1991, 11); s/he must find out what his/her body, the "other half" (85), did while memory stopped. Although memories are never returned to Sparrow, eventually s/he finds out that Mick was the horseman who rode the body. This retrieval of some memory triggers one kind of identification, and so the beginnings of an identity: Sparrow is a *cheval*, a horse, and so takes a position as victimized by a superior class. But Sparrow also must sort through the mystery of his/her "colorful origin" (12), the repressed memories of first consciousness. In a scene reminiscent of the monster's birth in *Frankenstein*, Sparrow was born when s/he awoke to an empty laboratory filling with water, fought a way out through dead bodies to the surface of Lake Pontchartrain in Louisiana (105–9), and chose a name (217). Sparrow thus remembers beginning the process of constructing the self, but has stopped that construction from fear of not being human. Sparrow must complete the new self before achieving the other tasks of the quest — toppling Tom Worecski's tyrannical rule.

One constructs an identity in Bull's novel, not by killing someone and taking his place, as in the traditional science fiction adventure novel, but through telling stories and making community. In the language that Sparrow and other characters use to talk about sexual identity, Bull demonstrates the impoverishment of language for this necessary task: because there are so many ways to talk about male and female, there are few to talk about other possibilities. Sparrow can be "it" (Bull 1991, 102 and 180), "hor . . ." (short for "horse" but with an obvious pun, 104), "neuter" (113), a "chameleon" (158), "him/her" (199, 200 and 204), or "Whatchacallit" (273). Since language as it currently exists (or even as it exists in Sparrow's future), does not offer an identity for Sparrow, s/he must make an identity for him/herself, creating a narrative language to replace the missing pronouns for a person who does not fit the male or female molds. "I couldn't imagine walking in that body," Sparrow says of a man in a dream s/he has, and of the woman, "I couldn't imagine walking in hers" (239).

Sparrow creates a new identity, however, also through language. "Identity magic is the oldest and easiest kind there is. It's what language is for" (Bull 1991, 210), says Josh, the doctor at the Hoodoo Engineers settlement who heals Sparrow. Josh is one accepting audience for whom Sparrow tries on this new identity: "I told him what I was and how I'd managed to end up blood-boltered in his front yard. Josh whistled and invoked gods in all the appropriate places" (220). Frances, because of her constructed identity as a horseman, is another: "I told the whole story [to Frances] without looking up. I had never told it to anyone. I'd been so careful never to even want to tell it that I'd mostly forgotten it myself" (108), reports Sparrow. Because the story of male and female constrain our tellings, Bull is pointing out, we do not hear the possibility of other kinds of identities. We have to learn to speak our own stories, not those imposed on us. Near the end, Sparrow records, "I've tried to faithfully reproduce the person who woke up on the river flats, and understand, and forgive" (276), but "life is not a finished story" (277).

Bull uses the androgynous narrator to move the science fiction novel from gender politics to identity politics. She employs the metaphor of making oneself by telling one's story to argue against an essentialist position even for this extreme test case of the person biologically (essentially?) both male and female. "The origin of my body and my mind didn't matter," Sparrow discovers; "I, the part of me that learned, that called on my memories, that knew I'd pulled a plant like this before, that had moved this hand to do it, was fifteen years old and innocent of evil or good. Neutral. From here forward, I was blank tape; what would be recorded there, and when, and why, was up to me" (Bull 1991, 214). The constructionist identity politics is underlined by Sparrow's unstated desire for Kris, the woman who taught

Sparrow to weed a garden at the community where s/he recovers, and his/her disappointment when s/he sees her with another woman in a lesbian romance (212).[44] Bull's is a curious but savvy move, to essentialize the political issue through the androgynous body, in order to argue for social construction of identity. "What happens if we take apart the binaries and build something else with a different language?" Bull asks us. Her answer is that we come to know how deeply constructed we are, and how much we may take a hand in our own constructions.

For Bull and for Sparrow, however, making community is just as important as making the self.[45] At first, Sparrow lives only by the Deal, a philosophy that baldly espouses free market trade and refuses binding exchanges: "Money, bright and folding, hard and soft, was running in its well-worn channels. Objects and services were passing from one hand to another, and by that alchemy were turned to gold, purifying with each transaction" (Bull 1991, 38).[46] Living by the deal, and afraid to acknowledge his/her bodily difference, Sparrow rejects community: "I have no friends" (150).[47] After sacrificing him/herself to unwanted sadistic sexual practices to help Frances to escape, Sparrow is rescued by friends and rewarded by membership in a community outside the city (209). When Frances responds to Sparrow's former sacrifice by refusing to let Sparrow go alone on the quest back to the city, Sparrow asks with anguish, "Why the hell do people have friends?" (250). Sparrow achieves his/her identity not as an individual but within a community, at the same time acknowledging the painfulness of social responsibility and caring.

The utopian island in the river beside the city, and the utopian commu-

44. In an e-mail comment to me after reading this section on her novel, Emma Bull cautioned,

> Your analysis of Sparrow's attitude toward Kris really startled me. Sparrow dislikes all physical contact, and is frightened and repulsed by sexual contact, even healthy sex (see *Bone Dance*, pg. 164, in which Sparrow involuntarily "eavesdrops" on Frances and Mick having sex in the next room). The scene in which Sparrow first meets Kris (207–8) is one of a series in which Sparrow is trying to rebuild the kind of purely superficial relationship to society that he/she had before coming to the Hoodoo Engineers. What disturbs Sparrow about the sight of Kris and her lover at the bonfire, what disturbs him/her about the whole evening's festivities, is the easy openness and friendship among all these people. In the case of Kris and her lover, add to that their ease of physical contact, which is almost impossible for Sparrow, and you have Sparrow's nose rubbed in all the pleasures of human community that Sparrow thinks will never be accessible to him/her.

45. In an e-mail comment to me, Emma Bull remarked, "I found that the strong sense of community that underlies Voudon and the other Afro-Diasporic religions made a lot of sense to me, and had a big influence on both the plot and the themes of the book."

46. In Bull 1991, on the deal, see also 12, 17, 51, 62. 76, 150, 158, 204, 232, and 245.

47. On Sparrow's refusal to acknowledge friends, see also Bull 1991, 153, and 205–6.

nity outside the city where Sparrow recovers share an appropriately utopian philosophy, hoodoo in which equitable spirits oppose markets and monopolies, trying to keep energy circulating in free gift exchange. These are the *loa*, the ancestors, one of whom claims to have made Sparrow, and they are handy spirits to have around for "this rough, hollow new world" (Bull 1991, 93), a new world that humans have not discovered but have made from their mismanagement. Combining old science and new, Bull imagines a utopian science practiced by the Hoodoo engineers (232–33, 247) that tries to undo the mistakes of the past, that rescues zoo animals and frees them back to the wild, that opposes the energy monopoly of the city boss in order to promote nonpolluting wind and solar technologies. In the *loa*, Bull provides symbols of a philosophy that disdains binary oppositions: "The people in the towers don't think about the spirits. They don't know how the world is shaped. And so they give it a shape, and try to make everything fit it. They separate the right from the left, the man from the woman, the plant from the animal, the sun from the moon. They only want to count to two. Ah!" (136) This Hoodoo utopian science advocates acceptance of difference and alternative sexualities by the androgynous symbol of Legba, Sparrow's patron (matron?).

Aided by the spirits, Sparrow and his/her community do free the city from the tyranny of Tom Worecski. But after the fight, the novel does not give us a romance ending. The only sexual relations described occur in the rape scene, where Sparrow sells his/her body to a sadist to rescue Frances (Bull 1991, 194). Although by the ending both Sherrea and Theo have admitted to crushes on Sparrow (160), the only relationships offered Sparrow at the end are a community of utopian Hoodoo friends, and partnership with Frances on her adventures. As in the science fiction master narrative of the male adolescent saving the world and earning self and community, romance is not the important achievement, but identity: Sparrow, a monster, isolated from others, finds a self and saves his/her world. However, the self is much more tentative and the world much more in flux than in a 1950s version of such a tale.

In the figure of the androgynous narrator, this novel provides a contemporary fantasy about potential entrapment in male or female roles, and celebrates a desire to be a third or neither (Garber 1992, 217). Bull transfers to issues of sexuality and identity the narrative strategies developed by women science fiction writers to treat gender and identity. I used a quotation from this novel to begin this chapter on the male narrator: "What if Sleeping Beauty woke behind the briers alone, in the dark, to the knowledge that the curse was not sleep but waking. . . . She/he/it would have no choice but to make something of the awakening. I do, as best I can" (Bull 1991, 276). For Bull, even memory is not trustworthy (276), and so narrative is as chancy a procedure as making an identity. Narrative is "three-quarters lying," admits Sparrow; "I can't have remembered everything; and the process of trying is like reconstructing a dream. You put the connective tissue in where it never existed, because without it, you've got, not a narrative, but a string of senseless images" (276). In creating subjectivity, Catherine Belsey reminds us, ideology masks as coherence and plenitude, when it is really inconsistent and contradictory (Belsey 1985, 54). Bull's androgynous narrator is a likely symbol of this apparent coherence but real contradiction in subjectivity entangled with ideology.

Angelika Bammer suggests that "Reality can only be changed by transgressing the limits of what has been declared possible" (1991, 97). She is speaking of utopias, but her observation applies equally well to the androgynous narrators of many science fictions by women. In twentieth-century science fiction women writers offer, instead of the traditional male gender of narration in the genre, gender reversed, gender ambiguous, or gender erased. They undermine the male narrator through conversion, parody, or revenge. They reverse the dominant gender or write multiple narrators that include the voices of females and ambiguously gendered aliens. They erase gender in aliens of unknown sex or in androgynous humans. All of these strategies, still falling under the rubric of "realistic" narrative techniques, demonstrate the creativity with which women, even under enormous constraint, resist the master narratives.

Epilogue
Virtual Women in Global Science Fiction

It is 1996. Science fiction has emigrated beyond Canada, Britain, the United States, and France. It is no longer a purely Western phenomenon. All over the world, women are writing science fiction, too.[1]

In this book, I have examined the conventions of science fiction as a genre as constraints for women writers in the West, and the writers' varied and creative solutions for overcoming these constraints. In response to a masculinist science that excludes women, women writers of science fiction have created myriad visions of utopian science. In response to the conventional character of the alien woman, women writers have taken her point of view and moved her to the center of their stories, in order to examine feminine experiences but also to analyze the processes of alienation. In response to the tradition of the male narrator, women writers have cross-dressed as male narrators, converting and punishing them and they have re-created gender to include alien sexualities and androgynous figures.

In the introduction, I have surveyed the criticism on science fiction by women and feminist utopias that explores these genres as liberatory for women, and introduced the constraints of the genre that work as obstructions for women writers. I explored Mary Shelley's *Frankenstein* as a model for later women's science fiction in handling these constraints. In Shelley's novel, Frankenstein's tragedy depends on the exclusion of women and of traditionally feminine traits from masculine science. The parallels between the monster and Safie present the woman as alien. And the convention of male narration is destabilized by multiple and competing male accounts, including one from the "abnormal" male monster.

1. Besides the stories I'm about to discuss in the epilogue, the first collection of Russian science fiction by women will be out soon, edited by Larisa Mihaylova of Moscow State University. In China, women regularly contribute science fiction stories to popular science journals; see, for example, Qinglan Wang and Yi Wang, "Dolphin Brand Soft Candy," in *Scientific Times* 1980. My thanks to Dali Tan for finding this short story, and to her parents for translating it for me.

In the chapter on "Utopian Science" we have explored the responses of contemporary women science fiction writers to the problems of masculinist science. How can women write science fiction, if science excludes women as agent-scientists and women's issues as worthy of examination, and further objectifies nature as feminine in order to control it? Using feminist science theories by Ruth Bleier, Elizabeth Fee, Hilary Rose, Evelyn Fox Keller, and Donna Haraway, I have set up a paradigm of the ways that women writers create a utopian science to allow them entry into the literary genre. In science fiction by women, women scientists participate in science, and redefine science and its discourses so that science responds to women's issues (such as reproduction); in addition, women writers see science as origin story and offer contesting accounts; moreover, women writers imagine a future science in partnership with nature, a science that incorporates subjective as well as objective analyses, and is organized as a decentralized rather than hierarchical institution. In analyses of Naomi Mitchison's *Memoirs of a Spacewoman*, Barbara Paul's *Under the Canopy*, and Octavia Butler's "Bloodchild," we looked at the differing ways that women writers place themselves in conversation with this paradigm of utopian science fiction in women's writings. Naomi Mitchison struggles with the terms of her scientific utopia for women as she builds it, distrusting and hoping at once, while Barbara Paul both elaborates a critique of masculinist science by testing it as a story for women, and also implicates white women in its imperialist discourses. In her short story, the African-American writer Octavia Butler imagines a future with all of the characteristics of the paradigm of feminist science which yet is a dystopia.

In a chapter on "The Woman as Alien," I examined the ways in which women writers adopt the generic trope of the woman as alien from men's science fiction in order to contest this marginalization of women. Using feminist psychoanalytic theories by Chodorow, Dinnerstein, Benjamin, and others, as cultural documents rather than as essentialist explanations of universal nature, I analyzed the paradigms of the heterosexual humanoid woman as alien caught in a sadistic earthman's script, the woman as machine representing the social role of women serving men, the woman as animal symbolizing the messy carnality of women's role as mother, and the minority woman as alien among us. In a discussion of Joan Slonczewski's *A Door into Ocean* and Carol Emshwiller's *Carmen Dog*, we looked at the ways that women writers adapt these generic paradigms to their individual politics. Slonczewski offers double ambiguous utopias of alien women: ones who have achieved equity, and ones who have developed a lesbian community. Her doubled utopia becomes a double bind that exposes the problems in contemporary feminist politics. Emshwiller uses the woman as animal to offer a loving comic parody of the women's movement.

In a final chapter on "Cross-dressing as a Male Narrator," I examined the ways in which women writers subvert the generic convention of male narration. Using feminist narrative literary theory by Christine Brooke-Rose, Patricia Yaeger, Judith Butler and others, and theories of cross-dressing by Marjorie Garber and others, I explored the paradigms through which women writers seem to accept yet actually subvert the constraint of male narration. Unlike mainstream fiction, where most writers write generally from their own gender, science fiction women writers still write two-thirds of their novels from male points of view. They subvert this convention in paradigmatic ways: cross-dressing as male narrators but converting them to feminist politics or punishing them with feminine stories; creating naive male narrators whose biases readers may feel superior to; interpolating women's voices inside of male narration and fragmenting the authorized male voice through multiple narrators — not only men and women, but also frequently aliens; fusing voices or points of view in communal narration; and constructing cross-dressed narrators who "pass" as male but reveal themselves as female or androgynous by the end. In a discussion of Cherry Wilder's *Second Nature* and Emma Bull's *Bone Dance* as fictions that en-gender narrative, we discovered ways that they exposed and resisted a universal male narrative voice, Wilder through multiple narrators, Bull through an androgynous narrator.

How do these science fiction conventions, and Western women's solutions to them, translate to other cultures? To conclude this study of science fiction by women, let us look briefly at new directions, at science fiction's outward impetus, examining one story from Argentina and one from India.

Angélica Gorodischer, born in 1941 in Buenos Aires, Argentina, has written a variety of science fiction and utopian stories, including *Trafalgar* (1967), *Las Pelucas* (1970), *Casta luna electrónica* (1975), and *Bajo las jubeas en Flor* (1988)(Agosin 1992, 330). Several of her stories are translated in Marjorie Agosin's collection of fantastic and science fictional stories from South America, *Secret Weavers: Stories of the Fantastic by Women of Argentina and Chile*. In one of them, "The Perfect Married Woman," we can follow the transmutations that the conventions of science fiction have undergone as it has emigrated to other cultures.

First, there is no male narrator in "The Perfect Married Woman," although Gorodischer uses one in another story — "Under the Flowering Tulips" (Agosin 1992, 259–80). Instead, "The Perfect Married Woman" is told from the third person point of view of the title character, a housewife in a small Argentinian town. Buried in the realistic narrative is a critique of Western science, but no utopian vision of a feminist science. The critique centers on the importation of Western technology to shore up the deadly routine of the South American housewife. The housewife cleans, knits, shops, cooks, washes clothes for her husband and son, irons twice a week, watches television, and reads *TV Guide* (243). She keeps track of the passage of days of the week by the television soap operas she watches (246). She lives in two realities, the drudgery of her housework, and "the life crises that she sees on

TV and reads about in *TV Guide"* (245). Western technology does not make her housewife's job easier; it simply marks the routine of it and offers escape from an otherwise fierce anger.

While not an alien woman, this housewife is an alienated woman, full of special powers. She is alienated by her routine of drudgery, so that husband, daughter, and son appear as a list of duties, rather than as companions. But she is also alienated by her unstated anger at her role. Her alienation is symbolized in this story by a special power. At times "doors behaved satisfactorily, though in general they were still acting dumb and leading to dining rooms, kitchens, laundry rooms, bedrooms and offices" (244). When they behaved "satisfactorily," she opened a door and it led, instead, to the Gobi desert (244), or some other exotic place—"she visited three monasteries, seven libraries, and the highest mountains in the world, and who knows how many theaters, cathedrals, jungles, refrigeration plants, dens of vice, universities, brothels, forests, stores, submarines, hotels, trenches, islands, factories, palaces, hovels, towers and hell" (245). The doors, like TV, offered her a virtual reality, one more rewarding than her scrubbing and ironing.

At times, the doors even offered her adventure, politics, the chance to change events with worldwide consequences, the chance to act. In one scene, she enters a bathroom, sees a man in the tub, and cuts off his head (245). In another scene, she enters a tent, sees a man with a woman on a bed and a sword in the corner, and beheads the man (245–46). These scenes are juxtaposed with and contrasted with her routine—taking her daughter to the doctor, mopping the patio (245–46). Her own alienation, her anger at the men who historically and presently have control of a life she does not control, expresses itself in these violent acts. Gorodischer magnifies the importance of this perfect housewife by our realization of the historical events she is influencing: the man in the bed is Holofernes—slain by a woman, Judith. Are the other murders also historical? Her violence thus makes us see that it is not the television or the doors that offer virtual reality, but the housewifely role. Her reality is her anger: "On Monday and Thursday afternoons, when she irons shirt collars, she thinks of the slit necks and the blood, and she waits" (246). Her anger changes events: she burns down a theater, pushes a man off a balcony, destroys a manuscript, buries the weapons of an army sleeping in a forest, and blows a hole in a dam (246).

The effects of her anger are fearsome and chilling. But the narrator has carefully kept the two sides of the doors separate, the one the routine of housework, boring but ordinary, the other the adventures, full of grim violence. In the last sentence, the narrator breaks through this separation: "Again, she runs the iron over the front of the shirt and remembers the other side of the doors that are always carefully closed in her house, that other side where the things that happen are much less abominable than the ones we experience on this side, as you can easily understand" (247). Here, the horror switches sides. It is not the murders that are abominable, explains the narrator matter-of-factly, but the killing boredom and waste of life and intelligence in the housewife's life. The narrator invites us all to understand, to sympathize with this anger — "you can easily understand." The anger expressed in the alternative reality is nourishing. The virtual reality of the gendered role of housewife is killing.

Manjula Padmanabran is currently writing and publishing science fiction in India. In her short story, "Unfaithful Servants" (1994),[2] Padmanabran adopts the doubled narration of the heterosexual romance to undermine the science fiction convention of male narration, as we have seen many Western women do. Her narration, however, begins on the other side of the story, not with the romance culminating in union (and conversion of the male), but after marriage, with disaffection and alienation between the couple. This alienation is represented in narration by the inclusion of sections from the point of view of holographs, virtual electrical copies of the husband and wife. These copies of the narrators are the title characters — the "unfaithful servants," who choose to love each other rather than to perform the murders they were created to do. Such a narrative device is particularly disturbing to gender because of its clouding of gendered boundaries: are holographs males and females, illusions of them, or machine-like its? In addition, Padmanabran carefully descends the social ladder through her points of view, critiquing hierarchy: Rauf's upper-class masculine point of view opens the story (Padmanabran 1994, 31–35), then we switch to feminine point of view with Uaan (35–36), then to the holographic male servant's point of view (36–39), a brief interlude of holographic shared point of view — male and female — (37) merging into a "they" (38), and finally a return to Rauf's (39–40). We have moved from upper-class male to female to lower-class it, returning to the upper-class male's point of view as readers who resist identification with him.

Also in Padmanabran's story, we see a "utopian" but not a feminist science, accompanied by a critique of the mechanical lives that increased technology without increased wisdom might bring. In this future India, the married protagonists' palace is parked in orbit above the earth, pressurized, warmed by solar heat, serviced by a shuttle (31). Technology has developed a "slumberizer unit" to help one sleep, and "Quik-Solv" to make suicide painless and effortless (35). The Western-like name for the suicide pill illuminates one target of Padmanabran's critique of science: the Western capitalist appropriation of science for marketing purposes, no matter the damaging effects to consumers.

This future science is equitable. The male and female protagonist to-

2. I wish to thank Madhurina Shah for finding this story by Padmanabran.

gether have perfected and marketed the invention of holographic illusions—
even holographic pets. Women are equal participants in science, and the
wife, Uaan is "design consultant," "technical advisor" (31), and eventually
partner in her husband Rauf's company (32). But the mere inclusion of
women in this hypertechological science has not made a difference to its
destructive effects. And, although Uaan and Rauf have fabulous wealth and
fabulous technology, they are not happy. Rauf is committing adultery and
Uaan is full of revenge.

In this short story, Padmanabran appropriates the science fiction convention of human as machine to apply it equitably to both her male and female
protagonists. At breakfast with his wife, Rauf is surprised when she disappears
with a "ZZZZZSSSSSSSSSST!" (31) In a particularly telling moment, Rauf
wonders if it was she he made love to or the holograph (33). She has made a
copy of herself that fools even Rauf and preempts his own design of a copy
of himself to cover for his absences during adulterous meetings. The holographic representations suggest the mechanized quality of a life of high
technology and the alienation that an ambitious, competitive, married couple
feel from each other as a result. Who is real? How can one trust? Indeed,
Rauf's suspicions mingle anxiety about his wife's revenge through adultery,
with fear of her revealing business secrets (32). Both have designed the
holographs in order to murder each other from a distance (36). In this future
capitalistic state, both the man and the woman have replaced themselves in
order to render themselves invulnerable, but instead, they have only rendered
themselves unhappy.

Eventually, the orbiting palace is blown up from the electrical currents
generated by the holographic copies' orgasm. Like Faye Weldon's military
academy, blown up by dissension between upper and lower classes, this event
is symbolic of the inevitable self-destruction of Western-style technology. The
story ends, however, not with this conflagration, but with the "return" of Rauf
and Uaan. From Rauf's point of view, we contemplate, "what had happened
. . . what had gone wrong" (40). He imagines, still, that his holograph
has destroyed his wife. Then he sees her, "quite alive, sitting less than ten
yards away, very still" (40). Separated by their technological environment,
Uaan "in her space suit" must turn on her communicator to speak to her
husband: "And he fancied he could even see her expression of sad amuse-
ment at the two of them, as her voice bridged empty space to say,
'ZZZZZSSSSSSSSSSST?' " (40) What does this ending represent? Is the real
Uaan dead in the house while the holographic Uaan carries on? Has Uaan
made an infinite series of replications of herself? Is this her joke, Uaan
performing as a holograph in order to stay alive, or to make a point about
their mutual attempts to destroy each other? Is this Padmanabran's comment
on Uaan's wifely role, that of a business partner the husband can trust (31–
32)—better performed by the holograph than the human? Who are the

"unfaithful servants" of the title — only the holographs, or also the wife? The very ambiguity underlines the virtual nature of human reality in a high tech culture. Virtually anyone can be inhuman, a machine.

Gorodischer and Padmanabran appropriate and adapt the conventions of science fiction and the solutions of Western women writers to them. They add their own concerns in their portraits of virtual housewives. Women across the globe are writing science fiction, taking up its conventions and transforming them to cultural critique, commenting on the virtual reality of women's gendered constraints.

Works Cited
Index

Works Cited

Agosin, Marjorie, ed. 1992. *Secret Weavers: Stories of the Fantastic by Women of Argentina and Chile.* Fredonia, N.Y.: White Pine Press.

Albinski, Nan Bowman. 1988a. "Utopia Reconsidered: Women Novelists and Nineteenth-Century Utopian Visions." *Signs* 13 (Summer): 830–41.

———. 1988b. *Women's Utopias in British and American Fiction.* New York: Routledge.

Aldiss, Brian, with David Wingrove. 1986. *Trillion Year Spree: The History of Science Fiction.* London: Victor Gollancz.

Anderson, Poul. 1966. *Planet of No Return.* 1956. Reprint. London: Dobson.

———. 1971. *Dancer from Atlantis.* Garden City, N.Y.: Nelson Doubleday.

———. 1979. *Ensign Flandry.* 1966. Reprint. Boston: Gregg Press.

———. 1984. *A Midsummer Tempest.* 1974. Reprint. New York: Tom Doherty Assoc.

Armitt, Lucie, ed. 1991. *Where No Man Has Gone Before: Women and Science Fiction.* New York: Routledge.

Arnason, Eleanor. 1986. *To The Resurrection Station.* New York: Avon.

———. 1987. *Daughter of the Bear King.* New York: Avon.

———. 1991. *A Woman of the Iron People.* New York: William Morrow.

———. 1993. *Ring of Swords.* New York: Tom Doherty Assoc.

Atwood, Margaret. 1987. *The Handmaid's Tale.* 1985. Reprint. New York: Fawcett.

Bammer, Angelika. 1991. *Partial Visions: Feminism and Utopianism in the 1970s.* New York: Routledge.

Barr, Marleen. 1987. *Alien To Femininity: Speculative Fiction and Feminist Theory.* Westport, Conn.: Greenwood Press.

———. 1992. *Feminist Fabulation: Space/Postmodern Fiction.* Iowa City: Univ. of Iowa Press.

———. 1993. *Lost in Space: Probing Feminist Science Fiction and Beyond.* Chapel Hill: Univ. of North Carolina Press.

Barr, Marleen, ed. 1981. *Future Females: A Critical Anthology.* Bowling Green, Ohio: Bowling Green State Univ. Popular Press.

Barr, Marleen, and Patrick Murphy, eds. 1987. *Feminism Faces the Fantastic. Women's Studies.* 14, no. 2 (Special Issue).

Barr, Marleen, and Nicholas Smith, eds. 1983. *Women and Utopia: Critical Interpretations.* Lanham, Md.: Univ. Press of America.

Bartkowski, Frances. 1989. *Feminist Utopias.* Lincoln: Univ. of Nebraska Press.

Beauvoir, Simone de. 1974. *The Second Sex*. Translated by H. M. Parshley. 1952. Reprint. New York: Vintage.

Behn, Aphra. 1698. "Adventures of the Black Lady." *All the Histories and Novels*. London.

Belsey, Catherine. 1985. "Constructing the Subject: Deconstructing the Text." In *Feminist Criticism and Social Change: Sex, Class and Race in Literature and Culture*, edited by Judith Newton and Deborah Rosenfelt, 45–64. New York: Methuen.

Benjamin, Jessica. 1988. *The Bonds of Love: Psychoanalysis, Feminism, and the Problem of Domination*. New York: Pantheon.

Benjamin, Marina. 1991. "Elbow Room: Women Writers on Science, 1790–1840." In *Science and Sensibility: Gender and Scientific Enquiry, 1780–1945*, edited by Marina Benjamin, 27–59. London: Basil Blackwell.

Bennett, Marcia J. 1984. *Shadow Singer*. New York, Ballantine.

Berg, Temma. 1989. "Suppressing the Language of Wo(Man): The Dream of a Common Language." In *Engendering the Word: Feminist Essays in Psychosexual Poetics*, edited by Temma Berg, et al., 3–28. Urbana: Univ. of Illinois Press.

Bewell, Alan. 1988. "An Issue of Monstrous Desire: *Frankenstein* and Obstetrics." *The Yale Journal of Criticism* 2, no. 1 (Fall): 105–28.

Birke, Lynda. 1986. "Changing Minds: Towards Gender Equality in Science?" In *Perspectives on Gender and Science*, edited by Jan Harding, 184–202. London: Falmer Press.

————. 1991. " 'Life' as We Have Known It: Feminism and the Biology of Gender." In *Science and Sensibility: Gender and Scientific Enquiry, 1780–1945*, edited by Marina Benjamin, 243–63. London: Basil Blackwell.

Bleier, Ruth. 1984. *Science and Gender: A Critique of Biology and Its Theories on Women*. New York: Pergamon Press.

————. 1986. "Sex Differences Research: Science or Belief?" In *Feminist Approaches to Science*, edited by Ruth Bleier, 147–64. New York: Pergamon Press.

Boston Lesbian Psychologies Collective, eds. 1987. *Lesbian Psychologies: Explorations & Challenges*. Urbana: Univ. of Illinois Press.

Brackett, Leigh. 1973. *The Hafling and Other Stories*. New York: Ace.

Bradley, Marion Zimmer. 1964. *The Bloody Sun*. New York: Ace.

————. 1972. *Darkover Landfall*. New York: DAW.

————. 1976. *The Shattered Chain*. New York: DAW.

————. 1978. *The Ruins of Isis*. New York: Simon and Schuster.

————. 1980. *Two to Conquer*. New York: DAW.

————. 1983. *Thendara House*. New York: DAW.

————. 1984. *City of Sorcery*. New York: DAW.

————. 1986. *Lythande*. New York: DAW.

Brewer, Maria Minnich. 1987. "Surviving Fictions: Gender and Difference in Postmodern and Postnuclear Narrative." *Discourse* 9:37–52.

Brooke-Rose, Christine. 1981. *A Rhetoric of the Unreal: Studies in Narrative and Structure, Especially of the Fantastic*. Cambridge: Cambridge Univ. Press.

Bryant, Dorothy. 1980. *The Kin of Ata Are Waiting for You*. In 1971 published as *The Comforter*. San Francisco: Moon.

Bull, Emma. 1991. *Bone Dance*. New York: Ace.

Butler, Judith. 1990. *Gender Trouble: Feminism and the Subversion of Identity*. New York: Routledge.

Butler, Marilyn. 1993. "The First *Frankenstein* and Radical Science." *TLS*, 9 Apr., 12–14.

Butler, Octavia. 1976. *Patternmaster*. New York: Avon.

———. 1977. *Mind of My Mind*. New York: Avon.

———. 1978. *Survivor*. New York: New American Library.

———. 1979. *Kindred*. Boston: Beacon Press.

———. 1980. *Wild Seed*. New York: Warner.

———. 1985. "Bloodchild." 1984. Reprint. In *The 1985 Annual World's Best SF*, edited by Donald A. Wollheim, 193–212. New York: DAW.

———. 1987. *Dawn*. See *Xenogensis*.

———. 1987–1989. *Xenogenesis: Dawn, Adulthood Rites, Imago*. New York: Warner.

———. 1988. *Adulthood Rites*. See *Xenogenesis*.

———. 1989. *Imago*. See *Xenogenesis*.

———. 1993. *Parable of the Sower*. New York: Four Walls Eight Windows.

Caldecott, Leonie. 1984. *Women of Our Century*. London: Ariel and BBC.

Carr, Jayge. 1979. *Leviathan's Deep*. Garden City, N.Y.: Doubleday.

Cavendish, Margaret, Duchess of Newcastle. 1668. *The Description of a New World, Called the Blazing World*. London.

Cherryh, C. J. 1978. *The Faded Sun: Shon'Jir*. Garden City, N.Y.: Nelson Doubleday.

———. 1979. *The Faded Sun: Kutath*. Garden City, N.Y.: Nelson Doubleday.

———. 1980. *Serpent's Reach*. New York: DAW.

———. 1982a. *Port Eternity*. New York: DAW.

———. 1982b. *The Pride of Chanur*. 1981. Reprint. New York: DAW.

———. 1984. *Chanur's Venture*. New York: DAW.

———. 1985. *The Kif Strike Back*. New York: DAW.

———. 1986. *Chanur's Homecoming*. New York: DAW.

———. 1992. *Chanur's Legacy*. New York: DAW.

Chesler, Phyllis. 1972. *Women and Madness*. Garden City, N.Y.: Doubleday.

Chodorow, Nancy J. 1978. *The Reproduction of Mothering: Psychoanalysis and the Sociology of Gender*. Berkeley: Univ. of California Press.

———. 1989. *Feminism and Psychoanalytic Theory*. New Haven: Yale Univ. Press.

Christian, Barbara. 1985. *Black Feminist Criticism*. New York: Pergamon Press.

Clareson, Thomas D. 1985. *Some Kind of Paradise: The Emergence of American Science Fiction*. Westport, Conn.: Greenwood Press.

Colie, Rosalie. 1974. *Shakespeare's Living Art*. Princeton: Princeton Univ. Press.

Cranny-Francis, Anne. 1990. *Feminist Fiction: Feminist Uses of Generic Fiction*. New York: St. Martin's Press.

Darwin, Charles. 1874. *The Descent of Man and Selection in Relation to Sex*. Rev. ed. Chicago: Rand, McNally.

———. 1899. *The Origin of Species by Means of Natural Selection*. 2 vols. New York: D. Appleton.

Davis, Angela. 1971. "Reflections on the Black Woman's Role in the Community of Slaves." *The Black Scholar* 3 (Dec.): 3–15.

Davison, Jane. 1980. *The Fall of a Doll's House: Three Generations of American Women and the Houses They Lived In*. New York: Holt, Rinehart, and Winston.

Defoe, Daniel. 1972. *The Life and Surprizing Adventures of Robinson Crusoe of York, Mariner.* London: Oxford Univ. Press.

del Rey, Lester. 1971. "Helen O'Loy." In *The Science Fiction Hall of Fame,* edited by Robert Silverberg. 1: 42–51. First published: *Astounding* (Dec. 1938). New York: Avon.

Dinnerstein, Dorothy. 1976. *The Mermaid and the Minotaur: Sexual Arrangements and Human Malaise.* New York: Harper and Row.

Donawerth, Jane. 1994. "Science Fiction by Women in the Early Pulps, 1926–1930." In *Utopian and Science Fiction by Women,* edited by Jane Donawerth and Carol Kolmerten, 137–52. Syracuse: Syracuse Univ. Press.

Donawerth, Jane, and Carol Kolmerten, eds. 1994. *Utopian and Science Fiction by Women: Worlds of Difference.* Syracuse: Syracuse Univ. Press.

DuPlessis, Rachel Blau. 1979. "The Feminist Apologues of Lessing, Piercy, and Russ." *Frontiers* 4 (Summer): 1–8.

———. 1985a. "For the Etruscans." In *The New Feminist Criticism: Essays on Women, Literature, and Theory,* edited by Elaine Showalter, 271–91. New York: Pantheon.

———. 1985b. *Writing Beyond the Ending: Narrative Strategies of Twentieth Century Women Writers.* Bloomington: Indiana Univ. Press.

Dussinger, John A. 1976. "Kinship and Guilt in Mary Shelley's *Frankenstein.*" *Studies in the Novel* 8, no. 1 (Spring): 38–55.

Easlea, Brian. 1986. "The Masculine Image of Science with Special Reference to Physics: How Much Does Gender Really Matter?" In *Perspectives on Gender and Science,* edited by Jan Harding, 132–58. London: Falmer Press.

Elgin, Suzette Haden. 1970. *The Communipaths.* New York: Ace.

———. 1971. *Furthest.* New York: Ace.

———. 1972. *At the Seventh Level.* New York: DAW.

———. 1980. *Communipath Worlds.* New York: Simon and Schuster.

———. 1981. *The Ozark Trilogy: Twelve Fair Kingdoms, The Grand Jubilee,* and *And Then There'll Be Fireworks.* Garden City, N.Y.: Nelson Doubleday.

———. 1984. *Native Tongue.* New York: DAW.

———. 1987. *The Judas Rose: Native Tongue II.* New York: DAW.

———. 1994. *Earthsong: Native Tongue III.* New York: DAW.

Ellis, Kate Ferguson. 1989. *The Contested Castle: Gothic Novels and the Subversion of Domestic Ideology.* Urbana: Univ. of Illinois Press.

Ellis, Sophie Wenzel. 1929. "The White Wizard." *Weird Tales* 14, no. 3: 297–314, 429–31.

———. 1930. "Creatures of the Light." *Astounding* 1, no. 2 (Feb.): 197–220.

Emshwiller, Carol. 1974. "The Childhood of the Human Hero." In *Nebula Award Stories Nine,* edited by Kate Wilhelm, 228–34. New York: Harper and Row.

———. 1990. *Carmen Dog.* San Francisco: Mercury House.

Faderman, Lillian. 1991. *Odd Girls and Twilight Lovers: A History of Lesbian Life in Twentieth-Century America.* New York: Penguin.

Fausto-Sterling, Anne. 1981. "Women and Science." *Women's Studies International Quarterly* 4, no. 1: 41–50.

———. 1985. *Myths of Gender: Biological Theories About Women and Men.* New York: Basic Books.

————. 1988. "Science and Feminism." Lecture, 29 Nov., Univ. of Maryland at College Park.

————. 1989. "Life in the XY Corral." *Women's Studies International Forum* 12, no. 3: 319–31.

Fee, Elizabeth. 1978. "Science and the 'Woman Question' 1860–1920: A Study of English Scientific Periodicals." Ph.D. diss., Princeton Univ.

————. 1981. "Is Feminism a Threat to Scientific Objectivity?" *International Journal of Women's Studies* 4, no. 4 (Sept.–Oct.): 378–92.

————. 1986. "Critiques of Modern Science: The Relationship of Feminism to Other Radical Epistemologies." In *Feminist Approaches to Science,* edited by Ruth Bleier, 42–55. New York: Pergamon Press.

Felice, Cynthia. 1978. *Godsfire.* New York: Simon and Schuster.

————. 1986. *Double Nocturne.* New York: DAW.

Felice, Cynthia, and Connie Willis. 1989. *Light Raid.* New York: Ace.

Fields, Barbara Jeanne. 1991. "Slavery, Race and Ideology in the United States of America." *New Left Review* 181:95–118.

Finch, Sheila. 1986. *Triad.* New York: Bantam Books.

————. 1987. *The Garden of the Shaped.* New York: Bantam.

Firestone, Shulamith. 1972. *The Dialectic of Sex: The Case for Feminist Revolution.* 1970. Reprint. New York: Bantam.

Fitting, Peter. 1987. "For Men Only: A Guide to Reading Single-Sex Worlds." *Women's Studies* 14:101–17.

————. 1992. "Reconsiderations of the Separatist Paradigm in Recent Feminist Science Fiction." *Science Fiction Studies* 19, no. 1 (Mar.): 32–48.

Forrest, Katherine V. 1984. *Daughters of a Coral Dawn.* Tallahasee, Fla.: Naiad Press.

Foster, Frances Smith. 1982. "Octavia Butler's Black Female Future Fiction." *Extrapolation* 23:37–49.

Foster, Hannah Webster. 1986. *The Coquette.* Edited by Cathy N. Davidson. 1797. Reprint. New York: Oxford Univ. Press.

Friend, Beverly. 1972–73. "Virgin Territory: Women and Sex in Science Fiction." *Extrapolation* 14:49–58. Revised, 1977, as "Virgin Territory: The Bonds and Boundaries of Women in Science Fiction." In *Many Futures Many Worlds: Theme and Form in Science Fiction,* edited by Thomas D. Clareson, 140–63. Gambier, Ohio: Kent State Univ. Press.

Gallop, Jane. 1989. "The Monster in the Mirror: The Feminist Critic's Psychoanalysis." In *Feminism and Psychoanalysis,* edited by Richard Feldstein and Judith Roof, 13–24. Ithaca, N.Y.: Cornell Univ. Press.

Gamble, Sarah. 1991. " 'Shambleau . . . and others': The Role of the Female in the Fiction of C. L. Moore." In *Where No Man Has Gone Before: Women and Science Fiction,* edited by Lucie Armitt, 29–49. London: Routledge.

Garber, Marjorie. 1992. *Vested Interests: Cross-Dressing & Cultural Anxiety.* New York: Routledge.

Gaskell, Jane. 1957. *Strange Evil.* New York: Simon and Schuster.

Gearhart, Sally Miller. 1974. "The Miracle of Lesbianism." In *Loving Women/Loving Men: Gay Liberation and the Church,* edited by Sally Miller Gearhart and William R. Johnson, 119–52. San Francisco: Glide.

————. 1984. *The Wanderground: Stories of the Hill Women.* 1979. Reprint. Boston: Alyson.

Gilbert, Sandra M. 1978. "Mary Shelley's Monstrous Eve." *Feminist Studies* 4, no. 2 (June): 48–73.

Gilbert, Sandra, and Susan Gubar. 1984. *The Madwoman in the Attic: The Woman Writer and the Nineteenth-Century Literary Imagination.* 1979. Reprint. New Haven: Yale Univ. Press.

Gillmore, Inez Haynes. 1988. *Angel Island.* 1914. Reprint. New York: New American Library.

Gilman, Charlotte Perkins. 1966. *Women and Economics: A Study of the Economic Relation Between Men and Women as a Factor in Social Evolution.* Edited by Carl N. Degler. New York: Harper and Row.

———. 1979. *Herland.* Introduction by Ann J. Lane. New York: Pantheon.

Gledhill, Christine. 1994. "Pleasurable Negotiations." In *Cultural Theory and Popular Culture,* edited by John Storey, 241–54. New York: Harvester/Wheatsheaf.

Gorodischer, Angélica. 1992. "The Perfect Married Woman." In *Secret Weavers,* edited by Marjorie Agosin, 243–47. Fredonia, N.Y.: White Pine Press.

Gotlieb, Phyllis. 1979. *O Master Caliban!* 1976. Reprint. New York: Bantam.

———. 1980. *A Judgment of Dragons.* New York: Berkley.

———. 1982. *Emperor, Swords, Pentacles.* New York: Ace.

———. 1983. *Son of the Morning and Other Stories.* New York: Ace.

———. 1985. *The Kingdom of the Cats.* New York: Ace.

Greer, Germaine. 1972. *The Female Eunuch.* 1970. Reprint. New York: Bantam.

Griffith, Mary. [also Mary Griffiths.] 1975. *Three Hundred Years Hence.* Introduction by David Hartwell. 1836. Reprint. Boston: Gregg Press.

Griffith, Nicola. 1992. *Ammonite.* New York: Ballantine.

Gubar, Susan. 1980. "C. L. Moore and the Conventions of Women's Science Fiction." *Science Fiction Studies* 7:16–27.

———. 1986. "Feminism and Utopia." *Science Fiction Studies* 13 (Mar.): 79–83.

Halpin, Zuleyma Tang. 1990. "Scientific Objectivity and the Concept of 'The Other.'" *Women's Studies International Forum* 12:285–93.

Hansen, L. [Louise] Taylor. 1930. "The City on the Cloud." *Wonder Stories* 2, no. 5 (Oct.): 426–31.

———. 1969. *The Ancient Atlantic.* Amherst, Wisc.: Amherst Press.

Haraway, Donna. 1978. "Animal Sociology and a Natural Economy of the Body Politic, Parts 1 and 2." *Signs* 4, no. 1: 21–60.

———. 1979. "The Biological Enterprise: Sex, Mind, and Profit from Human Engineering to Sociobiology." *Radical History Review* 20 (Spring–Summer): 206–37.

———. 1981. "In the Beginning Was the Word: The Genesis of Biological Theory." *Signs* 6, no. 3:469–81.

———. 1983. "The Contest for Primate Nature: Daughters of Man-the-Hunter in the Field, 1960–1980." In *The Future of American Democracy,* edited by Mark E. Kann, 175–207. Philadelphia: Temple Univ. Press.

———. 1985. "A Manifesto for Cyborgs: Science, Technology, and Socialist Feminism in the 1980s." *Socialist Review* 15, no. 2 (Mar.–Apr.): 65–107.

———. 1986. "Primatology is Politics by Other Means." In *Feminist Approaches to Science,* edited by Ruth Bleier, 77–117. New York: Pergamon Press.

———. 1989a. "Monkeys, Aliens, and Women: Love, Science, and Politics at the Intersection of Feminist Theory and Colonial Discourse." *Women's Studies International Forum* 12, no. 3: 295–312.

————. 1989b. *Primate Visions: Gender, Race, and Nature in the World of Modern Science*. New York: Routledge.

Harding, Jan. 1986. "The Making of a Scientist?" In *Perspectives on Gender and Science*, edited by Jan Harding, 159–202. London: Falmer Press.

Harding, Sandra. 1975–1987. "The Instability of the Analytical Categories of Feminist Theory." In *Sex and Scientific Inquiry*, edited by Sandra Harding and Jean F. O'Barr, 283–302. Chicago: Univ. of Chicago Press.

————. 1986. *The Science Question in Feminism*. Ithaca, N.Y.: Cornell Univ. Press.

————. 1991. *Whose Science? Whose Knowledge? Thinking from Women's Lives*. Ithaca, N.Y.: Cornell Univ. Press.

Harris, Clare Winger. 1928a. "The Menace of Mars." *Amazing Stories* 3, no. 7 (Oct.): 582–97.

————. 1928b. "The Fifth Dimension." *Amazing Stories* 3 (Dec.): 823–25, 850.

————. 1929. "The Artificial Man." *Science Wonder Quarterly* 1 (Fall): 79–83.

Hatlen, Burton. 1983. "Milton, Mary Shelley, and Patriarchy." In *Rhetoric, Literature, and Interpretation*, edited by Harry R. Garvin. *Bucknell Review*. 28, no. 2: 19–47.

Hein, Hilde. 1981. "Women and Science: Fitting Men to Think about Nature." *International Journal of Women's Studies* 4:369–77.

Henderson, Hazel. 1978. *Creating Alternative Futures*. New York; Berkley.

————. 1981. *The Politics of the Solar Age: Alternatives to Economics*. Garden City, N.Y.: Anchor Press.

Henderson, Zenna. 1963. *Pilgrimage. 1952–1961*. Reprint. New York: Avon.

Hite, Molly. 1989. *The Other Side of the Story: Structures and Strategies of Contemporary Feminist Narrative*. Ithaca, N.Y.: Cornell Univ. Press.

Hochschild, Arlie, with Anne Machung. 1989. *The Second Shift*. New York: Avon.

Hodges, Devon. 1983. "*Frankenstein* and the Feminine Subversion of the Novel." *Tulsa Studies in Women's Literature* 2 (Fall): 155–64.

Holland, Cecelia. 1975. *Floating Worlds*. New York: Simon and Schuster.

Hollinger, Veronica. 1989a. " 'The Most Grisly Truth': Responses to the Human Condition in the Works of James Tiptree, Jr." *Extrapolation* 30, no. 2 (Summer): 117–32.

————. 1989b. Science Fictions, Feminism, Criticisms. Paper delivered at Science Fiction Research Association Meeting, 25 June, at Miami Univ., Oxford, Ohio.

Holly, J. Hunter. 1966. *The Mind Traders*. New York: MacFadden-Bartell.

Homans, Margaret. 1987. "Bearing Demons: Frankenstein's Circumvention of the Maternal." In *Mary Shelley's Frankenstein*, edited by Harold Bloom, 133–53. Modern Critical Interpretations Series. New York: Chelsea House.

hooks, bell. 1984. *Feminism: from margin to center*. Boston: South End Press.

Horney, Karen. 1967. *Feminine Psychology*. Edited by Harold Kelman. New York: W. W. Norton.

Hovanec, Carol P. 1989. "Visions of Nature in *The Word For World is Forest*: A Mirror of the American Consciousness." *Extrapolation* 30, no. 1 (Spring): 84–92.

Hrdy, Sarah Blaffer. 1981. *The Woman That Never Evolved*. Cambridge, Mass.: Harvard Univ. Press.

Hubbard, Ruth, Mary Sue Henifin, and Barbara Fried, eds. 1982. *Biological Woman —The Convenient Myth*. Cambridge, Mass.: Schenkman.

Hughes, Monica. 1984. *The Keeper of the Isis Light*. 1980. Reprint. New York: Bantam.

Irving, Minna [Minnie Odell]. 1929. "The Moon Woman: A Tale of the Future." *Amazing Stories* 4, no. 8 (Nov.): 746–54.

Irwin, May. 1912. "My Views on That Ever-Interesting Topic — Woman." *Green Book Magazine* (Dec.): 1057–58.

Jacobus, Mary. 1982. "Is There a Woman in This Text?" *New Literary History* 14, no. 1 (Autumn): 117–54.

Johnson, Barbara. 1982. "My Monster / My Self." *Diacritics* 12, no. 2 (Summer): 2–10.

Jones, Alice Ilgenfritz, and Ella Merchant. 1991. *Unveiling a Parallel, A Romance*. Edited by Carol Kolmerten. 1893. Reprint. Syracuse, N.Y.: Syracuse Univ. Press.

Jones, Libby Falk and Sarah Webster Goodwin, eds. 1990. *Feminism, Utopia, and Narrative*. Tennessee Studies in Literature Vol. 32. Knoxville: Univ. of Tennessee Press.

Kagan, Janet. 1988. *Hellspark*. New York: Tom Doherty Assoc.

Kahle, Jane Butler. 1985. "Retention of Girls in Science: Case Studies of Secondary Teachers." In *Women in Science: A Report from the Field*, edited by Jane Butler Kahle, 49–76. London: Falmer Press.

Keller, Evelyn Fox. 1981. "Women and Science: Two Cultures or One?" *International Journal of Women's Studies* 4:414–19.

———. 1982. "Feminism and Science." *Signs* 7, no. 3:589–602.

———. 1983. *A Feeling for the Organism: The Life and Work of Barbara McClintock*. New York and San Francisco: W. H. Freeman.

———. 1985. *Reflections on Gender and Science*. New Haven: Yale Univ. Press.

———. 1986a. "How Gender Matters, or, Why It's So Hard for Us to Count Past Two." In *Perspectives on Gender and Science*, edited by Jan Harding, 168–83. London: Falmer Press.

———. 1986b. "Making Gender Visible in the Pursuit of Nature's Secrets." In *Feminist Studies, Critical Studies*, edited by Teresa de Lauretis, 67–77. Bloomington: Indiana Univ. Press.

———. 1989. "Nature's Secrets." Lecture, 30 Mar., Univ. of Maryland, College Park.

Kessler, Carol Farley. 1990. "Bibliography of Utopian Fiction by United States Women 1836–1988." *Utopian Studies* 1:1–58.

Kessler, Carol Farley, ed. 1984. *Daring to Dream: Utopian Stories by United States Women 1836–1919*. Boston: Pandora Press.

Khanna, Lee Cullen. 1984. "Frontiers of Imagination: Feminist Worlds." *Women's Studies International Forum* 7, no. 2: 97–102.

———. 1994. "The Subject of Utopia: Margaret Cavendish's *Blazing World*." In *Utopian and Science Fiction: Worlds of Difference*, edited by Jane Donawerth and Carol Kolmerten, 15–34. Syracuse, N.Y.: Syracuse Univ. Press.

———. 1995. "Utopias." In *The Oxford Companion to Women's Writing in the United States*, edited by Cathy N. Davidson and Linda Wagner-Martin, 892–94. New York: Oxford Univ. Press.

Killough, Lee. 1979. *A Voice Out of Ramah*. New York: Ballantine.

Kimberly, Gail. 1975. *Flyer*. New York: Popular Library.

King, Betty. 1984. *Women of the Future: The Female Main Character in Science Fiction*. Metuchen, N.J.: Scarecrow Press.

Klarer, Mario. 1991. "Re-Membering Men Dis-Membered in Sally Miller Gearhart's Ecofeminist Utopia *The Wanderground*." *Extrapolation* 32 (Winter): 319–30.

Kolmerten, Carol. 1994. "Texts and Contexts: American Women Envision Utopia, 1890–1920." In *Utopian and Science Fiction by Women: Worlds of Difference*, edited by Jane Donawerth and Carol Kolmerten, 107–25. Syracuse, N.Y.: Syracuse Univ. Press.

Kranzler, Laura. 1988–89. "*Frankenstein* and the Technological Future." *Foundation: The Review of Science Fiction* 44 (Winter): 42–49.

Kuhn, Thomas S. 1970. *The Structure of Scientific Revolution*. 2d ed. Chicago: Univ. of Chicago Press.

Lagon, Mark P. 1993. " 'We Owe It to Them to Interfere': *Star Trek* and U.S. Statecraft in the 1960s and 1990s." *Extrapolation* 34, no. 3 (Fall): 251–64.

Landau, Misia. 1984. "Human Evolution as Narrative." *American Scientist* 72 (May–June): 262–68.

Lane, Mary Bradley. 1975. *Mizora: A Prophecy*. Introduction by Stuart A. Teitler and Kristine Anderson. 1880–1881. Reprint. Boston: Gregg Press.

Lanser, Susan Sniader. 1988. "Feminism's 'Yellow Wallpaper' and the Transformation of Literature." Lecture, 11 February, at the Univ. of Maryland at College Park.

———. 1989. "Feminist Criticism, 'The Yellow Wallpaper,' and the Politics of Color in America." *Feminist Studies* 15, no. 3 (Fall): 415–41.

———. 1992. *Fictions of Authority: Women Writers and Narrative Voice*. Ithaca, N.Y.: Cornell Univ. Press.

Lee, Tanith. 1976. *Don't Bite the Sun*. New York: DAW.

———. 1977. *Drinking Sapphire Wine*. New York: DAW.

———. 1979. *Electric Forest*. Garden City, N.Y.: Nelson Doubleday.

———. 1981. *The Silver Metal Lover*. Garden City, N.Y.: Nelson Doubleday.

Lefanu, Sarah. 1988. *In the Chinks of the World Machine*. Published in the United States as *Feminism and Science Fiction*. Bloomington: Indiana Univ. Press.

Le Guin, Ursula K. 1972. *The Word for World Is Forest*. New York: Berkley.

———. 1975a. "The Day Before the Revolution." 1974. Reprint in *The Wind's Twelve Quarters*. 260–77. New York: Bantam.

———. 1975b. *The Dispossessed*. 1974. Reprint. New York: Avon.

———. 1976. *The Left Hand of Darkness*. 1969. Reprint. New York: Ace.

———. 1978. *Eye of the Heron*. New York: HarperCollins.

———. 1979. *The Language of the Night: Essays on Fantasy and Science Fiction*. Edited by Susan Wood. New York: G. P. Putnam's Sons.

———. 1987. *Always Coming Home*. 1985. Reprint. New York: Bantam.

———. 1989. *Dancing at the Edge of the World: Thoughts on Words, Women, Places*. New York: Harper and Row.

———. 1994. "The Matter of Seggri" *Crank!* No. 3 (Spring): 3–36.

———. 1995. "A Conversation with Ursula K. Le Guin." *Para-Doxa: Studies in World Literary Genres* 1, no. 1: 39–57.

Leith, Linda. 1980. "Marion Zimmer Bradley and Darkover." *Science Fiction Studies* 7:28–35.

Lerner, Gerda. 1979. *The Majority Finds Its Past: Placing Women in History*. New York: Oxford Univ. Press.

Levine, George, and U. C. Knoepflmacher, eds. 1979. *The Endurance of Frankenstein: Essays on Mary Shelley's Novel*. Berkeley: Univ. of California Press.

Lightner, A. M. [Alice Mary]. 1970. *The Day of the Drones*. 1969. Reprint. New York: Bantam.

Lipson, Jodi F. 1994. "Women in Science." *Outlook* 88, no. 3 (Fall): 6.

Longino, Helen, and Ruth Doell. 1975–1987. "Body, Bias, and Behavior: A Comparative Analysis of Reasoning in Two Areas of Biological Science." In *Sex and Scientific Inquiry*, edited by Sandra Harding and Jean F. O'Barr, 165–86. Chicago: Univ. of Chicago Press.

Lorde, Audre. 1984. *Sister Outsider: Essays and Speeches*. Freedom, Calif.: Crossing Press.

Lorraine, Lilith. 1930. "Into the 28th Century." *Science Wonder Quarterly* 1, no. 2 (Winter): 250–67, 276.

Lowe, Marian. 1981. "Cooperation and Competition in Science." *International Journal of Women's Studies* 4, no. 4 (Sept.–Oct.): 362–68.

Ludwick, Kathleen. 1930. "Dr. Immortelle." *Amazing Stories Quarterly* 3, no. 4 (Fall): 560–69.

Lynch, Jane Weedman. 1987. "*An Exercise for Madmen:* Barbara Paul's Look at Insanity." *Extrapolation* 28, no. 4: 340–44.

MacKinnon, Catharine A. 1982. "Feminism, Marxism, Method, and the State: An Agenda for Theory." In *The Signs Reader: Women, Gender and Scholarship*, edited by Elizabeth Abel and Emily K. Abel, 227–56. Chicago: Univ. of Chicago Press.

Mainiero, Lina, ed., and Langdon Lynne Faust, asst. ed. 1980. *American Women Writers: A Critical Reference Guide from Colonial Times to the Present*. New York: Frederick Ungar.

Marks, Elaine, and Isabelle de Courtivron, eds. 1980. *New French Feminisms: An Anthology*. New York: Schocken.

Marshall, Rachael, and Maverick Terrell. 1928. "The Mystery in Acatlan." *Weird Tales* 12, no. 5 (Nov.): 582–88, 715–16.

Martin, Biddy. 1988. "Feminism, Criticism, and Foucault." In *Feminism and Foucault: Reflections on Resistance*, edited by Irene Diamond and Lee Quimby, 3–19. Boston: Northeastern Univ. Press.

Maxwell, Ann. 1982. *Fire Dancer*. New York: New American Library.

———. 1983a. *Dancer's Illusion*. New York: New American Library.

———. 1983b. *Dancer's Luck*. New York: New American Library.

McCafferey, Larry, ed. 1990. *Across the Wounded Galaxies: Interviews with Contemporary American Science Fiction Writers*. Urbana: Univ. of Illinois Press.

McCaffrey, Anne. 1974. "Hitch Your Dragon to a Star: Romance and Glamour in Science Fiction." In *Science Fiction, Today and Tomorrow*, edited by Reginald Bretnor, 274–93. New York: Harper and Row.

———. 1979. *The Ship Who Sang*. 1969. Reprint. New York: Ballantine.

———. 1982a. *Dragonflight*. 1968. Reprint. New York: Ballantine.

———. 1982b. *Restoree*. 1967. Reprint. New York: Ballantine.

———. 1984. *Dinosaur Planet Survivors*. New York: Ballantine.

McCaffrey, Anne, and Margaret Ball. 1992. *PartnerShip*. Riverdale, N.Y.: Baen.

McIntyre, Vonda. 1978. *Dreamsnake*. New York: Dell.

———. 1983. *Superluminal*. New York: Pocket Books.

———. 1988. *Barbary*. 1986. Reprint. New York: Ace.

Mead, Margaret. 1961. *Coming of Age in Samoa: A Psychological Study of Primitive Youth for Western Civilization.* 1928. Reprint. New York: William Morrow.

———. 1975. *Blackberry Winter: My Earlier Years.* 1972. Reprint. New York: Washington Square Press.

Mellor, Anne K. 1987. "*Frankenstein:* A Feminist Critique of Science." In *One Culture: Essays in Science and Literature,* edited by George Levine, 287–312. Madison: Univ. of Wisconsin Press.

———. 1988. *Mary Shelley: Her Life, Her Fiction, Her Monsters.* New York: Methuen.

Merchant, Carolyn. 1980. *The Death of Nature: Women, Ecology, and the Scientific Revolution.* San Francisco: Harper and Row.

———. 1988. "Gender and Ecological Issues in Science and Technology." Lecture, 14 November, at the Univ. of Maryland at College Park.

Merril, Judith. 1963. *Out of Bounds.* 1960. Reprint. New York: Pyramid.

———. 1950. *Shadow on the Hearth.* Garden City, N.Y.: Doubleday.

Miller, Jean Baker. 1976. *Toward a New Psychology of Women.* Boston: Beacon Press.

Millett, Kate. 1987. *Sexual Politics.* 1969–70. Reprint. New York: Ballantine.

Mitchison, Naomi. 1973. *Memoirs of a Spacewoman.* 1962. Reprint. New York: Berkley.

———. 1975. *Solution Three.* New York: Warner.

Moers, Ellen. 1963–1977. *Literary Women: The Great Writers.* New York: Oxford Univ. Press.

Moffett, Judith. 1988. *Pennterra.* 1987. Reprint. Toronto and New York: Worldwide.

———. 1992. *The Ragged World.* 1991. Reprint. New York: Ballantine.

Moody, Judith. 1989. "Women and Science: Their Critical Move Together Into the 21st Century." *NWSAction.* 2, no. 2 (Summer): 1, 7–10.

Moore, C. L. 1975. *The Best of C. L. Moore.* Ed. Lester del Rey. Garden City, N.Y.: Nelson Doubleday.

Moraga, Cherríe. 1993. *The Last Generation.* Boston: South End Press.

Morris. Adelaide. 1992. "First Persons Plural in Contemporary Feminist Fiction." *Tulsa Studies in Women's Literature* 11:11–29.

Moylan, Tom. 1986. *Demand the Impossible: Science Fiction and the Utopian Imagination.* New York: Methuen.

Mukundan, Monisha, ed. 1994. *The Namasté Book of Short Stories.* Vol II. New Delhi: UBS Publishers' Distributors.

Mulvey, Laura. 1989. "Visual Pleasure and Narrative Cinema." In *Visual and Other Pleasures,* 14–26. Bloomington: Indiana Univ. Press.

Newman, Beth. 1986. "Narratives of Seduction and the Seductions of Narrative: The Frame Structure of *Frankenstein.*" *ELH* 53, no. 1 (Spring): 141–63.

Newman, Louise Michele, ed. 1985. *Men's Ideas/Women's Realities: Popular Science, 1870–1915.* New York: Pergamon Press.

Nicholls, Peter, ed. 1979. *The Science Fiction Encyclopedia.* Garden City, N.Y.: Doubleday.

Noble, David F. 1992. *A World Without Women: The Christian Clerical Culture of Western Science.* New York: Knopf.

Norton, Andre. 1963. *Witch World.* New York: Ace.

———. 1964. *Web of the Witch World.* New York: Ace.

————. 1965. *Three Against the Witch World*. New York: Ace.

————. 1966. *Moon of Three Rings*. New York: Ace.

————. 1967. *Daybreak—2250 A.D.* 3d ed. New York: Ace. First published 1952, as *Star Man's Son*. New York: Harcourt, Brace.

————. 1969. *Uncharted Stars*. New York: Ace.

————. 1970. *Ice Crown*. New York: Viking.

————. 1981a. *Breed to Come*. 1972. Reprint. New York: Ace.

————. 1981b. *Forerunner*. New York: Pinnacle.

————. 1981c. *Horn Crown*. New York: DAW.

————. 1985. *Secret of the Lost Race*. 1959. Reprint. New York: Ace.

Oates, Joyce Carol. 1984. "Frankenstein's Fallen Angel." *Critical Inquiry* 10, no. 3 (Mar.): 543–55.

O'Flinn, Paul. 1983. "Production and Reproduction: The Case of *Frankenstein*." *Literature and History* 9.2 (Autumn): 194–213.

Ore, Rebecca. 1988. *Becoming Alien*. New York: Tom Doherty Assoc.

————. 1989. *Being Alien*. New York: Tom Doherty Assoc.

————. 1990. *Human to Human*. New York: Tom Doherty Assoc.

Ortner, Sherry B. 1974. "Is Female to Male as Nature Is to Culture?" In *Woman, Culture, and Society*, edited by Michelle Zimbalist Rosaldo and Louise Lamphere, 67–87. Stanford: Stanford Univ. Press.

Padmanabran, Manjula. 1994. "Unfaithful Servants." In *The Namasté Book of Short Stories*, edited by Monisha Mukundan, 31–40. Vol II. New Delhi: UBS Publishers' Distributors.

Palmer, Jane. 1985. *The Planet Dweller*. London: Women's Press.

————. 1986. *The Watcher*. London: Women's Press.

Park, Severna. 1992. *Speaking Dreams*. Ithaca, N.Y.: Firebrand.

Parrinder, Patrick, ed. 1979. *Science Fiction: A Critical Guide*. London: Longman.

Paul, Barbara. 1978. *An Exercise for Madmen*. New York: Berkley.

————. 1980. *Under the Canopy*. New York: New American Library.

Pearson, Carol. 1977. "Women's Fantasies and Feminist Utopias." *Frontiers* 2 (Fall): 50–61.

Pfaelzer, Jean. 1983. "A State of One's Own: Feminism as Ideology in American Utopias 1880–1915." *Extrapolation* 24, no. 4 (Winter): 311–28.

————. 1984. *The Utopian Novel in America 1886–1896*. Pittsburgh: Univ. of Pittsburgh Press.

Pfafflin, Sheila M. 1984. "Women, Science, and Technology." *American Psychologist* 39, no. 10 (Oct.): 1183–86.

Piercy, Marge. 1976. *Woman on the Edge of Time*. Greenwich, Conn.: Fawcett.

Piserchia, Doris. 1974. *Star Rider*. New York: Bantam.

————. 1978. *Spaceling*. Garden City, N.Y.: Nelson Doubleday.

————. 1980. *The Spinner*. Garden City, N.Y.: Nelson Doubleday.

Poovey, Mary. 1987. " 'My Hideous Progeny': The Lady and the Monster." In *Mary Shelley's Frankenstein*, edtied by Harold Bloom, 81–106. Modern Critical Interpretations Series. New York: Chelsea House.

Rabine, Leslie W. 1985. "Romance in the Age of Electronics: Harlequin Enterprises." In *Feminist Criticism and Social Change: Sex, Class and Race in Literature and Culture*, edited by Judith Newton and Deborah Rosenfelt, 249–67. New York: Methuen.

Radway, Janice. 1984. *Reading the Romance: Women, Patriarchy, and Popular Litera-ture*. Chapel Hill: Univ. of North Carolina Press.

Randall, Marta. 1978. *Journey*. New York: Pocket Books.

————. 1980. *Dangerous Games*. New York: Pocket Books.

Reagon, Bernice Johnson. 1983. "Coalition Politics: Turning the Century." In *HomeGirls: A Black Feminist Anthology*, edited by Barbara Smith, 356–68. New York: Kitchen Table Women of Color Press.

Rice, Louise, and Tonjoroff-Roberts. 1930. "The Astounding Enemy." *Amazing Stories Quarterly* 3, no. 1 (Winter): 78–103.

Rich, Adrienne. 1980. "Compulsory Heterosexuality and Lesbian Existence." *Signs* 5:631–60.

Richardson, Brian. 1995. "I etcetera: On the Poetics and Ideology of Multipersonal Narratives." *Style* 28, no. 3: 312–28.

Riley, Dick, ed. 1978. *Critical Encounters*. New York: Frederick Ungar.

Roberts, Maria Mulvey. 1993. "The Male Scientist, Man-Midwife, and Female Mon-ster: Appropriation and Transmutation in *Frankenstein*." In *A Question of Iden-tity: Women, Science, and Literature*, edited by Marina Benjamin, 59–73. New Brunswick, N.J.: Rutgers Univ. Press.

Roberts, Robin. 1985. "The Paradigm of *Frankenstein*: Reading *Canopus in Argos* in the Context of Science Fiction by Women." *Extrapolation* 25, no. 1 (Spring): 16–23.

————. 1987. "The Female Alien: Pulp Science Fiction's Legacy to Feminists." *Journal of Popular Culture* 21:33–52.

————. 1993. *A New Species: Gender and Science in Science Fiction*. Urbana: Univ. of Illinois Press.

Rohrlich, Ruby, and Elaine Hoffman Baruch, eds. 1984. *Women in Search of Utopia: Mavericks and Mythmakers*. New York: Schocken.

Rose, Hilary. 1986. "Beyond Masculinist Realities: A Feminist Epistemology for the Sciences." In *Feminist Approaches to Science*, edited by Ruth Bleier, 57–75. New York: Pergamon Press.

————. 1987. "Hand, Brain, and Heart: A Feminist Epistemology for the Natural Sciences." In *Sex and Scientific Inquiry*, edited by Sandra Harding and Jean F. O'Barr, 265–81. Chicago: Univ. of Chicago Press.

————. 1994. *Love, Power, and Knowledge: Towards a Feminist Transformation of the Sciences*. Bloomington: Indiana Univ. Press.

Rose, Mark. 1981. *Alien Encounters: Anatomy of Science Fiction*. Cambridge, Mass.: Harvard Univ. Press.

Rosinsky, Natalie. 1982, 1984. *Feminist Futures: Contemporary Women's Speculative Fiction*. Studies in Speculative Fiction No. 1. Ann Arbor, Mich.: UMI Research Press.

Rossiter, Margaret W. 1982. *Women Scientists in America: Struggles and Strategies to 1940*. Baltimore: Johns Hopkins Univ. Press.

Rothschild, Joan. 1981. "A Feminist Perspective on Technology and the Future." *Women's Studies International Quarterly* 4, no. 1: 65–74.

Rousseau, Yvonne. 1992. "The Wilder Alien Shores: Or the Colonials Are Revolting." *Foundation: The Review of Science Fiction*. No. 54 (Spring): 15–36.

Rubenstein, Marc A. 1976. " 'My Accursed Origin': The Search for the Mother in *Frankenstein*." *Studies in Romanticism* 15 (Sept.): 165–94.

Russ, Joanna. 1968. *Picnic on Paradise*. New York: Berkley.

——. 1972a. "The Image of Women in Science Fiction." In *Images of Women in Fiction*, edited by Susan Koppelman Cornillon, 79–94. Bowling Green, Ohio: Bowling Green Univ. Popular Press.

——. 1972b. "What Can a Heroine Do? or Why Women Can't Write." In *Images of Women in Fiction*, edited by Susan Koppelman Cornillon, 3–20. Bowling Green, Ohio: Bowling Green Univ. Popular Press.

——. 1972c. "When It Changed." In *Again Dangerous Visions*, edited by Harlan Ellison, 253–62. Garden City, N.Y.: Doubleday.

——. 1975. *The Female Man*. New York: Bantam.

——. 1975–1977. *We Who Are About To . . .* New York: Dell.

——. 1980. *"Amor Vincit Foeminam:* The Battle of the Sexes in Science Fiction." *Science Fiction Studies* 7:2–15.

——. 1981–1983. "What Did You Do During the Revolution, Grandma?" In *Extra(Ordinary) People*, 117–44. London: Women's Press.

——. 1984. "Let George Do It." *Women's Studies International Forum* 7, no. 2: 125–26.

——. 1986a. *The Adventures of Alyx*. Published as short stories in various journals 1967–1970. New York: Baen.

——. 1986b. *The Two of Them*. 1978. Reprint. London: Women's Press.

——. 1995. *To Write Like a Woman: Essays in Feminism and Science Fiction*. Bloomington: Indiana Univ. Press.

St. Clair, Margaret. 1963. *Sign of the Labrys*. New York: Bantam.

——. 1967. *The Dolphins of Altair*. New York: Dell.

Sale, Kirkpatrick, with Carol Moore. 1987. "Ecofeminism — A New Perspective." *The Nation* 26 September: 302–5.

Sargent, Pamela. 1976. *Cloned Lives*. Greenwich, Conn.: Fawcett.

——. 1987. *The Shore of Women*. 1986. Reprint. New York: Bantam.

——. 1992. "On Peter Fitting's 'Reconsideration' in *SFS* #56." *Science Fiction Studies* 19, no. 2 (July): 271–76.

Sargent, Pamela, ed. 1975. *Women of Wonder: Science Fiction Stories By Women About Women*. 1974. Reprint. New York: Random House.

Schaef, Anne Wilson. 1985. *Women's Reality: An Emerging Female System in a White Male Society*. 1981. Reprint. San Francisco: Harper and Row.

Schnorrenberg, Barbara Brandon. 1982. "A Paradise Like Eve's: Three Eighteenth Century English Female Utopias." *Women's Studies*. 9:263–73.

Schocken, Susan, coordinator, with 1975 "Women and Science" class of the Univ. of Washington's Women's Studies Program. 1976. *Hypatia's Sisters: Biographies of Women Scientists Past and Present*. Seattle: Feminists Northwest.

Schweickart, Patrocinio. 1983. "What If. . . . Science and Technology in Feminist Utopias." In *Machina Ex Dea: Feminist Perspectives on Technology*, edited by Joan Rothschild, 198–211. New York: Pergamon Press.

Scott, Melissa. 1987. *The Kindly Ones*. New York: Baen.

——. 1995. *Shadow Man*. New York: Tom Doherty Assoc.

Scott, Sarah. 1986. *Millenium Hall*. 1762. Reprint. London: Virago Press.

Seal, Julie Luedtke. 1990. "James Tiptree, Jr.: Fostering the Future, Not Condemning It." *Extrapolation* 31, no. 1 (Spring): 73–82.

Seidelman, Susan, director. 1987. *Making Mr. Right.* Script by Floyd Byars and Laurie Frank. Orion Films.

Shelley, Mary. 1981. *Frankenstein.* 1818. Reprint. New York: Bantam.

Shepherd, Linda Jean. 1993. *Lifting the Veil: the Feminine Face of Science.* Boston: Shambhala.

Showalter, Elaine. 1977. *A Literature of Their Own: British Women Novelists From Bronte to Lessing.* Princeton, N.J.: Princeton Univ. Press.

Slonczewski, Joan. 1987. *A Door Into Ocean.* 1986. Reprint. New York: Avon.

———. 1989a. Interview on panel at Science Fiction Research Association Meeting, 25 June, Miami Univ., Oxford, Ohio.

———. 1989b. *The Wall Around Eden.* New York: William Morrow.

Slusser, George E., George R. Guffey, and Mark Rose, eds. 1980. *Bridges to Science Fiction.* Carbondale: Southern Illinois Univ. Press.

Slusser, George E., and Eric Rabkin, eds. 1987. *Aliens: The Anthropology of Science Fiction.* Carbondale: Southern Illinois Univ. Press.

Smith, Curtis C., ed. 1986. *Twentieth-Century Science-Fiction Writers.* 2d ed. Chicago: St. James Press.

Smith, Stephanie A. 1985. *Snow-Eyes.* New York: DAW.

Smith-Rosenberg, Carroll. 1986. *Disorderly Conduct: Visions of Gender in Victorian America.* 1985. Reprint. New York: Oxford Univ. Press.

Sparks, Muriel. 1987. *Mary Shelley.* 1951. Rev. ed. New York: New American Library.

Spector, Judith A. 1981. "Science Fiction and the Sex War: A Womb of One's Own." *Literature and Psychology* 31, no. 1: 21–32.

Spivack, Charlotte. 1987. *Merlin's Daughters: Contemporary Women Writers of Fantasy.* Contributions to the Study of Science Fiction and Fantasy No. 23. New York: Greenwood Press.

Spivak, Gayatri Chakravorty. 1985. "Three Women's Texts and a Critique of Imperialism." *Critical Inquiry* 12, no. 1 (Autumn): 243–61.

———. 1988. "Can the Subaltern Speak?" In *Marxism and the Interpretation of Culture,* edited by Cary Nelson and Lawrence Grossberg, 271–313. Urbana: Univ. of Illinois Press.

Stark-Adamec, Cannie. 1981. "Why Women And/In Science?" *International Journal of Women's Studies* 4, no. 4 (Sept.–Oct.): 311–17.

Stimpson, Catharine R. 1989. *Where the Meanings Are: Feminism and Cultural Spaces.* 1988. Reprint. New York: Routledge.

Stone, Leslie F. 1929a. "Letter of the Twenty-Fourth Century." *Amazing Stories* 4, no. 9 (Dec.): 860–61.

———. 1929b. "Out of the Void." Parts I and II. *Amazing Stories* 4, no. 5 (Aug.): 440–55, and 4, no. 6 (Sept.): 544–65.

———. 1929c. "Men With Wings." *Air Wonder Stories* 1 (July): 58–87.

———. 1929d. *When the Sun Went Out.* Science Fiction Series No. 4. New York: Stellar.

———. 1930. "Women With Wings." *Air Wonder Stories* 1 (May): 984–1003.

Suvin, Darko. 1979. *Metamorphoses of Science Fiction: On the Poetics and History of a Literary Genre.* New Haven: Yale Univ. Press.

Tepper, Sheri S. 1987. *After Long Silence.* New York: Bantam.

———. 1989. *The Gate to Women's Country.* 1988. Reprint. New York: Bantam.

Tillotson, Marcia. 1983. "'A Forced Solitude': Mary Shelley and the Creation of Frankenstein's Monster." In *The Female Gothic*, edited by Juliann E. Fleenor, 167–75, 298–300. Montreal: Eden Press.

Tiptree, James, Jr. [Alice Sheldon]. 1975. *Warm Worlds and Otherwise*. New York: Ballantine.

———. 1978. *Up the Walls of the World*. New York: Berkley.

———. 1988. "Houston, Houston, Do You Read?" Published as a short story in 1976 in *Science Fiction: The Science Fiction Research Association Anthology*, edited by Patricia S. Warrick, Charles G. Waugh, and Martin H. Greenberg, 434–74. New York: Harper and Row.

Tuck, Donald H. 1974. *The Encyclopedia of Science Fiction and Fantasy Through 1968*. 3 vols. Chicago: Advent.

Ulrich, Laurel Thatcher. 1990. *A Midwife's Tale: The Life of Martha Ballard, Based on Her Diary, 1785–1812*. New York: Random House.

Van Scyoc, Sydney J. 1975. *Star Mother*. New York: Berkley.

———. 1977. *Cloud Cry*. New York: Berkley.

Vonarburg, Elisabeth. 1992. *In the Mothers' Land*. Translated by Jane Brierly. New York: Bantam.

Walling, William A. 1972. *Mary Shelley*. New York: Twayne.

Wang, Qinglan, and Yi Wang. 1980. "Dolphin Brand Soft Candy." *Scientific Times* 1:219–20.

Waxman, Barbara Frey. 1987. "Victor Frankenstein's Romantic Fate: The Tragedy of the Promethean Overreacher as Woman." *Papers on Language and Literature* 23, no. 1 (Winter): 14–26.

Wehr, Demaris S. 1987. *Jung and Feminism*. Boston, Mass.: Beacon Press.

Weil, Simone. 1958. *Oppression and Liberty*. London: Routledge and Kegan Paul.

Weiler, Kathleen. 1988. *Women Teaching for Change: Gender, Class and Power*. South Hadley, Mass.: Bergin and Garvey.

———. 1991. "Freire and a Feminist Pedagogy of Difference." *Harvard Educational Review* 61, no. 4 (Nov.): 449–74.

Weinreich-Haste, Helen. 1986. "Brother Sun, Sister Moon: Does Rationality Overcome a Dualistic World View?" In *Perspectives on Gender and Science*, edited by Jan Harding, 113–31. London: Falmer Press.

Weldon, Fay. 1986. *The Shrapnel Academy*. New York: Viking Penguin.

———. 1991. *The Cloning of Joanna May*. 1989; New York: Penguin.

Wendell, Carolyn. 1979. "The Alien Species: A Study of Women Characters in the Nebula Award Winners, 1965–1973." *Extrapolation* 20:343–54.

Westkott, Marcia. 1986. "Historical and Developmental Roots of Female Dependency." *Psychotherapy* 23, no. 2 (Summer): 213–20.

Wilder, Cherry [Cherry Lockett Grimm]. 1982. *Second Nature*. New York: Simon and Schuster.

———. 1992. "The Profession of Science Fiction, 43: Far Fetched." *Foundation: The Review of Science Fiction*. No. 54 (Spring): 5–14.

Wilhelm, Kate. 1973. "Stranger in the House." 1967. Reprint. In *Abyss: Two Novellas*, 73–136. New York: Bantam.

Willis, Connie. 1992. *Doomsday Book*. New York: Bantam.

Wittig, Monique. 1969. *Les Guérilleres*. Translated by David Le Vay. New York: Avon.

Wolf, Naomi. 1991. *The Beauty Myth: How Images of Beauty Are Used Against Women*. New York: William Morrow.

Wolmark, Jenny. 1994. *Aliens and Others: Science Fiction, Feminism and Postmodernism*. Iowa City: Univ. of Iowa Press.

Woolf, Virginia. 1992. *Orlando*. 1928. Reprint. San Diego and New York: Harcourt, Brace.

Wyckoff, Hogie. 1980. "Sex Role Scripting in Men and Women" and "Banal Scripts of Women." 1974. Reprint. In *Scripts People Live*, by Claude M. Steiner, 196–234. New York: Bantam.

Yaeger, Patricia. 1988. *Honey-Mad Women: Emancipatory Strategies in Women's Writing*. New York: Columbia Univ. Press.

Yolen, Jane. 1984. *Cards of Grief*. New York: Ace.

———. 1989. *Sister Light, Sister Dark*. 1988. Reprint. In *The Books of Great Alta*, 1–205. New York: Guild America.

Zimmerman, Bonnie. 1990. *The Safe Sea of Women: Lesbian Fiction 1969–1989*. Boston: Beacon Press.

Index